Cohesion

The Making of Society

Robert G. Hercock

Published by Lulu Press

First edition Paperback - October 2009.

ISBN 978-1-4452-0914-2

Cover design by Robert Hercock, all images licensed from:
http://www.fotolia.com

Dedication

This book is dedicated to Mum and Dad.

Contents

Cohesion

The Making of Society

Preface

> *"It took just over a year after the first shots at Lexington for rebellion to turn into outright revolution. On 4 July 1776, in the austere chamber normally used by the Pennsylvania assembly, the Declaration of Independence was adopted by representatives of the thirteen secessionist colonies at the Second Continental Congress. Only two years before, its principal author, the 33-year-old Thomas Jefferson, had still addressed George III in the name of 'your subjects in British America'. Now the transatlantic or 'continental' Britons had become American 'Patriots'. In fact, most of the Declaration is a rather tedious and overstated list of wrongs supposedly inflicted on the colonists by the King, whom they accused of trying to erect a 'Tyranny over these States'. It bears all the hallmarks of a document heavily revised by an outsize committee. It is Jefferson's preamble that people remember today: 'We hold these truths to be self-evident, that all men are created equal, that they are endowed by their Creator with certain inalienable rights, that among these are life, liberty and the pursuit of happiness.'"*

(Ferguson, *Empire*, p.92)

This quote is of interest as it contains a snapshot in time of the formation of a new society. The birth of a new cohesive social entity, that we now call the United States of America. The birth of new societies has often been a violent, primeval process; almost like the emergence of new land itself from hot volcanic rifts. As is traditional in human affairs, the US Declaration of Independence was a little bloody, and occupied some tumultuous years; yet somehow from such pivotal moments in time, entirely new forms of unified cultural expression can emerge and form the foundation of whole new states and empires. However, as Ferguson rightly points out in his text, the real battle was between the Patriots and the local Loyalists, rather than with the remote British Crown itself. The battle was between two opposing world-views in the minds of the colonists themselves, each striving to hold a collective vision of the principles by which their society should function. What is of interest is how any such revolution results in a new cohesive whole. Ferguson articulates this succinctly:

"Perhaps the most remarkable thing about the Declaration of Independence was that the representatives of all thirteen colonies were able to sign it. Just over twenty years before, the divisions between them had seemed so wide that Charles Townshend had found it 'impossible to imagine that so many different representatives of so many different provinces, divided in interest and alienated by jealousy and inveterate prejudice, should ever be able to resolve upon a plan of mutual security and reciprocal expense."

Which sounds rather more like present-day US politics! It is quite ironic that the roles are now reversed, and it is the British Parliament that jumps when the White House calls. (Apparently, subservience has been redefined as a 'Special Relationship'.) So it is time to ask what is the theme of this book? The birth of the US is used as a prime example of a new society emerging out of diverse and disparate cultural groups. This book attempts to address some of the interesting questions that revolve around the formation and dissolution of human societies in general. Specifically whether, and how, we can shape the nature of cohesion present in modern societies. Some example questions we will review include: Why are complex systems able to form stable structures at all? Why are there companies, states and societies in such diverse forms? In particular we will attempt to understand what makes any culture, or organisation stable, and whether it is possible to increase the degree of social cohesion? The first two chapters lay the groundwork by introducing some key topics from the fields of Complex Systems, Networks, and computer-based modelling of social systems.

This book aims to address these questions and provide some ideas on how we may understand the principles that guide the development, stability and growth of complex social systems. The question which will be returned to is: *what forces create and sustain an integrated whole*? In other words, what exactly is 'cohesion', and why should we be concerned with its scientific investigation. The why is actually the easiest part. When economies, states and societies lose their cohesion, people suffer; to be precise a lot of people end up paying the cost. In the recession of 2008/09, as I write this text, one of the images that has resurfaced in the common media, is an iconic image from the 1930's Great Depression that depicts the suffering of a poor migrant mother and her children. Florence Owens Thompson, (born Florence Leona Christie), was the subject of Dorothea Lange's famous photo, *Migrant Mother* (1936). For me this image struck a deep chord and acted as an impetuous to complete this book. The tragic example of Mrs Thompson and her poignant image, might fairly stand as the epitome of all those who have suffered down the annals of history, in famines, wars, and economic busts. It is the tale of human endurance and perseverance in the face of overwhelming hardship and trials.

In chapters 3 and 5, we will attempt to address the vexing, (and topical,) question of why do economies collapse in such perpetual boom-bust cycles? However, the rest of the book is broader than just economics. We are looking for deeper clues as to what makes society work, i.e. what processes foster cooperation, altruism and harmony in society. Some of the specific themes that will be addressed revolve around the impact of trust, consultation and cooperation, in the building of cohesive communities and organizations. In particular, the power of trustworthiness, spiritual and moral values and cooperation, will be explored in detail. With specific examples from history, networks, commerce, warfare and computing used to illustrate their pervasive impact on social cohesion. The remainder of the chapters hangs together in a vaguely ordered, but not necessarily linear manner. (Linear thought, I strongly feel may be a requisite for accountants and actuaries, but becomes a strait-jacket when applied in the physical and social sciences.)

The text has also been heavily influenced by the work of Francis Fukuyama, although not by his infamous work, '*The End of History and the Last Man*', but by his lesser known piece on '*Trust – The Social Virtues and the Creation of Prosperity*'. This is a truly excellent book that deserves wider study. We will consider this work in more detail later, but in summary it highlights through a careful comparison of nation states economic development, the impact and pivotal role played by trust and social capital.

Who should read this book? Well firstly I would like to reach the curious general reader who has browsed through many pop-science texts and found them either baffling, or even more verbose than this volume. Second, I would really like to reach graduates of the social sciences, in order to convey some excitement and interest in applying Complex Systems theory to comprehending current social phenomena. Finally, if the text is of some small value to readers familiar with the fields of interest, that would be a bonus.

A few comments on the author are probably advisable at this point. I have a checkered scientific education and this will be reflected in the fluid expositions that will flow from chapter to chapter, like some meandering stream. (I also have a poetic bent, although having failed my high school English Literature exam, not a very gifted one.) So where am I coming from, well I have a deep and long-standing interest in the fields of Chaos and Complexity theory. Yes it is sad, but it keeps me off the streets, so a win-win situation for everyone else! Academically I started out in Physics, wandered through Electronics and finished with a PhD in Autonomous Robots; (the R2D2 kind not the car assembly kind). That was a fun time, designing and building bizarre mobile contraptions, with more silicon than an Intel Fab plant and more sensors than the Hubble telescope. I was then recruited by a major European telecommunications company (BT), and asked to research anything that would ideally lead to some profit. I have since spent several years researching AI, and Complex Systems, and their application to e-commerce and network security.

So I have far too many certificates and not enough social skills! Anyway, back to this book, my aim was to address a few key questions, currently being asked in many fields: from biology and economics to computer science and robotics. The crux of which is under what conditions do human social systems achieve stable and robust states.

This may appear to be overly ambitious, but such questions are of profound importance to the wider human race at the current time. We are in the midst of greater social, economic and technical change than at any time in history. Understanding how our current political, commercial and social systems operate, and whether they will retain any stability is rather important. To be honest, all is not well with the functioning of our modern globalized society, and its cohesion and stability are under serious threat from numerous factors; whether social, economic, demographic or climate change related. There are harsh consequences when we collectively fail to communicate. The current economic malaise, of 2009, is but a prelude to far worse, if we fail to learn the lessons of note.

Returning briefly to the early days of the United States, the character that most resonates with the theme of this book must be Benjamin Franklin. Franklin's life is well known as a printer, satirist, author, politician, scientist, inventor and diplomat. In relation to this work, his life is an exemplar of a social super-hub who bridged cultures, continents and class. Franklin was social cohesion in action. Via his founding scientific work on the nature of electricity he also helped lay the foundations for modern communications and technology; the themes for chapter four. In summary, Franklin was pivotal in forging the Union of the post-colonial states and in acting as a social bridge to the old world in England, and then as the US Ambassador to France. He was also one of the boldest anti-slavery advocates of his era. In contrast to many of the leading lights of the US independence movement, who merely paid lip service to the emancipation of the blacks. His contemporaries, however, clearly recognized the magnetizing influence such a figure could play in times of great change:

"He seized the lightning from Heaven and the scepter from the Tyrants." (Turgot)

In Franklin's life we witness an example of how at the right moment, it is the smallest of events, or actions of a single individual, that can catalyze the foundation of empires. Most of all his life embodied how the cohesion of great states is forged from the beliefs and values of a few souls. Those who value vision, action and belief in equal measure. In chapter six we address the influence that vision and beliefs still play on social cohesion. In chapter three we examine the vast subject of the rise and fall of civilizations, (somewhat briefly), and consider the forces that built and destroyed them. Beginning with: ancient Egypt, Rome, China, and the British Empire; before finally returning to the current unipolar world of the USA. Hence, the references to the birth of the United States act as a starting point for the voyage ahead.

Another major theme running through the text is how the power to communicate has shaped human society and provided the means to bind humanity together. From smoke signals, and the electric telegraph, through to fibre optics, and the Internet. As we stride into this new millennium the manifest boom in all forms of communication is bringing immense capabilities to form new social collectives and positive cultural developments. It is also shaking the historical edifices of party politics, tribal identities, race and the whole panoply of human society. We will explore the relative positive and negative impact of communications, and broader technology in general, on the cohesion of society. This book does not contain many answers, but posing the questions in a coherent and collected manner may still prove to be of some value. There will also be some nice quotes by famous people, and a few jokes to lighten the mood.

"In the beginning there was nothing, and it exploded."

Terry Pratchett, (on the big bang theory)

Acknowledgements

Of course the obligatory thanks are due to a menagerie of different people for their support, or inspiration. For inspiration, I thank Gene Rodenberry, Edward Wilson, James Burke, Carl Sagan, Buckminster Fuller, and William Gibson. For ideas and stimulating dialogue, I must thank Susan Ballati at SFI, Michael Mainelli at Z/Yen, Dave Rossetti at Cisco, Ed Gibson at Microsoft, Eric Ashdown at Accenture, and Iqbal Adjali at Unilever. For light entertainment value I must thank, Mark Shackleton, Ben Azvine, Andy Jones, Lesley Kipling, Ali Afnan, James Foadi, and Lynda Watson.

I must also thank my wife Nazila and our children, for tolerating the process.

Chapter 1

Cohesion: Patterns and Complexity

"The process of evolution may be described as differentiation of structure and integration of function. The more differentiated and specialized the parts, the more elaborate co-ordination is needed to create a well-balanced whole. The ultimate criterion of the value of a functional whole is the degree of its internal harmony or integratedness, whether the "functional whole" is a biological species or a civilization or an individual. A whole is defined by the pattern of relations between its parts, not by the sum of its parts; and a civilization is not defined by the sum of its science, technology, art and social organization, but by the total pattern which they form, and the degree of harmonious integration in that pattern."

(Koestler, 1989)

1. Introduction

The Cosmos is a symphony played with recurring leitmotifs at all scales. Fractal clouds of water vapour crown our ocean world, while families of galaxies cluster together in bizarre fractal geometries. Crescendos of supernovae and bass-note black holes reverberate across space-time, like the bass drums and horns in Berlioz's Symphonie Fantastique. Pulsars mimic cosmic metronomes keeping perfect time for the forging of stars across vast nebulae. We behold a cornucopia of living and socially complex structures across the earth, with infinite forms and patterns. Why? Of course evolution informs us of how organic complexity emerges from simpler forms. But why does any group of social agents, cohere into distinct groups? Surely the energy cost is immense in the face of the relentless second law of thermodynamics.

The field of Complex Systems, or Complexity Theory, has recently appeared precisely in order to develop a set of coherent theories for the formation and behaviour of all complex and self-organizing systems; (often abbreviated to CAS - Complex Adaptive Systems). However, as with all young branches of science its promoters are often over-exuberant, proclaiming it as an all-conquering paradigm shift. More cautious and experienced commentators have praised the high ambition of realizing new universal laws describing the *élan vital* of all life and complex structures, but advise caution in such grand ventures. Edward Wilson in his major work, *Consilience* (Wilson, 1998), provides just such a critique of the field of Complexity Theory; advocating a firmer basis in theory, and existing bodies of scientific knowledge.

However, it remains the case that a crucial requirement of modern science is the fusion of multiple disciplines into deeper and stronger interdisciplinary research threads. In this regard the institutes and research centres engaged in complex and nonlinear systems research represent the core of such work. Unfortunately, it also remains an almost hopeless case to acquire the research funding required for any fundamental interdisciplinary activity.

This text approaches the issue of complexity by focusing on one specific and crucial aspect of such systems, i.e. how do complex structures bind together? Specifically, what processes enable human social systems to form stable groups, whether the group is your local cricket club, a political party, tribe, city or nation state? The opening quote by Arthur Koestler is used precisely in order to frame the key question, which is laced throughout this text, i.e. what forces create and sustain an integrated whole? As stated in the preface, what exactly is cohesion and why should we be concerned with its scientific study?

By addressing this question we may assist in the complex social and technological challenges we face in the present century. It will be argued that distinct signs of global cohesive social and technological structures are in fact now self-assembling from the mismatched economic and political systems currently employed. If we can understand how and why such collectives emerge, then we may be able to steer the formation of healthier, stable and coherent societies. Failure to direct such emergent forces may lead to potentially bleak technological or sociological future scenarios. There are many potential paths facing humanity at this juncture in history, but selecting those that offer an aesthetically or morally sound option will be a greater challenge than that faced by any of our ancestors. (A topical example is the recent debate in British politics on whether to allow human-animal hybrid embryos. The science behind this communicates one message based on a simplistic cost vs. risk analysis, but the moral dimension has not been sufficiently addressed. Specifically, in the absence of any coherent religious motion on the debate, there is a serious imbalance towards the purely technical dimension.)

The focus of the text is on the physical forces acting on complex systems, which also includes the dimension of sociological and technological pressures. To be honest, there is a sub-agenda that reflects the authors optimistic perspective, i.e. that humanity can truly develop more integrated and cohesive societies. There are many related and critical questions which science is also beginning to consider. Firstly, how do complex systems form and grow, whether in morphogenesis within living organisms, or within company formation on the Nasdaq? A second related question is why do stable collectives of biological cells, or social units, break apart once formed? As in the ancient Chinese yin-yang symbology, creation appears to be intertwined with destructive forces. This theme will also be explored. Finally, are there any guiding heuristics we can utilize to assist in the creation and design of useful groups and structures? This text is therefore not solely about complex systems, although they form a connecting thread within many of the topics we will cover. The following introduces some of the themes we need to address. (One point to note is that the book often uses quotes from Wikipedia where basic historical references are required, and these are clearly cited. The Wikipedia experiment is one of the best examples of the power of collective information sharing, and reflects the open philosophy guiding the author in the formation of this text.)

1.1 Complexity Unbound

"The Greatest Challenge today, not just in cell biology and ecology but in all of science, is the accurate and complete description of complex systems". (Wilson, 1998, p.93)

This book addresses several subject areas that encompass various elements of the processes we are attempting to understand. This chapter provides a preliminary overview of the forces and patterns of interest; however let's start with a basic definition of complex adaptive systems.

"A Complex Adaptive System (CAS) is a dynamic network of many agents (which may represent cells, species, individuals, firms, nations) acting in parallel, constantly acting and reacting to what the other agents are doing. The control of a CAS tends to be highly dispersed and decentralized. If there is

to be any coherent behavior in the system, it has to arise from competition and cooperation among the agents themselves. The overall behavior of the system is the result of a huge number of decisions made every moment by many individual agents."
(Waldrop, 1994)

This definition is useful as it incorporates some core aspects of complex systems that are pivotal in understanding their wider societal impact. Firstly, they are in a state of constant change, never static; in a state of flux would be a suitable description. This quality echoes the words of the Greek philosopher, Heraclitus, whose famous expression aptly captures the nature of complex systems: "*You could not step twice into the same river; for other waters are ever flowing on to you.*" Secondly, the agents that compose such systems are constantly interacting in dynamic and unpredictable ways. Finally, the emergence of any large-scale coherent patterns or social structures is a result of the many interactions between the agents themselves, rather than something imposed by an exogenous grand designer. (The pervading philosophy in the CAS view of the world is a bottom-up approach, rather than a top-down model.) We will see in the following chapters how these properties shape coherent behaviour and phenomena across the spectrum of human society.

1.2 Principles and Forces

In order to address these questions we require some understanding of the underlying forces and common elements within complex systems. The issue is compounded by the need to describe sets of interlinked qualities, as opposed to traditional singular measures such as the entropy (i.e. the degree of order within a system) or the energy state of a system. There is within the scientific community an urgent technical goal to create metrics in order to adequately express the macro states within broad classes of complex system. (Recent work has considered the creation of new measures of entropy, such as Tsallis Entropy, but this is rather beyond the level of this text.) The following non-exhaustive list addresses some of the key features and mechanisms of interest within complex systems.

1.2.1 Patterns

An age-old puzzle is what defines a pattern? We would consider a rock as being a cohesive unit, but not in the sense that we are attempting to define here, i.e. a complex arrangement of matter that requires energy to sustain itself. (We will also query whether this is a sufficient definition). So what constitutes a pattern? Turning to the good old-fashioned paper dictionary, we find:

design: a repeated decorative design, for example on fabric

a zigzag pattern

regular form: a regular or repetitive form, order, or arrangement

a predictable pattern of behaviour

prototype: an original design or model from which exact copies can be made

This is not really useful as we are getting recursive logic, where patterns are defined by examples of other patterns! Let's consider a simplistic example. What is the difference between a rock and a whirlpool? Both are complex structures composed of vast numbers of atoms. However, a significant number of physicists and complex systems scientists study whirlpools, while few contemplate rocks, (except those with Zen leanings; of course Japanese Zen gardens may contain whirls of pebbles, but I digress). A whirlpool is of interest as a CAS, since it is a 'spatio-temporal' structure. It exists as a result of the interplay between its constituent matter and the energy flow which drives it. Remove the energy and the structure dissolves. Such is the way of life and all of the complex systems we are interested in for the purpose of this text. (A nice reference on the topic of patterns and complex systems is: *The Self-Made Tapestry, Pattern formation in nature* by Philip Ball (1999).)

The requirement for a constant flow of energy then is perhaps the best defining condition for any CAS that may be of interest. During the following chapters we will need to carefully elaborate and expand our definitions and worldview of complexity. For example, one of the central problems when reviewing the social domain is simply the ability to measure the degree of cohesion across a social group. What should be the defining parameters for measuring cohesion? For example, in the case of a company we could measure the turnover of staff as an indicator of morale, and hence group cohesion. However, as the scale and complexity of social structures increase, it becomes increasingly difficult to formalize. A city is clearly a persistent spatio-temporal system, which if viewed over a sufficient length of time, has the distinct appearance of a cohesive, pulsating, living entity. Yet its composition of citizens, shops, and businesses is constantly changing, day to day and year to year. One variable that does have more permanence is the transport networks that sustain and feed a metropolis. These evolve over time as well, but often new networks trace over the paths of earlier roads and byways. This aspect is why we need to spend some time in chapter two on the central role played by all forms of networks in sustaining cohesive patterns. In chapter four we look in more depth at the cohesive role played by transport networks.

Next is the critical question, if a social system is cohesive, over what time frame will it remain so? For example, North Korea has been stable for fifty years. Will it remain so? Probably not, based on the evolutionary path followed by most communist regimes. Such extreme regimes have proved to be stagnant and in stasis, rather than stable in a dynamic sense of the word. Fortunately, the physical laws of the universe seem to abhor stasis even more than a vacuum. The living and dynamic polity that surrounds such regimes swirls incessantly, and places an irresistible pressure to change and evolve on any social structure that holds itself rigid. We will return to the political domain in chapter three.

1.2.2 Harmony

The human mind clearly has preferences for ordered patterns and we seek such within our art, music, literature and indeed within scientific theories, where parsimony and order are highly prized elements of any substantial theory. (A great text in this regard is *It Must be Beautiful* (Farmelo, Ed., 2003), which contains a series of wonderful expositions by leading figures from each of the major scientific disciplines.) But what constitutes a harmonious pattern or arrangement?

"The term harmony originates in the Greek (harmonía), meaning "joint, agreement, concord". In Ancient Greek music, the term was used to define the combination of contrasted elements: a higher and lower note." (Wikipedia, 2009)

Frequently, as seen from the earlier definitions, we find that concepts such as harmony, or pattern, slip into recursion. Even more problematic is that our mental perception of groups or wholes is quite subjective; (the topic of Gestalt psychology is an interesting starting point for studies of pattern perception (Kohler, 1992).) We assign meaning to what we perceive to be spatially or temporally correlated, and our neural network brains are well evolved to this task. Part of why this is a difficult subject is reflected in the difficulty current digital computers have in reproducing human skills, for example face recognition or the visual processing of a scene. There is something quite subtle, analogue and complex in separating correlated signals from rich data environments, i.e. the real world.

So is harmony just a balancing of correlated elements? Or does it entrain something more fundamental? It is unlikely that we will soon realize an answer to this question, but in addressing the issue some insights may be gained into what defines a group or cohesive system. The text by Denis Noble is an excellent example of a scientific description of biological systems that uses harmony and musical metaphors to capture the dynamic and cohesive nature of all living systems (Noble, 2008.) Harmony is not just a delicate balance of elements therefore, but rather a subtle and constantly dynamic interplay between the threads within a greater whole. The following quote from one of Darwin's notebooks is a nice usage of the term in this context:

"What a magnificent view one can take of the world Astronomical & unknown causes, modified by unknown ones. Cause changes in geography & changes of climate superadded to change of climate from physical causes— these superinduce changes of form in the organic world, as adaptation, & these changing affect each other, & their bodies, by certain laws of harmony keep perfect in these themselves.—instincts alter, reason is formed, & the world peopled with Myriads of distinct forms from a period short of eternity to the present time, to the future."

(Darwin, Notebook D. p.36, [see ref. de Beer, 1960])

In chapter three we begin to address the question of what constitutes the hallmark of a cohesive or harmonious society. Indeed are they the same thing? (As indicated earlier, communist states were often very cohesive, but were they in harmony?). The fundamental issue is to understand in what ways a society, such as London, may be cohesive or harmonious in a multi-cultural sense. And are these properties mutually exclusive?

1.2.3 Integration and Diversity

From harmony we turn to the question of diversity, i.e. to what degree does the homogeneity of a system dominate its behaviour? Basically, how much variation or asymmetry is required to create novel forms, whilst maintaining the cohesion of the system as a whole? This is a crucial question in our attempts to understand cohesion, especially, vis-à-vis social diversity and cultural homogeneity. Is there a critical level of diversity required in order to maintain evolvability and plasticity within a complex system? For example, monocultures proved to be demonstrably fragile during the agricultural revolution of the 20th century. Is the same true of human society? Is Japanese society strengthened or weakened by being a single culture? Is the inverse therefore true for a highly diverse multicultural society such as the United Kingdom?

One example we will consider in chapter three is the cultural mix evolving within the suburbs of North America. Here the cultural diversity is acting in many complex ways, to both enrich society, and simultaneously create segregated enclaves along political, religious and racial lines. The ultimate expression of this process is best portrayed in the Cyber-punk literature, such as the novel *Snow Crash* by Neil Stephenson, where gated communities have evolved into '*Burbclaves*', which house completely ghettoized mini-cultures. The rise of the Internet and personal communication technologies are amplifying the driving forces behind these processes, but it remains to be seen how far this process will run. These topics are the focus of chapter three.

1.2.4 Tipping Points and Phase Transitions

One of the really tricky aspects of understanding complex systems is that they don't follow easily predicted paths. Typically they flow along nicely for a while and then jump suddenly into an entirely different state. The technical phrase to describe this is a "phase transition". It sounds abstract, but your mortgage repayments and the economy in general are often victims of just such a shift in market dynamics. The following is a brief technical description for those interested, or you can skip to the following section as it all makes sense later!

"A phase transition is an abrupt change in a systems behavior. A common example is the gas-liquid phase transition undergone by water. In such a transition, a plot of density versus temperature shows a distinct discontinuity at the critical temperature marking the transition point... In nonlinear dynamical systems, the transition from self-organizing to chaotic behavior is sometimes referred to as a phase transition (or, more specifically, as an order-disorder transition). The distinguishing characteristic of a phase transition is an abrupt sudden change in one or more physical properties.
(Wikipedia, 2009)

This concept of a step change in a social system is well captured in the popular concept of a 'tipping point'. The text by Malcolm Gladwell (Gladwell, 2002) is of particular interest in this context. One example outlined by Gladwell is from modern US societies, where the relative percentage of professional couples has a marked impact on the wider stability and prosperity of the surrounding community. What is of interest is that it requires a relatively small percentage change in these social units to have a massively positive, or negative, impact on the local society. Another rather topical example is the ongoing credit crisis and housing market woes being experienced globally; (as of mid 2009.) The bursting of such economic bubbles is a well-studied phenomenon, and research indicates that such processes demonstrate some of the properties of a phase transition, (simply on a larger scale than a boiling kettle (Haken, 2004.)

Politicians and economists often wish for a "soft landing" when the economy overheats, and they tweak interest rates and monetary policy in order to deliver this nice fluffy state of affairs. Unfortunately, the real economy is more like a 747 jumbo jet in mid-flight, and tweaking the rates is like giving the pilot only two big buttons marked up/down to press. He probably can land the plane, but 'soft' is not likely to be the right adjective! We return to this theme of transitions again within networks in chapter 2. (Actually a pilot did land a passenger jet once, using only his throttle to control his engines after the normal aileron control systems were destroyed by a missile over Baghdad: [http://wapedia.mobi/en/DHL_shootdown_incident_in_Baghdad].)

1.2.5 Exploitation vs. Exploration

Any society requires a degree of cultural homogeneity to provide a common context and trust between individuals. At the same time it also requires a flow of new knowledge, ideas, genes and social diversity in order to avoid stagnation and collapse. This effect is mirrored in all evolving physical systems, from ecosystems to commercial organizations. It has been most clearly described in the concise and excellent text *Harnessing Complexity*, (Axelrod and Cohen, 2000). This balance is also of interest in the design of computer programs that use a form of artificial evolution, termed Genetic Algorithms (GA) (Mitchell, 1998). In such GA models it becomes immediately obvious that a fine and difficult balance is required between shaping the population of evolving programs to the target problem, and allowing enough genetic diversity for the system to explore all of the problem space. This theme cuts across several chapters, but it is of most interest in the evolutionary development of societies and commercial enterprises. In commerce it is now an issue of basic survival to successfully balance the exploitation of existing offerings, against investment in research for new products, which is both costly and time-consuming. One of the less visible, but ultimately critical developments is the accelerating migration of R&D programmes from western states to the emerging BRIC countries. Across Asia, China and India state-of-the-art research facilities have been developed and invested in, by both governments and corporate groups. The power house of 21st century innovation will therefore be these new centres of thought. When coupled with the parallel total shift in manufacturing capability, this paints a desperate picture for the economic prosperity of many western states that have failed to sustain investment in their own research efforts. More on this topic is captured in chapter five.

1.2.6 Symmetry and Asymmetry

One well-studied aspect of the driving processes in complex systems is that of symmetry breaking. In particular most CAS frequently require some point of asymmetric interaction in order to enable work to be done and novelty generated. It appears to be a key to many processes of complex pattern formation; from snowflakes to Islamic carpets. (A useful introductory reference on the topic is the book, *The Self-Made Tapestry,* [Ball, 1999].) A useful example of trust and asymmetry comes from work in which small asymmetries in the pay-off matrix for a Prisoners Dilemma problem lead to highly complex spatial patterns (Nowak and May, 1992). We will return to this topic in chapter three. It is also interesting to see that for complex structures to emerge within a CAS, its constituent elements need to be in a state of imbalance. A question we might then ask is what does this imply for a society and the impact of cultural diversity?

1.2.7 Polarization and Differentiation

One of the most interesting aspects of cohesive systems is the spontaneous differentiation into complex sub-structures. The apex of this process is cell-differentiation in multicellular organisms. The transformation of a single cell into an elephant, or a bee, is a pretty cool trick. No, we don't understand the detail of how this is accomplished, even when we possess a genomic map for some organisms. The recent work by the systems biologist Denis Noble (Noble, 2008) beautifully illustrates the sheer complexity of the problem. An interesting example of this is the first cloned cat (Copycat!), which has marked variation in the patterns of its fur when compared to its genetically identical parent. As well as marked behavioural differences. Such examples deflate the misplaced belief that an organism's genes completely determine its condition and actions. This is especially important in the area of socio-biology, where vocal proponents such as Richard Dawkins, attempt to enshrine genes as the primary determinants of human evolution. The following quote from Noble illustrates a more comprehensive perspective on the formation of life, than that advocated by the Neo-Darwinist camp:

"Much more than the genome is involved in the development of an organism. If there is a score for the music of life, it is not the genome, or at least not that alone. DNA never acts outside the context of a cell. And we each inherit much more than our DNA. We inherit the egg cell from our mother with all its machinery, including mitochondria, ribosomes, and other cytoplasmic components, such as the proteins that enter the nucleus to initiate DNA transcription. These proteins are, initially at least, those encoded by the mother's genes. As Brenner said, 'the correct level of abstraction is the cell and not the genome'." (Noble, 2008, p.41).

Finally, no text on complex systems and patterns can fail to mention the early work by Alan Turing on pattern formation in organisms and CAS (Turing, 1952.) In addition to laying the foundation of computer science and breaking German encryption ciphers, he also found time to do seminal work on equations that describe reaction-diffusion systems. Such equations describe how patterns emerge, from how the skin of a zebra displays stripes, to how spiral waves emerge in complex chemical reactions. The interest in such mechanisms is not that we may possess some theory for how complex patterns emerge from simple interactions, but that when they do the host structure can often retain its identity or function. Increasing differentiation is subsumed or incorporated within the adapting structure. We will be returning to the themes of polarization and differentiation in later chapters as they play a major role in group formation in CAS. It pertains to the question of why human populations become so easily polarized into opposing or conflicting groups. A number of researchers have recently addressed this issue and produced very detailed models, which may explain such behaviour, (Epstein *et al.*, 1996). This topic really matters, as human beings are still busy demonizing each other and planning genocide based on social polarization. Chapter three will look in detail at the historical consequences of this behavior in terms of the rise and fall of civilizations. Basically, these apparently abstract concepts often possess profound social consequences, for example, in the formation and isolation of multi-racial communities within the UK. We will return to this under the theme of societies and cultures.

1.2.8 Energy and Dissipation

All physical systems obey the second law of thermodynamics. Any composite system is continuously struggling to maintain its form and cohesion. To maintain structure an input of energy is required. It has been one of the longstanding mysteries of life that it appears to flagrantly violate this principle within localized regions of space-time. Like a stage magician, life conjures complex forms out of apparent thin air, using a sleight of hand to steal energy from the surrounding matrix of the universe. What is of interest in a social context is that energy and dissipation are also essential to the sustained existence of complex social structures. One example of the social dimension of this is in the sudden market shocks that periodically impact the global market. Economists rush to offer blasé explanations such as interest rates or oil price shifts, yet the cause may be an endogenous (internal) shifting of the forces at play in the system, with no single principal cause.

A far more useful question to ask is, do we need the destructive side of CAS? Are disruptive forces in fact essential to sustain change and evolvability in a finite system? This theme will be reflected upon throughout the book. A controversial and extreme example of this is the argument that wars are ultimately constructive, as they accelerate technological development and sweep away dysfunctional social/political organizational systems. The prime cited examples are the formation of the UN after World War II, and the League of Nations following the First World War. (The author's personal view is that there must be cheaper and less bloody methods to reshape human society.) One interesting analogy from biological systems is the process of apoptosis, within which cells in the body undergo a programmed self-destruction in order to preserve the overall functioning of the host organism. If a system has no mechanism for a phased renewal of its component parts then stasis or disintegration will result. Of course disambiguating these processes in the social context can be tricky. Is a revolution a state of violent chaos, or a useful mechanism for restructuring society into a renewed cohesive state?

1.2.9 Feedback

A precursor to Complex Systems was the field of Cybernetics, which originated in the 1940s in parallel with von Neumann's work on game theory. Cybernetics is of interest as it is a subject that gets continuously rediscovered every decade or so and given a new name! Each time the basic concept of a feedback driven system is studied, a new sub-field is spawned, yet the original work on Cybernetics remains in essence as the foundation. One of the preeminent and most lucid early writers on the topic was W. Ross Ashby, a brilliant English psychiatrist and founder of Cybernetic thinking. A nice example, which sets the scene for our later consideration of Complex Adaptive Systems, can be taken from his classic text, *An Introduction to Cybernetics*:

"Science stands today on something of a divide. For two centuries it has been exploring systems that are either intrinsically simple or that are capable of being analysed into simple components. The fact that such a dogma as "vary the factors one at a time" could be accepted for a century, shows that scientists were largely concerned in investigating such systems as allowed this method; for this method is often fundamentally impossible in the complex systems. Not until Sir Donald Fisher's work in the '20s, with experiments conducted on agricultural soils, did it become clearly recognised that there are complex systems that just do not allow the varying of only one factor at a time—they are so dynamic and interconnected that the alteration of one factor immediately acts as cause to evoke alterations in others, perhaps in a great many others. Until recently, science tended to evade the study of such systems, focusing its attention on those that were simple and, especially, reducible." (Ashby, 1956, p.5).

His excellent book has now been made available online and can be found at http://pespmc1.vub.ac.be/ASHBBOOK.html.

The key point is that from control theory we understand that any system can only maintain stability (and hence structure) via a feedback loop. This applies equally to CAS and offers one basic method to understand their behaviour. Unfortunately, it appears to be frequently forgotten in the social sciences and economics. Even worse, and simply inexcusable, is the degree of ignorance within the military communities of the Western powers, who fail to understand that any action taken will lead to recursive and unpredictable consequences, due to complex and multiple feedback paths; (more on that in chapter two.) However, identifying the feedback paths and mechanisms within complex systems can be extremely difficult. If a company maintains healthy operation over many decades in the face of constant competition and bear markets, what are the key feedback processes that enabled it to survive? Was it focusing on profit, or a focus on strong social cohesion and morale within the organisation. (Gladwell's *The Tipping Point* (2002) provides some examples of adaptive companies, as does the major reference work in the commercial domain, *Built to Last* (Collins and Porras, 2005).) This aspect will be illustrated in chapters four and five on technological and commercial development.

Another example of human feedback is the process of flood control. Major flooding occurs with increasing frequency as we attempt to engineer rigid flood defences and give rivers nowhere to go when they rise. Smart thinking says take down the levees, and give the river room to flood agricultural areas, where it will deposit useful silt anyway. This is a classic case where we mistakenly apply linear thinking to the management of a fundamentally complex adaptive system. The summer of 2007 again witnessed serious flooding across the UK. Why? Because we have neglected basic maintenance of the rivers and waterways. In politics, sewage and river dredging are very low priorities. (Even if dredging up political sewage on your opponents is a somewhat higher priority.)

1.2.10 Trust and Trustworthiness

A subtle, but vital dimension of complexity is a principle that primarily applies in the human social and political domains, i.e. that of trust between agents and institutions. It has corollaries in the physical sciences, but is of key interest as a force acting upon social systems. The author's guiding hypothesis is that inter-agent trust is a primary catalyst for social cohesion. Trust is the dynamic glue that binds the fabric of human society together, politically, socially and economically (Putnam, 2001, Fukuyama, 1995.) It is a key element in the evolution of human social structures from hunter-gatherers to city building civilizations. If this book conveys nothing else it is my intention to emphasize this point. That is, that trust, and the parallel quality of trustworthiness, are the very bedrock of cohesive human societies, in all dimensions of life, political - private, public, and commercial. We will allocate some time to developing the themes of trust and trustworthiness in the following chapters.

1.3 Book overview

This section briefly outlines the principal contents of the remaining chapters. This is a useful process from an educational perspective as it helps set the scene and provides some context as you read the text. (I also strongly recommend the study texts by Tony Buzan (Buzan, 2006), as they provide very practical and effective techniques for learning any subject. I therefore include some of Buzan's methods in the style and presentation of this text in order to make it more digestible, such as the use of mind maps at the end of each chapter, as an overview method.)

There are three common themes that thread the chapters together. The first of these is the effect of trust on the cohesion of systems. Second is the theme of bridges as a physical and literal metaphor for the linking together of disparate elements to build a cohesive whole. Third is the role of security and defence mechanisms within CAS as a force for sustaining cohesion. Of course this later theme also leads to violent disruption, but this will be part of the discourse as we progress.

Chapter 2 *Networks*

The second chapter introduces the important topic of network theory and its key role in many CAS. The study of network dynamics, topology and behaviour is currently very topical and many recent texts have addressed this subject, for example *Linked*, (Barabasi, 2003.) The text by Watts (Watts, 2004) is also an excellent introduction to the subject and recommended for any serious study of complex network systems. The need to include a chapter on the subject here is simply that it underlies so many of the arguments in the subsequent material on social, biological, and technological cohesion. For example, we will look at the cohesive role of networks in the domains of security and defence, social networks and in physical transport networks. We will also cover the distinction between physical and abstract networks, as each form plays multiple roles in binding complex systems together.

The chapter covers not just how networks transfer information across systems, but also how this information may be constructive or destructive, as in the case of violent conflicts. On a technical level the chapter aims to communicate some of the excitement that is driving a rapidly emerging scientific field that has vast implications for how we design everything, from telecommunication networks to rail links and air routes. Of course the greatest exemplar of this is the Internet, which gets a section of its own and appears again in the exposition on technology in chapter four. There is some techie detail on network theory, feel free to skip it, if it doesn't float your boat! This is followed by a sub-theme on resilience and robustness in complex systems, which is more interesting and worth a dip. Finally we have a piece on the history of communication networks in warfare, which is of more general interest.

Chapter 3 *Societies and Collectives*

This chapter attempts to analyse the degree of social cohesion present both today and over the history of human civilization, (a somewhat non-trivial exercise.) The goal of this is to predict what future forms human collectives will take. In particular, we look briefly at the factors influencing the lifespan of several civilizations throughout history. Beginning with ancient Egypt, then Rome, China, the British Empire and finally studying the current hegemony of the USA. Specifically, are there some obvious signatures that characterize the emergence of a civilization and, more importantly, signs that signal its demise?

We then introduce the concept of modelling civilizations and societies using artificial computer-based agent simulations. Again, feel free to skip this part if it gets a bit too technical. It descends into an historical review of Artificial Intelligence for the purpose of introducing computer modelling of human societies. It also looks at the inherent limits of artificial models for understanding large-scale human activities. This is followed by the crux of the text, a review of the driving factors that impact the cohesion of current societies. We look at the major forces shaping family, political, religious and cultural cohesion. The chapter then looks at the topics of trust and consultation; as two of the thematic threads that hopefully bind the text into a whole.

The final section asks the pertinent question, what will be the lifetime of current western and oriental societies? Don't expect an answer to this, just the author's personal opinion, with a smattering of facts and figures to justify the stance. At least you have been forewarned, unlike most texts that sell themselves on the pretext of offering the 'truth'. Escaping one's cultural roots is never an easy task, although, having travelled to over twenty countries, and lived and worked in China, I feel partly able to see beyond my immediate cultural horizon. (China is a land whose culinary achievements certainly broaden the occidental mind!)

Chapter 4 *Technology Nexus*

This chapter considers a number of technical developments in the telecommunications and computing domain, in order to illustrate how self-organizing processes can build highly complex structures from basic elements. Such structures may be defined as emergent. Hence the theme of interest is how technologies have shaped the structure and growth of human societies, in particular what makes communication and IT technologies such powerful catalysts for social change. Some of the key technologies and associated issues of interest that are touched upon are:

- Libraries and electronic webs
- Information Networks
- Computing
- Robots and Artificial Intelligence

The history of communications is reviewed from ancient times, as this illuminates the power of this process in human history. A particular emphasis is placed on the role of communication networks in warfare, as these represent the spear-head of human communication processes (pardon the pun!) The technology piece then flows from the communication domain, lasers, and silicon into computers, AI, the smart-phone, and software. The rationale for the treatment of these topics is the sheer scale of the impact they are having, i.e. the computing revolution makes all of the facets of globalization possible. These technology forces are also shaping the future in profound ways that we simply do not understand. As a fan of the Cyber Punk genre of fiction, I frequently turn to the works of William Gibson and Neil Stephenson in order to grasp the potential social consequences of the knowledge revolution.

The chapter also covers the issues surrounding security in the cyber age, as this has been the focus of the author's personal research for several years. In particular, it throws light on our understanding of what makes a network, or complex system, stable under attack conditions. For example, the way in which computer viruses mirror the behaviour of biological pathogens, has underscored the need for interdisciplinary research and the holistic nature of complex adaptive systems.

Finally, technology-driven networks are, of course, morally neutral. They can transmit spam, or porn, or even integrate military command networks. Alternatively, they are clearly enabling innovative new social interactions, (e.g. the Facebook, Twitter and MySpace effect), and lowering economic costs. We have not been at such a technological juncture, since the invention of movable type and the Gutenberg press around 1439. The full consequences of that revolution would have been equally impossible to foresee in the mid-15th century.

Chapter 5 *Corporate Cohesion*

The motivation for this chapter is to understand how companies form and dissipate. Again the twin themes of diversity and cohesion will be analysed in this context, as they have a significant impact on all aspects of commercial activity, from the size of companies to the degree of competition within a market. A number of sub-themes are also considered, including:

- Monopolies and mergers
- Optimization vs. resilience
- Globalization and networks
- Agent-based modelling of commerce
- The adaptive enterprise

The second point is of most interest, as it relates to the topic of cohesion across complex systems. Specifically, to what degree does any system require reserves of energy and resources in order to sustain itself? It appears to be a common principle in most organizations to use cost-cutting as a first line response to external pressure. The chapter then looks at transport and communication networks again, but from a commercial perspective. It ends with a brief set of case studies that illustrate some of the techniques adopted by good companies that have enabled them to survive and grow. And conversely some examples of companies that have failed to adapt.

Chapter 6 *Conclusion: Building Bridges*

This summary chapter is an overview of cohesion and in particular expounds on the bridge theme for understanding cohesive forces. The aim is to show how a single overarching theme, i.e. cohesion can illuminate the domain of complex systems. Such an effect may be best defined as one of *consilience*. It looks at the dynamic balances inherent in CAS that leads to cohesive states, e.g. between security and stability, and growth versus decay. The contentious topic of social engineering is then reviewed and whether it is possible to engineer stable societies. This leads nicely into the domain of revolutions and the clash of civilizations.

We complete the chapter by then embarking on a visionary walk to divine possible future scenarios for human society in terms of our potential for cohesive development. In particular, we return to the importance of trust as a mechanism to reinforce the bonds of society. We may lose contact with terra firma at this point, but hopefully the previous six chapters contained enough pragmatic content for you to not ask for your money back!

1.4 Dreamers

We have spoken of principles, symmetry, forces and harmony. We will examine these at play in networks of all forms, both physical and social, and in engineering structures, such as bridges. In writing this work I was partly inspired by the lives of two men in particular, Isambard Kingdom Brunel and Buckminster Fuller. Both men embodied these same principles in their work and achievements. Brunel, the engineer supreme and master of ships, rail networks and bridges. Fuller, the dreamer and architect, whose geodesic domes, marked the transition in the 1950's from old-world design, to a new age of free-form structures, and were an embodiment of future vision. (As such, they frequently crop up as city spanning domes in Sci-fi movies.) This section briefly reflects on elements from both of their lives, as they help frame the journey we are exploring. In particular, they echo the ethos of cohesion and structural harmony that we are seeking to capture.

Isambard Kingdom Brunel

At the beginning of the 19th century the world was still vast and disconnected. Not much had really happened for the preceding four millennia. Oh, we had put up a few pyramids and the Coliseum, and even printed the odd book, but our distant ancestors would still have felt quite at home, if they were magically transported through time to the year 1800. Yet within a mere century, the earth had moved. The same ancestors dropped in the year 1900, would have felt mind-numbing culture shock. As if by the wave of some omnipotent hand, humanity had mastered the physical world overnight. Little of the modern world that we see around us today did not have its roots or origin in the 19th century. (This includes the computer I am typing this on, as many would regard its grand-father, as the Victorian genius Charles Babbage.)

One of the leading architects of this world-shaking revolution was Isambard Kingdom Brunel. He achieved fame as the Chief Engineer of the first major river tunnel in the world; constructed under the Thames in London and completed circa 1843. As with many of Brunel's works, the tunnel was not an immediate financial success - it was first run as a shopping mall and tourist attraction, charging just a penny a visit. But, just like his vast iron ships, it proved the technology was possible, and others followed where he led. The tunnel was followed by bridges, the most amazing example of which, I feel, is the Maidenhead Railway Bridge over the Thames in Berkshire. This was the flattest, widest brick arch bridge in the world. What boggles the mind is that it is still carrying main-line trains to the west of England, over its two arches, with each span totalling 39 m, and a wide enough to carry four tracks. This supreme example of engineering now carries modern trains that are approximately 10 times as heavy as those of Brunel's age. Not bad for someone who infamously said:

"I am opposed to the laying down of rules or conditions to be observed in the construction of bridges lest the progress of improvement tomorrow might be embarrassed or shackled by recording or registering as law the prejudices or errors of today."

(Isambard Kingdom Brunel)

Most men would consider the creation of the greatest tunnels and bridges in history a sufficient lifetime's achievement, but not Brunel. Brunel's vision was epic. He envisaged passengers purchasing a single ticket at London Paddington station, and then travelling from London to New York, changing from the Great Western Railway to The Great Eastern Steamship at the Terminus in Neyland, South Wales. So his next task was to design and create the greatest ships the world had ever seen. He started with the SS Great Western in 1837. The largest steamship in the world, it halved the journey time to New York from 34 to 15 days. Not good enough says Brunel, let's build an even larger all-iron ship with a propeller. The SS Great Britain could do the London to New York run in 14 days!

This still wasn't good enough, so Brunel built an iron ship 700 feet in length and able to sail to Australia and back without refueling, the SS Great Eastern. Unfortunately, as a passenger carrying ship it was a complete and utter disaster. In 1859 Brunel suffered a stroke and died just before the Great Eastern sailed for New York. Then on its maiden voyage, which was due to begin on 16th June 1860, once the passengers had boarded, the Captain announced they would not sail until the 17th as the crew were drunk! It's most valuable phase was probably towards the end of its service, when it was used as a cable-laying ship for the first successful transatlantic telegraph. This nicely brings us to the modern age of electronic communications, a point which we will return to in chapter four.

Buckminster Fuller

Fuller's life is one of early tragedy and later vindication as a visionary of the 20th century. It is a story that is infrequently told these days, which I feel is shameful, and this state of affairs will now be rectified here. Fuller was a maverick from childhood, always inventing new contraptions and seeking to push the boundaries of knowledge. In 1922 his first daughter died aged four from meningitis, a tragedy that nearly drove him to suicide. His first efforts at establishing a new housing business ended in total bankruptcy, after which he determined to undertake a new quest and personal voyage. In his own words:

"In 1927, at age thirty-two, finding myself a "throwaway" in the business world, I sought to use myself as my scientific "guinea pig"...in a lifelong experiment designed to discover what – if anything – a healthy young male of average size, experience, and capability with an economically dependent wife and newborn child, starting without capital or any kind of wealth...or university degree, could effectively do that could not be done by great nations or great private enterprise to lastingly improve the physical protection and support of all human lives, at the same time removing undesirable restraints and improving individual initiatives of any and all humans aboard our planet Earth."

(Fuller, 1981, p.124)

He really liked long sentences! He was perpetually optimistic and travelled the globe incessantly, meeting and conversing with everyone he could. One of his lesser idiosyncrasies was to wear three wrist watches, one for the current zone, one for the zone he had departed, and one for the zone he was going to! His life is truly inspiring as an example of the difference a single human being can make through sheer force of will, and an optimistic vision of life. In relation to the cohesion theme, his principal contribution (one of many), the geodesic dome, is a brilliant example of structural beauty, harmony and balanced forces. In his major summary work, *Critical Path*, he explains how, as a young man he witnessed firsthand the succession of technological revolutions that were then birthing the modern world, such as the motor car and the first powered flight at Kitty Hawk.

"I was convinced that, unannounced by any authority, a much greater environmental and ecological change was just beginning to take place in my

generation's unfolding experience than had occurred cumulatively between my father's, grandfather's, great-, and great-great-grandfathers four previous generations. I had read their diaries, expense accounts, or letters containing descriptions of their lives in their successive undergraduate days in the Harvard classes of 1883,1843,1801,and 1760, respectively. They all told of days-long walking or driving trips between Cambridge and Boston. I realized intuitively that the subway, which opened in my 1913 freshman year to connect Harvard Square in Cambridge to Tremont and Park streets in Boston in seven minutes, was a harbinger of an entirely new space-time relationship of the individual and the environment." (Fuller, 1981, p.130)

Fuller clearly perceived the quantum shift in man's relation to the scale of the planet as a result of the revolution in communication and physical transport networks, that occurred at the beginning of the 20th century. He passionately believed in the future potential of humanity to achieve a prosperous and united world order. And, equally, that we stand at a treacherous crossroads in our potential evolution, depending on our capacity to embrace such a global vision.

His concept of tensegrity structures, such as the geodesic dome, is even now being applied in state-of-the-art examples of architecture. And in particular, it is being used in novel bridges, such as the new Kurilpa Bridge in Australia, which links us back to one of our sub-themes again, and the work of Brunel. (Tensegrity is a fascinating concept, a mash-up of the words tensional and integrity. It refers to structures with an integrity based on a synergy between balanced tension and compression components. In addition, biological structures i.e. muscles and bones, and even cell membranes at the micro-scale, are immensely strong due to the balance of tensioned and compressed parts. The muscular-skeletal system is hence a synergy of muscle and bone. (Wikipedia, 2009).) Fuller thought deeply in a holistic and systems oriented manner. He also thought big; really, really big, with detailed designs for mile-high towers, vast cities and mile-wide airships; (whimsically termed Cloud 9's)! Reading his works however, is not an easy task, due to his bizarre penchant for initiating new fused and twisted technical terminology; for example using 'world-around', rather than 'world-wide'. In an almost Descartes-like manner, he wished to fundamentally revise how people conceived of the world, and themselves, with new trigonometric projections for maps, linguistic expressions and engineering concepts. However, Fuller's story demonstrates that, as we will encounter in later chapters, one person can make a fundamental difference.

Summary

So we have raised some questions about the vexing issues of social cohesion and the evolution of human civilization. As ever, nature guards its secrets with jealous care. Fortunately, we have the legacy of Turing, Von Neumann and many other great minds on hand, to draw on in our attempts to fathom the complex processes within the formation and dissolution of human societies. In charting this wild territory we can at least now construct microcosms within our desktop computers that may open vistas unreachable by the finite calculating might of the unaided human brain.

The motivation for the book is therefore to illuminate how complex social systems, via aggregation and self-organization, maintain their existence. The following chapters are designed to stimulate, entertain and occasionally provoke the reader. A number of questions can now be readily formulated that will act as the template for this book:

- What defines a cohesive system?
- How is any balance between attractive and repulsive forces achieved?
- What makes a coherent society, culture or company?
- And more importantly, can we engineer cohesive, (yet diverse), societies?

At this point a note of caution and modesty is required. These questions have troubled philosophers and scientists for millennia, and will almost certainly continue to do so for a long time to come. Consider this book as a route map, or tourist guide, to some of the more interesting or entertaining issues surrounding complexity and cohesion. A final word on the topic of bridges sets the scene for our journey:

"The bridge, behind him now, perhaps forever, is a medium of transport become a destination: salt air, scavenged neon, the sliding cries of gulls. He has glimpsed the edges of a life there that he feels is somehow ancient and eternal. Apparent disorder arranged in some deeper, some unthinkable fashion."

(William Gibson, *All Tomorrow's Parties*, p.273)

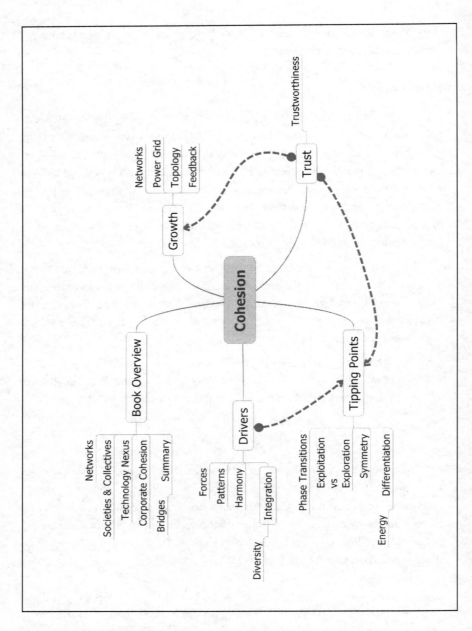

Mind map for chapter one.

Chapter 2

Cohesion: Networks

"All things by immortal power

Near and far, Hiddenly

To each other linked are,

That thou canst not stir a flower

Without troubling of a star".

(Francis Thompson, 1859-1907)

1. Introduction

The Invasion of Iraq 2003:

Once the invasion began, breakdowns quickly became the norm. For the movement of lots of data—such as satellite or spy-plane images—between high-level commanders and units in the field, the military employed a microwave-based communications system originally envisioned for war in Europe. This system relied on antenna relays carried by certain units in the advancing convoy. Critically, these relays—sometimes called "Ma Bell for the army"—needed to be stationary to function. Units had to be within a line of sight to pass information to one another. But in practice, the convoys were moving too fast, and too far, for the system to work. Perversely, in three cases, U.S. vehicles were actually attacked while they stopped to receive intelligence data on enemy positions. "A lot of the guys said, 'Enough of this shit,' and turned it off," says Perry, flicking his wrist as if clicking off a radio. "'We can't afford to wait for this.'"

One Third Infantry Division brigade intelligence officer reported to Rand that when his unit moved, its communications links would fail, except for the GPS tracking system. The unit would travel for a few hours, stop, hoist up the antenna, log back onto the intelligence network, and attempt to download whatever information it could. But bandwidth and software problems caused its computer system to lock up for ten to 12 hours at a time, rendering it useless.

Meanwhile, commanders in Qatar and Kuwait had their own problems. Their connectivity was good—too good. They received so much data from some of their airborne sensors that they couldn't process it all; at some points, they had to stop accepting feeds. When they tried to send information to the front, of course, they found the line-of-sight microwave-relay system virtually disabled. At the command levels above Marcone's—the brigade and even the division levels—such problems were ubiquitous. "The network we had built to pass imagery, et cetera, didn't support us. It just didn't work," says Col. Peter Bayer, then the division's operations officer, who was south of Marcone's battalion on the night of April 2 and 3. "The link for V Corps [the army command] to the division, the majority of time, didn't work, to pass a digital image of something."

("What went wrong in Iraq", *Technology Review*, 2004).

The above quote indicates how vital the role of communication networks has become for the most pivotal aspects of human endeavour, such as large-scale conflicts. What is apparent is that there are major gaps in our understanding of the behaviour of large-scale complex networks. In particular, with regard to the dynamic behaviour and evolution of such networks. The first part of this chapter provides a brief introduction to networks and their key properties. The core theme of the chapter however, is to understand how large-scale networks are engineered for desirable properties; such as resilience, transport efficiency and stability. These apply whether we are considering air traffic networks, computer networks, or the economic interactions between companies and individuals. These processes are also of interest in the wider realm of human social networks. The following examples illustrate the breadth and impact of the subject.

Back in 1998, one US utility executive John Casazza predicted that, "*blackout risks will be increased*", if plans for deregulating electric power transmission in the US proceeded as planned by the federal authorities. So on August 14 2003, a massive blackout that covered much of the Northeast United States was of little surprise to the engineers responsible for the system.

They understood that the new rules had fundamentally altered the behaviour of the power grid. Such failures of the power-transmission system are a direct result of a clash between the physics of the power grid and the foolish economic constraints that now regulate it.

"In the four years between the issuance of Order 888 and its full implementation, engineers began to warn that the new rules ignored the physics of the grid. The new policies "do not recognize the single-machine characteristics of the electric-power network," Casazza wrote in 1998. "The new rule balkanized control over the single machine," he explains. "It is like having every player in an orchestra use their own tunes."

Some of the smarter minds in the utility business however, do understand that the system requires a complete overhaul and modernization. A leading figure in this aspect is Prof. Massoud Amin, a tall and imposing Iranian émigré to the US, whose research has highlighted the scale of the problems facing all nations with insatiable appetites for energy consumption. One solution Amin advocates is the need to build a real-time sensing and information network across the power grid. This is essential if operators are to have any chance of reacting to the lightning fast cascades and failures that now strike across the power grid.

"But perhaps even more important, the power grid must be made smarter. Most of the equipment that minds the flow of electricity dates back to the 1970s. This control system is not good enough to track disturbances in real time as they happen or to respond automatically to isolate problems before they snowball. Every node in the power grid should be awake. A smarter power grid that automatically responds to problems could reduce the rising number of debilitating blackouts. Furthermore, the information that operators receive at central control stations is sparse and at least 30 seconds old, making it impossible for them to react fast enough to stop the large cascades that do start. A self-healing smart grid one that is aware of nascent trouble and can reconfigure itself to resolve the problem could reduce blackouts dramatically."

(Amin & Schewe, 2007)

This quote is interesting as it advocates the need for an intelligent and self-aware utility network, in which AI systems become the managing components of the system. The ultimate extension of which will be a smart power monitoring node in every home, that reacts to fluctuations in demand

and energy costs in real-time, and coordinates with centralized AI systems to help stabilize the total system. This is in rather stark contrast to the current situation, as reflected in the following quotes from operators on August 14th 2003:

"PJM: " I'm still seeing flow on both those lines. Am I looking at state estimated data?"

AEP: " Probably."

PJM: " Yeah, it's behind, okay. You're able to see raw data?"

AEP: " Yeah; it's open. South Canton-Star is open. . . We have more trouble

more things are tripping. East Lima and New Liberty tripped out.

Look at that. . . . Oh, my gosh, I'm in deep . . ."

PJM: "You and me both, brother. What are we going to do?"

PJM: Pennsylvania–New Jersey–Maryland operator

AEP: American Electric Power operator

The security evangelist Bruce Schneier speculates, quite convincingly, that this power failure cascade was possibly a side effect of a computer worm that was infecting many global computer networks at the same time: http://www.schneier.com/essay-069.html. This example is used to illustrate the necessity for policy makers to understand the physical laws that govern large-scale complex networks, such as utility and power distribution. Unfortunately, most policy makers in the US and Europe have Law or Politics degrees. Yes they take advice from panels of technical experts, of course they do. Would be silly not to! Well actually no, they receive the advice having commissioned it. And that's where a choice is made to either accept the consensus of the technorati, or save money and look good on CNN. (In the USA for example, the money spent on R&D for updating the power grid is less than that spent on sewage disposal improvement!) The consequences impact every member of society and will increasingly do so at ever greater economic cost.

A second very topical example, that drives the renewed interest in network structure and behaviour, is the need to understand and predict the operation of terrorist organizations. Post 9/11 and the barbaric attacks on the World Trade Centers, the intelligence communities of the West realized that they possessed a large volume of information on the terrorists responsible prior to the event. But the data was widely dispersed and fragmented across multiple agencies. The correlations were simply not visible. By turning to large-scale data analysis and visualization it became apparent that you could uncover such terror cells and the connections between them. Figure 2.0 is an example of some work in this domain, by one of the leading researchers, Valdis Krebs. Unfortunately, while it is a trivial task to assemble such a network diagram after the event, doing so in advance is not quite so simple. As Krebs puts it:

"As the network structure emerges, a key dynamic that needs to be closely monitored is the activity within the network. Network activity spikes when a planned event approaches. Is there an increase of flow across known links? Are new links rapidly emerging between known nodes? Are money flows suddenly going in the opposite direction? When activity reaches a certain pattern and threshold, it is time to stop monitoring the network, and time to start removing nodes." (Krebs, http://www.orgnet.com/prevent.html.)

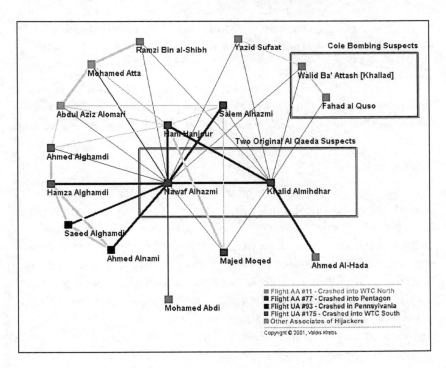

Figure 2.0 Example network visualization showing social network between a group of terrorist suspects. (Reproduced with permission: Krebs, 2002)

The key aspect here is the point that most networks of interest are complex in both time and space. The rest of the chapter aims to provide a basic

29

introduction to the science and properties of networks. We are also gaining a deeper knowledge of this topic from studies of naturally occurring networks. From gene regulatory networks, to the mammalian lymphatic system, and complex webs of interactions in whole ecosystems. Of specific interest is how large networks, both natural and artificial evolve over time, as seen from the terrorist example.

This resurgent interest in networks stems from the belief that it may provide universal laws and theories for complex systems as a whole. Laws that have to date proved elusive. Within the field of CAS researchers have been desperate to find universal laws, or constructive theories, that can integrate broad domains within what is otherwise a highly disparate enterprise. The study of network dynamics has recently emerged as a possible conceptual framework to allow a cohesive linking of the many sub-disciplines within CAS. For example, within biology the role of networks is increasingly seen as a crucial operational mechanism in cell structure, function and evolution. Early work by Stuart Kaufmann introduced network processes in the context of genetic regulation:

".. much of the order seen in development arises almost without regard for how the networks of interacting genes are strung together. Such order is robust and emergent, a kind of collective crystallization of spontaneous structure."

(Kaufmann, 1996)

Kaufmann pioneered some of the earliest work on the application of network theory to complex biological systems; (his text, *'At Home in the Universe: The Search for Laws of Self-organisation and Complexity'* is a fascinating introduction to the topic.) Among those properties that have been most thoroughly investigated is the resilience of a network to node failure. Several authors (Albert *et al.*, 2000) have pointed out that different connection rules give rise to architectures that react to such perturbation in very different ways. For example, Albert Barabsi and his team have quantitatively demonstrated that scale-free networks, typically characterized by a strong hierarchical structure, are very resistant to random node failure, while they remain sensitive to directed attack against key relays.

The core of this chapter will focus on communicating an overview of networks and hopefully assist the reader to apply the knowledge to understand network behaviour, whether in a social, defence, health, or technology domain.

Section 2 describes some basic concepts in the theory of networks that will be required for the rest of the text. Section 3 introduces the important aspect of resilience in networks and how economics and transport efficiency impact air traffic and computer networks. Section 4 provides a specific application domain, i.e. networks in military systems.

2. Network Dynamics

A critical development in recent years has been the emerging field of Network Dynamics, which centers on the study of complex networks and their dynamic and topological properties. In chapter five the power of network formation will be considered in the light of computing and communication networks. First, however, we need to answer what properties of networks are important in the theme of system cohesion?

"In networks it is not the number of connections one has, but where the connections lead to that creates advantage. In networks the golden rule is the same as in Real Estate -- location, location, location. In real estate it is physical location -- geography. In networks it is virtual location -- determined by the pattern of connections surrounding a node."

(Krebs, http://www.orgnet.com/booknet.html)

The first question, of course, must be what is a network? A basic definition is a set of edges (links) and nodes (vertices). A network may therefore be defined in the abstract as the relationship of a set of edges to nodes. A network may be conceptual as in social networks, virtual such as a collection of web pages, or physical such as a telephone network. In the simplest case a network is represented as a *graph* that consists of a set of n *vertices* (nodes) connected by a set of m *edges* (links). The edges can be *directed* or *undirected* giving directed or undirected graphs. An edge may be directed or undirected. Often we ignore this property and presume all edges are undirected, as is the case for most physical networks that transport some material or information. It becomes important however, when we need to analyse the mathematical properties of networks.

The *degree* of a network, k is the number of edges connected to a vertex v and is therefore equal to the number of nearest neighbours. Of particular interest is the range of values in the vertex degree, described by the *degree distribution*, which is characterized by the *distribution function* $P(k)$. $P(k)$ gives the probability that a randomly chosen vertex in the graph has exactly k edges, or equivalently k nearest neighbours. (We will see why this matters in the section on network types, but a simple case is when we are studying the topology of large networks like the Internet, and the distribution of edges to nodes becomes critical in understanding the behaviour of the network as a whole.)

Clustering

This one is easy, a *cluster* is a connected set of vertices, disconnected from other clusters of the graph. If the graph only contains one cluster, the graph is *connected*. A little more tricky, is the *clustering coefficient* C, this is the probability that the two nearest neighbours of a vertex (node) are also nearest neighbours to one another. On the net graph, such a relation forms a *triangle*. A high *clustering coefficient* is indicated visually by a large number of triangles on the graph. A simple example is within a social network where vertices are people and net edges represent some form of relationship or interaction between them. In this case C corresponds to the probability that two of one's friends are also friends with each another.

Classes of Networks

There are several major classes of network that have been modeled and analyzed in detail. These include: random networks, small-world and scale-free networks. We will briefly review the form of each and their key properties. Of course this is not an exhaustive set and the reader might wish to consider a detailed text on the subject, (e.g. Watts, 2004).

Random Networks

The mathematician Paul Erdős and his colleague Alfréd Rényi played a pivotal role in developing the model of a random graph, a graph in which either a fixed number of edges are randomly distributed among all the pairs of a set of nodes, or, alternatively, a graph in which every pair has the same independent probability of being connected. This mathematically tractable, but simplistic model forms the starting point for the study of more complex networks and acts as a useful reference point. The first and rather obvious point is that Random networks possess no distinct structure, i.e. there is no tendency to form clusters (cliques). Also there is no centralization, hence no topological bias is present in a random graph. Compared to social networks, random graphs also possess a low level of clustering and small differences in degree among the vertices.

Small-World Networks

Of far greater interest is the concept of a small-world network. The concept of a 'small-world' dates from the now famous experiment by Stanley Milgram. In 1967, the social psychologist Stanley Milgram, sent letters to a few hundred randomly selected individuals in Nebraska and Kansas, USA, with the aim of sending the letters to one of two "targets" in the Boston area. The recipients were told to send the letter to a person they knew on first-name basis, an acquaintance, and who they thought was more likely to know the target than they were themselves. Subsequent recipients followed the same procedure. The information given about the target was their name, address and occupation. The letters were traced by requesting that each participant send Milgram a postcard. The result was that the average length of the resulting acquaintance chains was about six. This is commonly referred to as the "six degrees of separation" principle and was the first evidence that the world is indeed "small", (Kleinberg, 2000).

As an aside to this topic, serious controversy surrounded Stanley Milgram for much of his professional life as a result of a series of experiments on obedience to authority which he conducted at Yale University in 1961-1962. He found that 65% of his subjects, ordinary residents of New Haven, were willing to give apparently harmful electric shocks-up to 450 volts, to a protesting victim, simply because a scientific authority commanded them to. The victim was, in reality, a good actor who didn't actually receive shocks, and this fact was revealed to the subjects at the end of the experiment. But, during the experiment itself, the experience was a very real and gripping one for most participants. The trauma it induced in the actual subject of the experiment led to widespread condemnation of Milgram and a major review of all medical and psychological experiments involving human subjects in the USA. However, Milgram succinctly expresses this result:

"...The social psychology of this century reveals a major lesson: often it is not so much the kind of person a man is as the kind of situation in which he finds himself that determines how he will act." (Milgram, 1974)

Returning to the theme of the chapter, the small world hypothesis has since been verified in a number of experiments, (for example The Small World Project at, http://smallworld.columbia.edu/results.html.) Hence two arbitrary people are connected by only six degrees of separation, when the diameter of the corresponding graph of social connections is not much greater than six. Small-world networks have been the subject of detailed study by Duncan

Watts and Steven Strogatz. They appear to be 'small' because they have a small average path length, like random or complete graphs. Yet they can be highly clustered, like regular lattices.

Their model (Watts and Strogatz, 1998), was one of the first models with both the property of high clustering coefficient and the small-world effect. In their model the network is created from a simple one-dimensional lattice in a loop. Every vertex is then connected to the nearest neighbour, and to at least one next nearest neighbour in the one dimensional lattice. Then, one by one, every edge is rewired with probability p, in such a way that long range connections appear, i.e. many edges are used to connect locally and a few edges are used for long range connections. Ok you say, so what? The interest comes from the properties the resulting topology displays. Basically for a small probability of rewiring, where the local properties are almost unchanged, the average shortest path length is similar to that for random networks. In terms of a social network, these short cut edges begin to explain the short acquaintance chains in the experiment by Milgram.

The small-world phenomenon is clearly a significant process in the organization and evolution of a very broad class of complex systems. It is particularly relevant to our theme, as it partially explains how many systems achieve a high degree of cohesive functionality and identity, even when the scale, or dimension of the system would imply that this should not be the case. (As in the case of the World Wide Web.)

Scale-Free Networks

Another interesting form of network topology is known as a *scale-free* network. This concept was developed by Albert-Laszlo Barabasi and his group at the University of Notre Dame, around 1998. Their research into the topology of the web indicated that rather than possessing a random graph topology, it actually displayed the properties of a scale-free network, i.e. a few nodes had far more links than most other nodes. When the degree distribution of the web was plotted it displayed a familiar power-law distribution. Consequently when such a network is subject to failure, it responds very differently, depending on whether it is the highly connected 'hub' nodes that have failed or a node with average connectivity.

"Systems as diverse as genetic networks or the World Wide Web are best described as networks with complex topology. A common property of many

large networks is that the vertex connectivities follow a scale-free power-law distribution. This feature was found to be a consequence of two generic mechanisms: (i) networks expand continuously by the addition of new vertices, and (ii) new vertices attach preferentially to sites that are already well connected. A model based on these two ingredients reproduces the observed stationary scale-free distributions, which indicates that the development of large networks is governed by robust self-organizing phenomena that go beyond the particulars of the individual systems."

(Barabasi & Albert, 1999)

These highly connected vertices dominate the topology of the network, by forming super-hubs, which are not a feature of random and small world networks. Barabási and Albert argued that the scale free nature of these networks originated from two generic features of many real-world networks: First, most real networks are open systems that *grow* by the addition of vertices. Second, the edges are not randomly connecting vertices. There is a *preferential attachment* process, which favours attachment to vertices with higher degree. This manifests itself in effects such as the rich get richer, and that being popular is attractive, (if you have some friends its easier to add new ones.) A personal example of a scale-free network effect occurred when I recently visited the Judge Institute in Cambridge and booked a hot desk space. Even though my visit only lasted a few hours an executive from a major oil company noticed my name and company id on the desk and emailed me to initiate a business networking session. This never happens at my normal lab desk in rural Suffolk, but the Judge Institute is a cosmopolitan centre for business studies, and hence a network super hub in commercial space.

Power of Growth

In the past few years, the non-linear properties of technological networks have received increasing attention from the complex systems community. This is for a very good reason: thanks to the incredibly fast development of the Internet, the growth of a self-organized artificial network could actually be monitored for the first time in history. Indeed, there are evidences that many other human artifacts, from transport and telecommunication networks to social relationships, exhibit a similar emerging architecture (see e.g. Watts and Strogatz, 1998; Newman, 2001.) Yet these structures growth usually occurs at a relatively slow pace, making the underlying dynamics both more difficult and less attractive to study.

In fact the network growth process itself also plays a role in the emergence of the power-law signature of scale-free networks. Heated arguments have erupted between the leading researchers in this field. Such as the criticism (Adamic and Huberman, 1999), regarding the work of Barabasi and Albert. For example, it is debated whether the World-Wide-Web and its underlying infrastructure, (the packet-based Internet), do obey the same growth dynamics, even though they share global topological features like the power-law frequency distribution of nodes according to their connectivity.

Resilience in Networks

One useful question to consider would be, is a resilient network by definition cohesive? If so then from network theory, we now have a useful set of metrics to determine if a given complex system is cohesive and to what degree. Of course this presumes that it is fundamentally defined by the set of underlying networks that link its constituent components. The later chapters will consider if this assumption holds true. This section however, looks at the engineering of large-scale complex systems and how to build resilient networks. The first question therefore is what is a resilient network? The concept of resilience was first developed in the ecological and social sciences, where it is critical for survival and growth. Ecologists define resilience as *the capacity of a system to tolerate disturbances while retaining its structure and function.*

We can define a resilient network as one that maintains a degree of integrity when subjected to stress or attack in some form. There are a number of quantifiable metrics we can apply to determine the integrity of a network, including: average path length, cluster coefficient, and network diameter as outlined in the previous section. However these are static measures and do not capture the ability of many real world networks to exhibit adaptive and pro-active regenerative behaviour. For this we need to include temporal measures of the time required to reconstruct edges or nodes, and the degree of memory possessed within the network to enable reconstruction. One apparent solution is to design with a degree of plasticity and adaptability. The problem lies in deciding where to permit adaptability and how much. Too little and the system is brittle and rigid, too much and it is easily degraded and subverted, or insensitive to management/control processes. As usual the devil is in the details! Another dimension of the problem is that many real networked systems also exhibit *redundancy*. This may be in the form of multiple pathways between nodes in a network, or replication of resources at the nodes themselves. It is certainly a ubiquitous feature of biological systems, which have been shaped and molded by intense evolutionary pressure to survive. One example is the lymphatic network in mammals, which is a fully distributed set of lymph nodes, each of which acts to produce and transport lymphocytes, the key component in the defence system of vertebrates.

Topology and Resilience

Let's first consider the impact of topology on the resilience of a network. If vertices are removed at random, that is: independently of their degree k, what we find is the giant component gradually disintegrates as more and more nodes are missing. Yet recent work (Callaway *et al.*, 2000) has shown that this dislocation process is far from trivial and is highly sensitive to network topology. In particular, (Albert *et al.* 2000) argue that the scale-free architecture is intrinsically much more resilient to node failure, because its hierarchical structure implies that only a few highly connected nodes are responsible for network cohesion. Another problem is that physical networks may support a multitude of logical networks layered on top of them. Real networks are not simple abstract links and nodes; they exist as a stack of virtual, logical, and multiple physical network layers. This is one factor that makes them such challenging objects of study and why they display such complex behaviour over time.

This is highlighted in recent work by (Kurant and Thiran, 2006), who demonstrated how multi-layer networks may be even more susceptible to node failure than single layer networks.

"A layered perspective may completely change our view on the error and attack tolerance [1] of many complex systems. For example, a failure of a single physical edge affects all logical edges that are mapped on it. If the paths defined by the mapping cannot be changed then every affected logical edge is (temporarily) eliminated. In the context of rail-way networks, this would mean a cancellation of all trains traversing the faulty rail track. Consequently, a tiny, seemingly unharmful (from a one-layer perspective) disruption of the

physical graph might destroy a substantial part of the logical graph, rendering the whole system useless in practice." (Kurant and Thrian, 2006.)

A specific example they provide is based on a simulated attack or failure of the European rail network, in which a deletion of only 3% of the physical edges results in a loss of more than 50% of the train connections. Basically, the service provided by the network is then reduced by half, although the networks physical connectivity is barely touched; (i.e. the largest component size remains at about 95% of the original size). This is illustrated in figure 2.1.

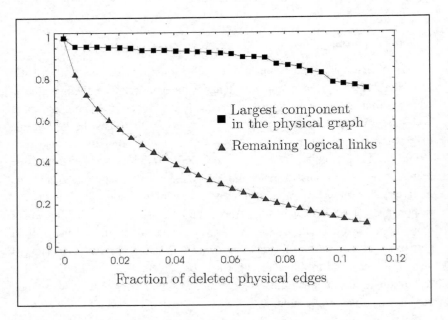

Figure 2.1 Robustness of the European railway network from a two-layer perspective. When a simulated attack destroys a small fraction of the most loaded physical edges, the plot shows the size of the remaining largest connected physical component (squares) and fraction of remaining logical links (triangles). (Kurant and Thiran, 2006)

This example result, i.e. that rail networks are inherently fragile and susceptible to disruption, is certainly validated from personal experience when travelling across the UK by rail. Approximately 50% of all my rail trips are delayed or disrupted! Of course the underlying reason for this is years of neglect and poor investment, however as the cited research indicates, such behaviour is fundamental and inherent to this form of multi-layer network design. (A favourite pastime of the poor folk in Suffolk is jumping under trains on the East coast train line, thus amplifying the problem. As well as forming another bizarre example of clustering in the cases of suicides; another well known network effect; [see Malcom Gladwell's description in Tipping Point].)

This research is important as it highlights the enormous complexity of interdependent networks and the challenges surrounding our comprehension of such systems. It is therefore of core interest to our main theme of cohesion. If we consider that individual human beings are normally elements in multiple network layers, the loss of one individual may fracture a disproportionate slice of society, if they have a high degree of connectivity. (Of interest is that the UK has recently established a new Technology Strategy Board, which has wisely started a preliminary research programme into the interdependencies of the nation's critical infrastructure and its supporting networks.)

More recent studies have indicated that dynamic behaviour, such as resilience and the transmission of information, across social networks is far more complex than early work suggests. For example, work by Damon Centola shows how there is a major difference in the dynamic properties of social networks, depending on whether a node is activated by a single neighbour changing state, or whether a node requires multiple neighbours to change state. The first case is termed 'simple propagation', and the multi-neighbour case is termed 'complex propagation'. For example, herding behaviour in stock markets, riots, lynch mobs, and grass root collectives, require multiple local participants to join in before the response threshold of a given individual is triggered. Such social cascades are thus best triggered in locally dense networks, where the probability of the same message or trigger being received from multiple contacts is maximized. Basically humans follow a simple heuristic, i.e. if one of my friends is doing something crazy ignore them, if most of my friends are following a trend then it's probably good, so join in! Unfortunately, this applies to mob behaviour equally as well as positive community activities. The work by Centola investigates the mathematical basis for why contagion spreads like this through social networks. It appears that life is rarely ever simple.

Robust Architectures

Evolution is an ever present force shaping all complex systems, especially networks. It is therefore common to find that for a broad range of natural and artificial networks, we find recurrent solutions to achieving robustness, that many complex systems have adopted. One of the most ubiquitous is a 3-tier design. In this approach a system is composed of a rigid inner core that can change, but at a relatively slow time scale compared to the rest of the system. This is surrounded by a middle layer that adapts at a higher rate and finally an outer layer that adapts rapidly to real-time events. An interesting overview and perspective on this concept is provided by the Centre for resilience at Ohio State University:

"In a world of ever-increasing complexity, connectivity, and turbulence, it is time to abandon the mechanistic view of the enterprise as a controllable artifact, and to view it instead as a living system embedded in a dynamic network. We can define the resilience of an enterprise in terms of its behaviour as a living system:.. At the strategic level, managers are concerned with robustness of the enterprise over time scales that are measured in years. Here, functional resilience involves understanding strategic threats or opportunities and developing creative and powerful responses (e.g., innovative products). Structural resilience involves organizing the enterprise to reduce vulnerability to change and increase versatility (e.g., diversifying through acquisition). At the tactical or operational level, managers are concerned with continuity of the enterprise over shorter time scales. Here, functional resilience involves agility in recognizing and resolving problems (e.g., emergency response), and structural resilience involves establishing safeguards against disruption (e.g., alternate supply channels). While adaptation in natural systems usually requires genetic evolution, human enterprises can anticipate change and respond more rapidly.."

(http://resilience.osu.edu/EnterpriseResilience.html)

Hence the three layer approach has been widely applied at the human organizational level. Within technical systems this design method has also been applied to the architecture of large-scale software applications. The 3-layer design pattern that has emerged to address these problems is to separate the architectural components as follows:

Front-end (text, forms, etc.) - delivering and presenting the data, getting input from the user. This layer, generally referred to as the client has many types, for example: browser, Java application, MS Excel, etc.

• **Middle** - programs to connect the front-end with the back-end. These programs can be written as scripts, or servlets running inside applications servers.

• **Back-end** – the actual system data stored in a database

This design method works extremely well up to a certain scale, for example the design of a single enterprise e-commerce web portal.

However, beyond this point, large-scale software systems have proved notoriously difficult to design and operate, with frequent over-budget development and poor or inadequate performance on delivery, (notable examples being the London Stock Exchange Taurus project; and in the USA, the Federal Aviation Authority (FAA) has attempted over fifteen years, to install an "all States" Air Traffic Control system.) We clearly do not yet understand the complete ensemble of interactions between the human, technical and information networks that comprise such large-scale ICT systems.

3. Example Networks

We can now review some examples of networks with the aim of understanding what, if any, are the common features between resilience and efficiency. The networks of interest are: the air transport network, and the infamous Internet. An interesting feature these networks have in common is the process of 'packetization'. The material, or information, to be moved is wrapped in a standard container, which then enables the dumb network principle to operate. Within the air transport network we have containers for cargo, and even the human passengers have adopted a standardized carry-on wheeled suitcase. So tagged packets, (or suitcases), can greatly simplify the construction of a robust and efficient network. The simple concept of standardizing the container for goods has enabled a revolution in the efficiency of a broad range of transport networks.

Air Transport

The global air transport network is an astounding phenomenon. Every day over 4 million passengers are safely carried to their destination. In the UK alone in 2006 over 2.3 million tonnes of air cargo was shipped. Most of which even arrived in the correct destination. (Although, I do still have a small blue suitcase currently en route to Bangkok!) If we look at the topology of the underlying air transport network we see a distinct pattern known as a hub and spoke model. It is also a classic example of a scale-free network, as discussed in the topology section. Hence we would expect it to display the same properties of transport efficiency and sensitivity to removal of the key hubs. Its form reflects the economic pressures acting on the airline industry as it slowly evolved from the early 20th century until today.

Resilience of the Air Transport system

Unfortunately the hub and spoke model is also very susceptible to disruption. In the UK the top 4 airports handle the vast majority of the air traffic. A nice illustration of this problem occurred in the summer of 2005. An unexpected 3 day strike by the Heathrow catering staff caused a complete shut-down of the airport. It was also an interesting example of interdependencies in networks with a hub focus, as many passengers expected problems with BA for summer flights; (a recurrent event, as I have personally experienced), and had booked on alternative airlines. However, the dispute between BA and the catering supplier caused a support strike by baggage handling staff, which resulted in delays to all flights as they all used the same baggage system. The result was total chaos and over 100,000 people stranded at Heathrow for several days and a 50 million pound loss to BA. Network interdependencies matter and can be hard to see or predict.

In the global airline network we therefore see a clear trade-off for efficiency at the expense of resilience. The projected growth in air travel over the next 20 years may prompt a rethink of this process, as the economic impact of closures and secondary costs of super hubs begins to erode the efficiency advantage of this topology. However, the growth of air traffic is relentless, in China alone the government plans to invest over $60 billion in new hub and secondary airports up to 2020. A nice example of the heated political debate than surrounds the development of major airport hubs is captured in the following article in the Guardian newspaper, 17th June 2008:

"A Conservative government is likely to block a third runway for Heathrow airport, David Cameron indicated yesterday as he criticised Gordon Brown for "pig-headedly" pressing ahead with the scheme. In his first big environment speech of the year, the Tory leader called on the government to make Heathrow "better, not bigger" and denied that the party was abandoning its green agenda. "I think the whole country can agree that the

most important priority for Heathrow is making it better, not bigger,"
Cameron told environmental group leaders. "And yet Gordon Brown is pig-
headedly pursuing a third runway just to try and prove a political point. What
a ridiculous way to plan for the future.""

The hub model offers efficiency up to a finite size limit, but beyond that the environmental and ground congestion problems begin to severely erode the economic benefits.

The Internet

Since everyone already knows everything about the Internet ad nauseam, we will keep this short. We will return to the net in chapter four, where we consider the wider role of technology and communications on social cohesion. The following is a brief historical perspective simply to set the scene.

The genesis of the Internet was deep in the days of the Cold-War, in the 1960's. The first concepts of a computer network for general communication between users on multiple computers were floated by Licklider of MIT in August 1962. These were discussed in a series of memos describing a Galactic Network concept. By October 1962, Licklider was appointed head of the Behavioral Sciences and Command and Control programs at ARPA, the United States Department of Defense Advanced Research Projects Agency, where his ideas began to spread and get noticed. Independently, Paul Baran had worked on secure networks at the RAND corporation. The intent was to create a highly resilient communications network that could enable a military network to withstand a nuclear attack. Baran's work, described two essential concepts:

- first, use of a decentralized network with multiple paths between any two points;
- and second, dividing complete user messages into what he called message blocks before sending them into the network.

The first idea enabled the system to bypass any single points of failure, and enabled the network to automatically and efficiently work around any failures. The second idea was the foundation for an efficient packet based transport model. As usual, UK scientists, at the National Physics Laboratory, were also busy developing similar ideas, and as usual, through lack of state or private investment, failed to realize any commercial development of the work.

Topology

Here is where it gets a little more interesting. The problem is we don't know what the topology of the net actually is. As indicated earlier, the work by Barabasi, and a host of others suggests the net has a scale-free edge distribution. The importance of this is that scale-free networks, i.e. those having a hub and spoke topology, display the following key properties:

a. Extreme resilience under random failure.
b. Extreme brittleness under targeted attack.

Basically, a scale-free network can withstand the random removal of a large number of nodes without collapse of the network into isolated islands or clusters. In contrast the same topology has a nasty flip side. If a malicious individual attacks and removes the hub nodes, then even with the removal of a small fraction of the nodes, the net as a whole quickly fragments into disconnected sub-nets. This is the common property shared by both the air traffic system and the web (but not the Internet), both possess a scale-free topology and these mutual properties of resilience and fragility. In the case of airports, many smaller airports may be shut down due to bad weather, security alerts or staff strikes, in any 24 hour period, and little disruption occurs to the global system. However, if for any reason two or three major airport hubs are shut down, then severe world-wide disruption to air traffic quickly ensues. (For example take out Heathrow and Chicago O'Hare, and lots of poor travelers are going to have a very bad day.)

As mentioned in the history section, the net had a requirement for extreme resilience to disruption as part of its original conception as the Arpanet. (A nuclear strike is pretty extreme!) Hence it should be no surprise that it has evolved into the most resilient man-made system ever created. Sorry, yes I know your broadband connection is flakey as pastry; I work for a major ISP provider. However, the underlying TCP/IP control layer and router network is very stable and robust against failure. Within the commercial world the underlying belief is that while a local router or system may go offline, the Internet as a whole is a persistent and dependable system. Hopefully this will prove to be the case in the foreseeable future. Although, I do worry about the unforeseeable future!

What makes the Internet Robust?

This section briefly reviews some of the key design features that confer such resilience on the Internet. We have just looked at the key topology features that affect the robustness of the net. In addition there are several underlying design properties that confer its massive resilience, i.e.:

1. Packet-based division of data. This works by breaking your file into small pieces of approximately 1kbyte and transmitting these sequentially via the network. This stream of packets is then reassembled at the receiving node into the original file. Kind of like the Star Trek transporter. (Just more reliable!)

2. Hour-glass design, i.e. the Internet is based on a stack of separate protocol layers, and the middle IP layer was designed to be as simple as possible, helping to isolate the upper and lower management layers, and provide great flexibility to evolve.

3. Dynamic Routing. This is the ability to route around failed nodes.

In chapter 5 we will consider the future evolution of the net and where it is beginning to show its age. What is not commonly discussed is how fragile the core routing of the Internet is, i.e. the process known as Border Gateway protocol (BGP). This controls routing of all packets between the major domains of the net known as Autonomous Systems, each of which is typically owned and run by a major ISP. The BGP system was designed long before computer hackers appeared and has almost no defence mechanism; it is a real headache for the companies that provide the core net routing services, such as Cisco. (This is now common knowledge and certainly known to the Black Hat community, so no secrets are being divulged).

Network Efficiency

However there is more to a network than just resilience. A network requires both resilience and transport efficiency, as edges and nodes have a real economic cost and finite transport or processing capacity. There is also a fundamental trade-off between these two dimensions. In artificial networks we can engineer high-levels of resilience and the ability to cope with attacks. Principally by the use of massive redundancy in the design of the network. However, this is expensive in terms of resources and may lead to a sub-optimal design in terms of transport efficiency or some related criteria.

Musical Networks and eDonkeys

The file-sharing phenomenon is now in full swing, and most users of the internet have at least sampled, a few tracks via the more infamous file-sharing channels, e.g. eDonkey, Morpheus or newer BitTorrent clients. In fact the bandwidth consumed by file-sharing is now a major concern for all of the ISPs. Some estimates guess that up to 60% of all network traffic is now a product of such applications. Many strongly worded letters have been mailed to the worst offenders threatening removal of net access or legal action by the media companies. In the authors opinion this is an unstoppable tide, and the content providers must simply offer better legal alternatives. Unless a shift in mind-set can be created such that a majority of people begin to see digital media as having physical value, as much as CDs in cases or DVDs.

What is actually interesting about file-sharing is the amazing resilience of the host peer-to-peer (P2P) networks that carry the shared files. In the beginning of course was Napster, the first internet-based file sharing scheme, created by Shawn Fanning, at Northeastern University in Boston. This service operated from summer of 1999 to summer 2001, at which point it was closed by a court order. The system offered the first user friendly and simple means for searching for online music, mostly in violation of copyright at the time. What mattered however is that while the files existed on many distributed user systems, the directory service run by Napster was managed on a few centralized servers. Hence when the court order closed the servers, the whole system ceased to function. Basically it was a hub style topology, and hence as discussed earlier, not resilient to targeted attacks.

Of course, that was just the beginning of the story, as the internet is in essence a perpetual social revolution. Even before the shutdown of Napster the world's Geeks had been busy coding a fully distributed alternative, called Gnutella. As soon as Napster disappeared, a number of Gnutella based clients spread rapidly across the network, based on open-source code. These new P2P clients now formed the basis of file-sharing activity and have proved virtually impossible to close down. Since both the data files and the directory mechanisms are fully distributed there is no central server to target. While P2P software offers a great way to find music and media, the protocols used to locate and transfer data are frequently inefficient and consume large amounts of net bandwidth.

From a social perspective the emergence of P2P networks reflects the increasing quantity and value of resources at the edge of networks. The association established between peers creates a logical connection of peers and forms a peer overlay network on top of the underlying network architecture. As P2P networks are dynamic complex systems involving distributed and continuously changing peers and resources, how to construct appropriate peer connections to support efficient resource sharing is a significant challenge. In particular if the number of edges is too small, all nodes may not be reachable in acceptable time. However if the number of edges is too large then any flooding or broadcast algorithm will generate a heavy bandwidth load from excessive query messages.

Network Economics & Feedback Loops

The subject of P2P networks brings us nicely to the topic of network economics. Basically transport costs deeply affect the emergent structure and dynamics of all networks. This section is about how the economic processes operating on, and within networks, fundamentally affect the resultant network structure. For example, urban development and most cities in high GDP states, reflect the dominance of the car and its associated road network. This encourages more dispersed urban structures that arguably have weaker levels of social cohesion. A powerful example of this effect is discussed in an article from The Economist, 'The Big Sort', June 2008. This article cites the analysis from a new book on the topic by Bill Bishop. Bill's reading of the statistics from across the USA since the 1970's appear to indicate that very strong social and cultural clustering has occurred. The conclusion is that this is fueling the increasingly polarized nature of US politics, as liberals and conservatives, (the primary axis of separation), rarely interact and receive their information from similarly polarized media and internet feeds. Or as one liberal minded person expressed it, *"We hate each other cordially"*. The supply of cheap personal transport, frequent career shifts and work mobility combine to enable people to select new neighborhoods based on very precise cultural indicators, (type of church, bumper stickers, schools etc). The result is that folk seek out like-minded company. Hence the modes and interactions of transport and employment networks have had a profound impact on the micro-scale patterns of social cohesion.

We will return to this hot topic in chapter three where we examine the insights revealed by computer simulation of such processes. Specifically, we consider if such models allow us to predict the future evolution of such socio-cultural patterns. This particular feedback between transport and cultural dynamics is likely to be radically shifted in the near future, as the price of oil soars, and US drivers face far higher petrol costs. In the vast US sub-urban hinterland, the almost total reliance on private cars and lack of public transport, such fuel costs will finally force a rethink in residential developments, and more importantly shifts in personal choices.

As illustrated by the tale above, the essential thing about networks is that they are both a consequence of, and causal effect acting on the interactions between agents or entities. In the real world, the cost of edges matters. In addition, positive and negative feedback cycles driven by agent activity on the network, can lead to rapid and even chaotic changes of state in the patterns of behaviour expressed by the total system. Basically, systems are cohesive when the individual benefits of belonging to the system outweigh the costs of being a member. Put another way, agents, whether individually or collectively, care how much they pay to link to a resource, or to communicate. (A fascinating, if a little dated, reference on the whole area of chaos, feedback, and complex systems, is Kevin Kelly's: *Out of Control, the New Biology of Machines*, (Kelly, 1994.))

Network Evolution

In fact, all networks physical or virtual will evolve, over a sufficient timescale. The best example is the multiple overlapping networks that constitute a city. A more subtle issue is how the information flows across a network result in modifications to the network itself. This is best exemplified in virtual networks such as the web, where usage patterns rapidly affect the structure of the network. The question is how do patterns of agent activity impact a networks structure? This is clearly a process of co-evolution, with the network shaping each agent's behaviour, and in turn being shaped by the resulting agent interactions. Which is precisely why it is rather complex!

The complexity of global economic networks has clearly eluded the minds of the world's financiers since 2006 and the latest credit crisis. In January 2008 at the infamous Davos gathering, Lord Levene, chairman of Lloyd's of London, is quoted as saying,

"If I had predicted a year ago that Merrill Lynch and Citigroup would sink into the red and have to be bailed out by the sovereign funds of the developing world, people would have wondered what I'd been smoking", (Guardian 24-1-08, p.51.) Quite. An even more poignant remark was apparently made at the

same meeting by Cheng Siwei, vice-chairman of the National People's Congress of China, regarding the current economic crisis:

"Asians save today's money for tomorrow, while Americans spend tomorrow's money today".

4. Social Networks

Since the earliest research on networks, there has emerged a vast literature on the application of network theory to modelling and understanding human social networks (e.g. Jackson & Watts 2002). Social scientists have known of the importance of the network patterns that link individuals and groups together for many years. However, it is only the advent of the modern computer, and recent theoretical developments, that have made it possible to map and visualize such networks. Whether it is how news of job vacancies spreads through a community, or how criminal gangs exchange information and operate, the flow of information across social networks has become a hot scientific topic. More importantly it is a highly interdisciplinary domain that merges mathematics, computer science, physics, statistics, biology and anthropology! It is also of significant political interest as the figure on terrorist networks at the start of the chapter indicates; understanding social networks now has global security implications.

In the *Tipping Point*, Gladwell also conveys clearly how cultural networks and cliques ebb and flow around individuals and their respective social fabric. His stories of individuals and their roles in creating social epidemics, via networks, is a valuable insight into the human level dynamics that forms the structure of social networks. The best example being Paul Reveres ride at the beginning of the war of independence, from which one man's personal social network reshaped history.

The goal of science in this field, is to understand in a quantitative fashion, precisely how and why information flows across social networks and the underlying physical constraints. For example, at what point does a new idea begin to spread in a population. Research work by Vespiganni, and in parallel by Barabasi's team, indicates that many human social networks are clustered small worlds, but with a scale-free distribution across the personal networks that individuals possess. In English that means most people have a few dozens of contacts, but some are super-hubs with hundreds, or even thousands of contacts. When these individuals catch or create a new idea (or meme) it spreads rapidly as an epidemic across a large swathe of the surrounding population. Sometimes the meme is harmless like skateboarding or fashion statements. Sometimes it has greater consequences, such as cult formation like the Aum sect that carried out the Tokyo subway attacks. More importantly our personal networks are also the most likely vector for the transmission of infectious diseases.

As Barabasi points out, a disease like AIDS was greatly accelerated in its spread due to the early activity of a few highly promiscuous men, who had large numbers of sexual partners. These individuals acted as super-hubs, allowing the virus a free and easy ride across an extensive social network. The result of the theoretical studies is to show that if we wish to slow the spread of any epidemic process, we need to selectively target these hubs. In the virus case that means targeting vaccines or treatments on these specific individuals.

Interestingly, many crime statistics also display evidence of super-hubs at work. Frequently the majority of criminal cases in a particular urban area are the result of a handful of criminals, or even a single individual. (Detailed studies have questioned whether the statistical distribution for crime does actually follow a power law, but the figures certainly support a highly non-uniform distribution of cases. In data analyzed by a lead researcher in this area, Paul Ormerod, out of a sample of 400 youths from the city of Cambridge, in the UK, the majority had zero or one offence, a handful had up to 3 convictions, while 2 individuals had over fourteen convictions over the same time period.) Since the actual ratio of offences to convictions in the UK is approximately 4:1, then the most active pair of villains would have probably committed over 56 crimes each, over this time period.

Blogging Space

A recent facet of social networks is the phenomenon of '*blogging*'. The term blog is an abridged version of **web log**, i.e. an online diary/commentary, created and maintained by one of more individuals. The term blog was originally coined by Peter Merholtz in 1999, on his blog Peterme.com. Initially dismissed by the established mass media as just another internet fad, the top blog sites are now the cutting edge of news and debate online, and attract mass audiences. The personal blog is the most common format where an individual maintains a detailed running commentary on their favourite topic or subject matter, often to a fanatical extent. The collective blog space online is commonly referred to as the 'Blogosphere'; a simply great expression of this flowering virtual space. Many sites have arisen that are now dedicated to cataloging and tracking the activity of blogs in this space; for example tailrank.com aims to index and make visible the best, or most popular, blogs available.

Once again there appears to be a power law distribution in the popularity, or number of links to a given blog page. The vast majorities of blogs are limited in scope and attract few viewers or web links to them. However, a very small number, out of the millions of blogs, become highly visited with millions of subscribers and a large number of links to them. (The most popular blog in 2006 was reported by the Technorati site, as that of an attractive Chinese actress, Xu Jinglei, with 50 million page views.) It is also not unexpected that such a free form mode of communication has become the object of censorship and restrictions in many Asian and developing states. Even so, the power of the medium to enable individual expression often overrides these constraints.

One brilliant recent work by John Kelly and Bruce Etling, used computational social network mapping in combination with human and automated content analysis to analyze the Iranian blogosphere. They constructed a network visualization of blogs related to politics and culture for Iran. In the resulting map the size of the dot represented the number of other blogs that link to it, i.e. a measure of its popularity. The position of each dot is a function of its links with its neighbors. The result of these simulated physical forces is that large groups of blogs cluster up into densely interlinked network neighborhoods. Blogs that share a lot of common neighbors will be close together in the map, even when they do not link directly to one another. As they clearly articulate:

"Our research indicates that the Persian blogosphere is indeed a large discussion space of approximately 60,000 routinely updated blogs featuring a rich and varied mix of bloggers. Social network analysis reveals the Iranian blogosphere to be dominated by four major network formations, or poles, with identifiable sub-clusters of bloggers within those poles. We label the poles as 1) Secular/Reformist, 2) Conservative/Religious, 3) Persian Poetry and Literature, and 4)Mixed Networks. The secular/reformist pole contains both expatriates and Iranians involved in a dialog about Iranian politics, among many other issues. The conservative/religious pole contains three distinct sub-clusters, two focused principally on religious issues and one on politics and

current affairs. Given the repressive political and media environment, and high profile arrests and harassment of bloggers, one might not expect to find much political contestation in the blogosphere.

However, we identified a subset of the secular/reformist pole focused intently on politics and current affairs and comprised mainly of bloggers living inside Iran, which is linked in contentious dialog with the conservative political sub-cluster. Surprisingly, a minority of bloggers in the secular/reformist pole appear to blog anonymously, even in the more politically-oriented part of it; instead, it is more common for bloggers in the religious/conservative pole to blog anonymously. Blocking of blogs by the government is less pervasive than we had assumed. Most of the blogosphere network is visible inside Iran, although the most frequently blocked blogs are clearly those in the secular/reformist pole. Given the repressive media environment in Iran today, blogs may represent the most open public communications platform for political discourse. The peer-to-peer architecture of the blogosphere is more resistant to capture or control by the state than the older, hub and spoke architecture of the mass media model."
(Kelly and Etling, 2008)

The methods they used to capture this image of the blogosphere are briefly summarized here, but a full ready of the paper is highly recommended.

"Using links captured from the Iranian blogosphere over a period of seven months, we map the structure of the network in two ways. First, we identify large scale groupings of densely linked blogs in the network. Second, clustering methods are used to discern patterns in the links from these blogs to all other Internet resources (not only blogs), defining attentive clusters of bloggers who link to similar things, thus sharing informational worlds. Several types of content analysis are used to help interpret the cultural and political meaning of the Iranian blogosphere's structure. We worked with a team of Persian speakers to read and code hundreds of blogs using two questionnaires. We analyzed the frequencies of words and phrases in the posts of Iranian bloggers. And we spent hours sitting with culturally knowledgeable Iranians, looking at dozens of blogs in key positions on the map, as well as dozens of the news sites, organizations, and other online resources these bloggers link to. The results, quantitative and qualitative, portray a diverse network of online discourse, in which one can see the richness of Iranian culture and the clear footprint of political contention."

(Kelly and Etling, 2008)

This intricate research process reveals some interesting points that relate strongly to the cohesion theme of the book. Firstly, via smart data-analysis techniques it is now possible to discover and make visible complex social clusters and sub-groups, within a society. More than that, it also enables a fine-grained study of the social and political interactions that bind a society together. This capability is nothing less than a revolution in our understanding of the ways in which societies evolve and function. Clearly, the bloggers world is a highly valuable channel for political expression in virtually every state. How it will evolve however remains an unanswered question. I suspect it has already reached a steady state in which a small, but ever changing core of high profile denizen bloggers exist in conjunction with a swarm of brief, yet passionate, blogging fireflies. One web site that provides some cool visualizations of the blogosphere is maintained at:

http://datamining.typepad.com/gallery/blog-map-gallery.html

One final quote from this work is a useful footnote:

"Perhaps the most remarkable thing about the larger network of bloggers is its sheer diversity. As in the American blogosphere, the cartoonishly simple portrayal of political attitudes and human characters found in mass media fade in the face of the complex variety of real human voices."

(Kelly and Etling, p.17.)

Facebook *et al*

The obvious arena in which electronic communications is facilitating new human to human interactions is the wave of social networking web sites. For example, according to a recent Nielsen Online report, Facebook is now generating a billion user minutes of interaction per month. We need to consider how such extraordinary growth has taken place and enabled such a powerful conduit for new social interactions. Once again considering the theme of the book, i.e. social cohesion, the question is, do such sites enhance or diminish social cohesion?

At one level Facebook and MySpace *et al* clearly create an additional information flow between people, and enable social connections to a far richer and more diverse pool than before. While such effects were already well advanced with the use of email and instant messaging, these were primarily single channel person to person links. The use of social network sites makes multi-cast and media rich social interactions, not just possible, but simple enough for children to use. Hence, Facebook for example has witnessed exponential growth in its first four years, since February 2004, and now boasts over 80 million users globally.

Let's return to the key question, will these sites increase or decrease social cohesion? Well the basic aim of any social networking site is to create an online community. In this respect they have clearly succeeded beyond most pundits expectations. So can we first understand what the factors that enabled such dynamic growth are? The first generation of sites, such as Classmates.com, offered only flat lists of friends. The second generation allowed true social network structures that followed the six degrees rule, e.g. LinkedIn.com. The third generation sites are now social media sites, and these enable richer multi-media and multi-way group interactions, e.g. Facebook, MySpace or Bebo. So using Gladwell's terminology, these sites are 'sticky'. People go where the content is, and especially where that content has a close affinity to their personal interests and pre-existing social connections. What we have therefore is a situation with positive feedback, as users add their personal content to a site and invite their friends, the value of the site increases to them and their contacts.

4.1 Rats, Students, and Net Addicts

Yet some psychologists are now raising the counter arguments against the benefits of social networking. The most obvious of these is the addictive nature of such sites. One self-confessed Facebook addict from Bristol is quoted as saying,

"I'm definitely addicted to Facebook. It takes over your life. I have the site set as a bookmark. Its really hard not to be tempted to login."

This effect is building on the well known, but poorly understood process of browsing and email addiction already present in society. A nice example from a student of psychology is cited below:

"Like lots of people who sit in front of a computer all day, I am addicted to email. This worries me for two reasons. The first is the sheer strength of my compulsion. I must hit the 'get mail' button at least a hundred times a day. Sometimes, if I don't have any new mail, I hit it again immediately, just to check. I interrupt my work to check my mail even when I know that I'm not going to find anything interesting and that I should just concentrate on what I

am supposed to be doing. When I come back to my office it's the first thing I do. If I'm prevented from checking my mail for more than a few hours I get a little jumpy and remain that way until I have. This is all rather sad, but the second reason I am worried by my email addiction is that I work in a psychology department and we're supposed to understand how these things work. Now email isn't a drug - it doesn't deliver a chemical into your bloodstream. Yet it is clearly addictive. I'm a normal rational person (which is to say I'm just normally maladjusted) and I know that I don't need to check my email as often as it do - certainly not immediately after checking it the first time for Goodness' sake! - but still I am compelled."

The same researcher has also deduced the correct answer as to why this addiction is so strong. It is due to a very well known psychology process: 'variable interval reinforcement'. This effect was originally investigated in studies of animal and human behaviour from the 1920's to the 1980's when 'Behavioural' psychology went out of fashion. Lead by the psychologist Burrhus Skinner, creator of the infamous 'Skinner box' a laboratory tool for conditioning behaviours, usually in rats or pigeons. The animals would be required to press a lever to receive a food pellet as a reward. The interesting discovery that he made was that if an animal was only reinforced, i.e. given the reward at random or irregular intervals it pressed the level more frequently than if it received consistent rewards. The following example from Skinner is interesting:

"I watch a hungry pigeon carefully. When he makes a slight clockwise turn, he's instantly rewarded for it. After he eats, he immediately tries it again. Then I wait for more of a turn and reinforce again. Within two or three minutes, I can get any pigeon to make a full circle. Next I reinforce only when he moves in the other direction. Then I wait until he does both, and reinforce him again and again until it becomes a kind of drill. Within ten to 15 minutes, the pigeon will be doing a perfect figure eight."

A more bizarre example of the application for such a process occurred during World War II, when Skinner proposed the idea of using pigeons in guided-missile control; three birds were conditioned to peck continuously for a few minutes at the image of a target on a screen. Then they were supposed to be placed in a harness in the nose of a missile, facing a screen on which the target would appear when the missile was in flight. By pecking at the image moving on the screen, the pigeons would send corrective signals that moved the missiles fins and kept it on target. The missile, called the Pelican (seriously), was never used in warfare. The genius Skinner apparently commented; *"our problem was no one would take us seriously."*

However, Skinner also had many critics, such as Noam Chomsky who published a scathing review of Skinner's Verbal Behaviour research. His main criticisms were that Skinners work lacked scientific rigor, by not adhering to a falsifiable hypothesis. It had limited value when extended to humans and most of all that such work was misused by totalitarian regimes, in conducting similar human experiments and programmes of social engineering.

Returning to the present day however, it is interesting how closely the interaction between people and computers matches the original Skinner conditioning work. Considering the social impact of the web and email it is amazing that so little human psychological studies have been performed on its impact on behaviour. Hopefully this will be corrected in the near future. Similar studies reinforce the conclusion that the net is addictive, such as work by Kimberly Young, an assistant professor of psychology at the University of Pittsburgh at Bradford, which has led to the American Psychological Association, labeling this new disorder, Pathological Internet Use (PIU). The following quote is a nice example:

"Checking email is a behaviour that has variable interval reinforcement. Sometimes, but not everytime, the behaviour produces a reward. Everyone loves to get an email from a friend, or some good news, or even an amusing web link. Sometimes checking your email will get you one of these rewards. And because you can never tell which time you check will produce the reward, checking all the time is reinforced, even if most of the time checking your email turns out to have been pointless. You still check because you never know when the reward will come.

I have just proved to myself how automatic my email checking behaviour has become. I am writing this in a hotel room which doesn't have internet access. When sorting through my email (you don't need a connection to delete email you've replied to, or are never going to reply to) I still hit the 'check mail' button at the rest points of the read-consider-delete cycle I am performing. My reflective self knows that there is no internet connection, so there is no way in hell I'm going to have new email - but that knowledge doesn't filter down to the part of me hitting the 'check email' button. The habit, engrained in my mind by operant conditioning, is isolated from conscious knowledge, and in part from deliberate control; it can start without me thinking about it or even me wanting it to."

Ok, let's return to the issues around social networking sites in particular, as these represent the most prominent example of addictive net behaviour. There are also a number of wider topical issues that result from the use of social network sites. The major single concern is that of user privacy. These concerns range from the processes in place to remove user's data when they delete their account. To the more serious end of the spectrum, where other individuals or groups use web-scraping techniques and shell scripts to harvest large quantities of users personal data. Even though many sites like Facebook make it possible for users to set stronger privacy settings, many fail to do so. Either through ignorance of the issues, or simply due to a lack of concern. One highlighted example hit media attention in Jan 2008, when Sociologists at the University of California, Los Angeles (UCLA), and Harvard University, admitted using such methods to gather large volumes of personal data. One of the lead researchers, Andreas Wimmer, professor of Sociology at UCLA, commented that:

"We're harvesting information from Facebook. We have all the information on an entire class of students. We are gathering that data and transforming it into a dataset that can be easily used for all kinds of analysis...It's a wealth of data on who relates to whom, and who becomes friends with whom, that is quite unprecedented. Compared to the usual survey data it's a huge leap forward in terms of the precision with which relationships are recorded."

From one perspective, this is a great resource and tool for social scientists, whose consequent research may be of value to wider society and policy makers. Certainly from the author's scientific viewpoint such data is immensely valuable. However, this stance alone is simply naïve and any social networking site needs to enforce minimum levels of privacy that protects user's data. The best option should be an opt-out policy where a user needs to manually and expressly reduce the level of protection they have on a site to allow wider sharing of their personal data. What is interesting however, is the simple fact that most users don't care about the information they post on a web site. This result in itself is a fascinating new element of human psychology and group behaviour.

So what might be the impact on social cohesion of these sites? Well looking again at the value of scientifically analyzing the personal data that can be gathered, it is clear that it can lead to some positive policy developments, for example:

"If you look at the entire picture of who is hanging out with whom - or what are the principles of group formation in this college, then you see that the most important thing is co-residence, who people have been thrown together with in the same dorm...It seems that since this 'opportunity' structure matters so much, what this college and a lot of others are doing, is mixing people from different backgrounds - racial, social-economic etc - in their dorms and their residences. It really helps to establish ties across these various divides."

(Prof. Wimmer, UCLA.)

Hence in this case a direct and measurable increase in cohesion may be achieved. One of Prof. Wimmers co-authors in related work, Prof. Christakis at Harvard is also using analysis of social networks to understand health dynamics, and behaviours, i.e. the process by which they form (*connection*) and the way they operate to influence behaviour (*contagion*), (Christakis and Fowler, 2009). His recent work in the New England Journal of Medicine examined the spread of smoking behaviour in social networks. This highlighted the result that people quit in droves. Hence, the decision to quit smoking was not made purely as an individual choice, but actually reflects choices made by entire groups of people connected to each other across their extended social network. His web site [http://christakis.med.harvard.edu/] offers a superb graphical animation showing this process, and is highly recommended for a visit.

How social networking will evolve in the immediate future is hotly debated, however, Facebook in particular may have some longer term commercial issues, i.e. the websites relatively low 0.02%-0.04% ad click-through rate. (In comparison the MySpace ad click-through rate is closer to 0.1%.). Either way this is likely just the beginning of many new facets of human interaction that the internet has already, and will yet enable. Finally, on a positive note, some less conservative organizations, such as the Greater Manchester Police, are using a Facebook application to help the community to report and be notified of crime in the area. The remainder of this chapter focuses on a quite different application in order to highlight some of the network issues discussed so far.

5. Network Centric Warfare: and other Follies

This section returns to the topic highlighted at the start of the chapter, i.e. the application of networks to military operations. There are several reasons for selecting this domain. Firstly it has been a dominant force directing the flow of human history; second it has utilized and driven the development of communication networks, as exampled by Arpanet. Third, in its current incarnation it is at the cutting edge of network theory and applications. In chapter three we consider the historical dimension of military communications and physical transport networks. Before we begin however, it is worth noting the human dimension of conflict, with reference to a story from my own family.

In early 1938 as the fault-lines in European politics were beginning to crack, my own grandfather took a pickaxe, strode out into the tarmac area behind his council house and started digging. The neighbours gathered round and asked what he was doing, but he said little. They all had quite a good laugh. After a couple of days, however, there was a crude bomb shelter in the back yard, made of corrugated iron sheets with layers of earth piled on top. The local council sent someone round, to order him to fill it in and repair the area; as the space was actually common ground between the rows of back-to-back terrace housing. The kind you see in old films of life in a grim northern British town. But my Grandfather's robust and direct response to the young man from the council, convinced him that better to leave well alone; as a pickaxe handle wrapped round your skull, tends to offend. Granddad was not an educated person, having worked in the Sheffield mining industry as a shift superintendent, but he had lived through the First World War, and could read the signs well enough. He knew without a doubt that Germany would wage war again, and that modern aircraft would likely bring an aerial bombardment of British cities. Returning to the topic, we first need a basic understanding of what Network Centric Warfare (NCW) is supposed to be, and then we can examine where it may miss the target, (pun intended.) This section will therefore outline the main aspects of NCW and its relation to networks; interspersed with a socio-political dialogue on its implications and failings. We will also consider how each of the network aspects reviewed in the chapter have impacted the historical evolution of military systems; i.e. network dynamics, resilience, efficiency, social behaviour and economics. One of the most insightful and experienced voices in the US defence arena, and someone who actually understands the issues at stake, is retired marine, Lt. General Paul

Van Riper. Van Riper now teaches at the US National Defence University, and in an interview in 2004 after the second Gulf war, said:

"I have no truck with those who talk about terms like transformation. It clearly indicates they don't know what they're doing. All it is is a slogan rather than getting to the hard problems. ... These ideas have never truly been vetted, and yet they're being sold to our headquarters, our services, as the way we want to fight in the future. This intellectual renaissance that I've referred to repeatedly that occurred after Vietnam has not been revived. Rather than trying to think our way through the problem, we're trying to buy our way. So we had to buy our way in terms of technology; we buy our way in terms of some of these ideas without the underpinnings of real bases that you can fight on. ... I see a very close parallel to what happened after the end of the Second World War. At the end of the Second World War, the focus was on atomic weapons, the technology. Today, the analogous idea is on information technology. We believe that's the cure-all for everything."

(Van Riper, 2004)

We will return to the Van Riper story later, as it is most illuminating, but first let's cover the basics. (For a detailed review of Van Ripers' role in US Network Operations, Gladwell's text Blink has a whole chapter devoted to the matter.)

Networks at War

"The consensus seemed to be that if really large numbers of men were sent to storm the mountain, then enough might survive the rocks to take the citadel. This is essentially the basis of all military thinking."

(Terry Pratchett, *Eric*)

So the goal of current US military planners is something known as Network Centric Warfare (NCW). The idea is that robotic planes (UAV) and ground vehicles with complex sensing, targeting, imaging, and communications capabilities will support teams of networked soldiers. Hence, NCW (also known as 'force transformation'), is intended to solve the problem of "asymmetric warfare" in the 21st century, where U.S. forces are not directly confronted by conventional massed armies, but rather need to destroy terrorist cells, or stabilize regions via peace-keeping operations. The UK and associated Western military forces have also adopted the same philosophy to varying degrees. In the UK it is known as Network Enabled Capability (NEC); also referred to as a poor mans NCW, as its goals are a vastly reduced subset of those envisaged by NCW. (A very useful web site with some free ebooks that detail current NCW thinking is: http://www.dodccrp.org/.)

One example of the process of linking the US and UK network strategies and systems, is a mini war-gaming exercise, held each year at Portsdown West, on the picturesque south coast of England. Called the Coalition Warrior Interoperability Demonstrator, (CWID for short as the military love acronyms more than any other human collective), it is a showcase event in which the prime defence contractors, and military units attempt to string their respective systems and networks into a single coherent whole. The grand vision, being a unified and omnipotent view of the battlespace; at any given time. A small army of technicians and uniformed geeks spend endless months, huddled in an array of rain and wind-swept tents, attempting to make this vision a reality. The participants are driven on and sustained by a large volume of caffeine, pro-plus, and profuse swearing. During the actual demonstrations, various generals, and defence VIPs turn up and peruse the technologies on offer; a bit like PC World for the army. The only difference is that this kit costs several order of magnitude more bucks than your home laptop; and the only style option is camouflage green.

Whichever technology is used however, it all rests on the premise that a smaller lightly armored force can have the same effect as a more heavily armored group, if it is networked into a *cohesive* unit. However, this all requires vast amounts of complex software and computing hardware to work perfectly in a hostile environment. (Ideally, you should also only confront an enemy lacking the same level of technological sophistication. Some pygmy tribes of the Upper Congo basin would be ideal for this requirement). A number of texts have highlighted the dangers inherent in the NCW approach, most notably by a distinguished US strategist Alfred Kaufman. The fundamental error that has recurred through modern military history is an over reliance on technological solutions at the expense of the human element. Recent experiences in the second Gulf conflict have reinforced this point. For example, US forces were busy welding even more armour onto their heavy-armour vehicles, to increase protection against simple rocket propelled grenades. Even though the prevailing US defence policy was to migrate to lighter armoured vehicles, using speed and agility to survive! The following quote from the leading author of all military thinkers, von Clausewitz, should be recalled by those engaged in the contemplation of conflict:

"We come now to the region dominated by the powers of intellect. War is the realm of uncertainty . . . . War is the realm of chance. . . . Two qualities are indispensable: first, an intellect that, even in the darkest hour, retains some glimmerings of the inner light which leads to truth; and second, the courage to follow this faint light wherever it may lead. The first of these qualities is described by the French term, coup d'oeil; the second is determination."

Returning to the Van Riper story, in his 2004 interview, Van Riper recalls how after the Vietnam disaster, (at least from a US not Vietnamese perspective), many US military officers returned to the basics of strategy and dusted off the works of von Clausewitz and Sun Tzu. And the essence of all such military theory is this: for every meticulously crafted plan you design, the enemy always has a craftier and dirtier one. Above all, the greatest enemy in conflict is complexity, either in your procedures, strategy, or technologies. In contrast, the most lethal and widespread weapon of the past century has been the Kalashnikov assault rifle; itself an object lesson in simplicity.

Smart Corporals and Dumb Generals

To make NCW work the only way is to make the customer king. And the customer is the poor idiot sat on the front line who is facing imminent annihilation if the network fails. One approach then is to place a greater degree of trust in the NCOs and lower echelon officers, and make the network responsive to their requirements. This is sometimes referred to as the "Strategic Corporal" concept, as it is envisaged that an NCO empowered by access to advanced network technology and modern weapon systems could decisively influence the outcome of a major conflict by their local actions. Of course generals hate this concept and complain that they will lose strategic vision if the lower ranks are empowered. Which is precisely why they tend to be the major road block to the full realization of NCW. It is exactly the same principle that made the internet itself truly useful, i.e. the dumb network concept, where content and effect reside on the edges of the network; with the end users. (It is also why concepts such as thin clients, in the civil ICT domain, never realized their promise, as they fundamentally disempowered the end user.) A computer becomes a useful artifact only when the user takes personal control of it, and in the language of Richard Dawkins, it becomes '*an extended phenotype*'.

Technology Matrix

The bleeding edge of defence technology, is the current focus on enabling Autonomous networks and systems. The media-grabbing side of this is battlefield robots and drones that are increasingly armed and used to engage the enemy, (as in Afghanistan with heavily armed Predator UAVs), or that operate as reconnaissance units. While current UAVs and ground robots are normally remote controlled, the vision is for them to have limited autonomy in the not too distant future.

Ok, so what are some of the problems in such a reliance on ICT and networks for defence strategy? Well one perennial problem is that of Cyber Security, i.e. how to secure such networks against your opponent, or hackers. When the stakes are high, even developing nations can put together a powerful cyber attack capability. Even when facing a foe such as the Taliban with minimal cyber resources, your mighty NCW is at risk when shop keepers are selling USB memory sticks containing classified details of your forces, outside the command HQ for $20 a pop; (as was the case in Kabul in 2007.) If your network security does fail, then the network and its assets become a giant vulnerability at best, and at worst a weapon to be used against you. During the Cold-War life was so much simpler, as tight control could be maintained over the flow of information and vast resources existed in defence budgets to secure all electronic assets, primitive though they were.

We return now to the topic of network topology and its impact on the behaviour of large-scale complex networks. The US and UK have invested significant resources in studies to understand how complex ICT networks behave and the effect of different topologies on this behaviour. One example is work by the leading authors in this field, who suggest, *"The richest and most resilient network structure...appears to be a hybrid that looks at the global level like a scale-free network, but at the intermediate level is composed on small-world networks, and at the local level fully connected social networks."* (Alberts and Hayes, 2006, p. 107)

Group Cohesion

This section will drop the technology and look at the human dimension of warfare in general, as it is illuminating to the major theme of the book, i.e. social cohesion, and specifically the sub-theme of trust. The analysts, soldiers and junior officers know exactly what the technology can do for them, as they are the PlayStation and mobile phone generation. The major battle being fought is therefore between those truly familiar with the technology and those who place contracts with the defence corporations. There is more profit in selling a new custom battlespace command network than in enabling a secure text channel to soldiers standard mobile phones; or allowing intelligence analysts to use open-source web services and blogs. The secret of mission success however, is social and technical cohesion, not raw technology. The point about the Blitzkrieg and the success of the Battle of Britain radar system was not the technology or the network, rather the resulting social and collective cohesion that resulted from the integration of man and technology. This is a subtle point to communicate. It is about the emergence of a new higher level of system organization. This is the real power of networks. Of course this concept has been extensively covered within the discipline of Cybernetics in the 50's and 60's and Complexity theory in the 90's. However, it is extremely difficult to quantify at what point a complex system undergoes a transition and achieves a degree of cohesion that empowers it to achieve qualitatively new behaviours. This is precisely the effect sought by US and other military commanders. Unfortunately it is rather tricky to specify in a spreadsheet or Gantt chart.

A large body of work does exists in military literature extolling the power of group cohesion. In this context cohesion has been defined as: *"...the bonding together of members of an organization/unit in such a way as to sustain their will and commitment to each other, their unit, and the mission."* http://www.au.af.mil/au/awc/awcgate/ndu/cohesion/ch01.pdf. This is the élan-vital that is desired by the leaders of all organizations, i.e. a pervasive sense of morale that energizes human beings. Such a cohesive process is difficult to engineer and even harder to enforce. It has to emerge. What can be done is to establish positive conditions to encourage its growth.

"...the North Vietnamese Army endured the most concentrated firepower ever directed against an army for seven continuous years. When Van Tien Dung spoke of "moral superiority" within the ranks of the North Vietnamese Army, he was referring to what many analysts consider the creation of one of the most cohesive armies ever fielded. The attention paid within that army to organization, leadership, care of the soldier, and development of military cohesion and psychological control within the smallest units has not been equaled by other modern armies. The North Vietnamese Army was able to endure some of the greatest stress of combat and hardship because of its

extensive development of the human element." "The failure to consider the human element in war adequately and an overemphasis on weapon capabilities, numbers of troops, and other concrete factors are caused by the difficulty in quantifying the human element, whereas the more tangible factors are easily counted, totaled, and compared..."

(Henderson, 1985)

One of the key ingredients to achieve morale is Trust, (the capitalization is intentional), which will be covered in some detail in chapter three. In brief Trust is the dynamic glue that binds a complex social or organizational network together. It is the corner stone of group morale and efficient agent interactions. If you are managing any organization, commercial team or military force, the first step must be to create policies and processes that build and reinforce Trust. Everything else follows.

"The North Vietnamese soldier generally had great confidence in his immediate leaders. He trusted them, respected their abilities, and generally believed that under their direction he and his fellow soldiers could successfully meet the situations and environment encountered by their unit. Leadership in the North Vietnamese Army emphasized personal and continuing face-to-face contacts between leader and soldier. This relationship was the primary one in both the soldier and the leader's life, taking precedence over all others, and it was expected by each to continue to be such so long as both remained in the Army."

Iraq and the Middle East

We now come to the current quagmire that is the West's involvement in Iraq and Afghanistan. Firstly, oceans of words have been disseminated that address why the current conflict arose and the post 9/11 debate rages on. Returning to the Paul Van Riper story, his major claim to fame was as commander of the Red team in the biggest war game ever mounted. This was called Millenium Challenge '02. Run in the summer of 2002 it cost over $250 million and was designed to test the effectiveness of the US military machine against a rogue dictator in a non-specific Gulf state. (It is politically incorrect in such games to actually name a state, as it may cause offence!) Lt General Riper was given the task of commanding the Red team, i.e. the military forces of the rogue state. To cut a long story short Van Riper thought carefully about the situation, and made the following logical move. Since his Red team forces were no direct match for the combined air, land and seas firepower of the entire USA, his only option was to launch a devastating pre-emptive strike using suicide speed boats and primitive, but deadly Chinese cruise missiles. In the ensuing simulated war games, his attack took the Blue team completely by surprise, and resulted in sixteen key US Navy battleships being struck or heavily damaged. Thus ending the game in a bizarre win for the rogue state. Of course, this was not the answer the Pentagon had in mind, and on the eve of the actual Iraq invasion not something they wished to be discussed. Hence the game was re-run and all of the surprise tactics of Van Riper were disabled, rendering his forces powerless. Not surprisingly, the second outcome was an overwhelming victory for the good guys. Thus justifying the future operation, as it was about to unfold in the Gulf, in March 2003.

It is fortunate for the US and its allies indeed, that Saddam and his team were not as inventive as Van Riper. Had the Iraqis deployed such tactics and only inflicted a fraction of the damage Van Riper achieved, it would have changed the course of the war. If nothing else, it would have significantly boosted the morale of the political groups and states in the region who are so vehemently opposed to the US. The failure of the Iraqi leadership and military we may attribute to the severe lack of cohesion and trust that existed between all strata of that political/cultural system. This cultural failure was the greatest ally of the Western forces, not their technologically superior weapons.

"Including culture in strategic assessments has a poor legacy, for it has often been spun from an ugly brew of ignorance, wishful thinking, and mythology. Thus, the U.S. Army in the 1930s evaluated the Japanese national character as lacking originality and drew the unwarranted conclusion that that country would be permanently disadvantaged in technology. Hitler dismissed the United States as a mongrel society and consequently underestimated the impact of America's entry into the war. American strategists assumed that the pain threshold of the North Vietnamese approximated our own and that the air bombardment of the North would bring it to its knees. Three days of aerial attacks were thought to be all the Serbs could withstand; in fact, seventy-eight days were needed...as the military histories of the Ottoman and Roman empires illustrate. In both cases it was training, discipline, esprit, and élan which made the difference, not the individual soldiers' origin. The highly disciplined and effective Roman legions, for example, recruited from throughout the Roman Empire,."

(De Atkine, 2002)

Basically, without the cohesion supplied by empowered NCOs, units tend to disintegrate in the stress of combat. One final example of over reliance on smart weapons comes from the conflict against Serbia. During the massed missile strikes on Belgrade and its air defense radar positions in the spring of 1999, the Serbs realized that the missiles would lock onto any wireless emitter in the correct frequency range. It just so happens that any household microwave oven is a powerful emitter of radio energy in the same frequency band. So the Serbs switched hundreds of domestic microwaves on near targeted facilities, with the doors wedged open, or just ripped off, and the safety micro-switch disabled to allow the oven to still work. It is almost impossible to get an accurate estimate of how effective this tactic was, as the details are still classified, but Google around a bit and you get the impression that it worked quite well. The UK forces should have learnt better by now, since they invented similar ludicrously simple counter measures in the Second World War, when they dropped aluminum strips (chaff) from bombers to fool German radar.

This section utilized the example of military networks and strategy, as it encompasses a broad spectrum of technological and social network effects, and the influence of cohesion on their interplay. It is also illustrative in terms of the human costs that result from a failure to see the operation of cohesive forces within the networks of interest. It is to be hoped that as the 21st century unfolds, humanity will finally learn the value of peaceful cooperation. The prospects for our mutual survival do not bode well if we fail to learn.

Summary

The recent explosion of interest in network dynamics has provided a useful set of analytical tools to apply to complex systems. It also provides an abstract yet fundamental level of description, which was previously missing. Some aspects of the field, for example small-world networks, are also quite intuitive and hence easy to communicate to a wider audience. Similarly the utility they offer to this text is to help focus our understanding of how complex social, biological, technological and commercial structures bind together. In particular, a deeper understanding of the delicate interrelation between CAS and networks is vital to the theme of cohesion. The topic will occur repeatedly throughout the remainder of the book, due to its ubiquitous underpinning of the topics we will address. The key idea was presented earlier, where we considered the factors they make a network resilient. It is almost oxymoronic to state, but we are clearly interested in those networks that are persistent over some measurable time-scale. The spontaneous emergence of particular network patterns, such as the three-layer design, can teach us a great deal about how networks operate and sustain themselves.

In this chapter we also briefly reviewed the impact of cohesion on military networks and processes as one applied example. It illustrated how social networks and group cohesion have greatly impacted the efficiency of armies throughout history. And especially since the advent of modern communication networks, beginning with the telegraph in the 19th century. Although in most successful cases the technology played a secondary role to the skills and social processes operating within the military units.

At present the American defence system is probably the most complex engineered set of networks after the Internet itself. The NCW vision is of interest as it attempts to consider the whole panoply of the social, cultural, technological, and communication networks within its scope. The US and UK are also investing in defence-based research to understand the fundamental properties of CAS. It remains to be seen whether the western military powers will realize the digital nirvana they currently envisage, in which evil-doers are simply erased by a software command, flashing over their command and control networks. History may very well prove otherwise.

It is pertinent to remember that communication networks for civil or military use, are in no sense a new invention: Herodotus wrote, *"There is nothing in the world that travels faster than these Persian couriers....Neither snow nor rain nor heat nor darkness of night prevents them from accomplishing the task proposed to them with the very utmost speed"*

Even this early example was a complex amalgam of pre-existing roads fused together, illustrating how networks undergo dynamic growth and adaptation. It is also an illustration of the moral spectrum of applications we can find for network structures. The Royal Road carried both commercial traffic, and permitted the rapid deployment of the armies of Persia. (A fact that my Iranian friends constantly remind me was apparently a significant contribution to world civilization!)

Of course no single scientific tool can provide all of the answers. The network concepts presented in this chapter simply provide a template by which we understand some of the processes in cohesive systems. However, far more questions remain unanswered, or even stated, as in any branch of science. We do not understand the dynamic behaviour of CAS on networks, or processes of network growth and decay, or what really separates brittle from resilient networks. In many real-world cases, as we will visit in subsequent chapters, we can't even define where the network begins or ends. For example, as is the case for ecological systems and food webs. We have just started down a very long road, but one that will be of critical importance in this century. Chapter three will introduce the realm of social systems and raise some questions as to how and when they exhibit cohesive phenomena.

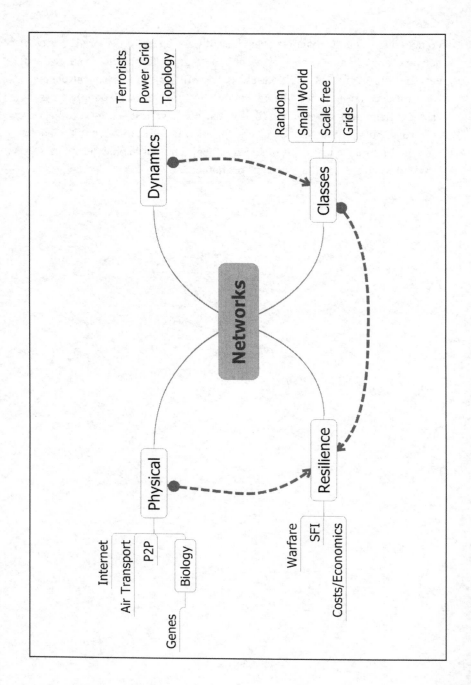

Mind map for chapter two.

Chapter 3

Cohesion: Societies and Collectives

"Clothes make the man. Naked people have little or no influence on society."
(Mark Twain)

1. Observations in Geneva

The ingenuity of Homo sapiens is nowhere more apparent than strolling along the Rue de la Servette in Geneva. Every other shop window is festooned with watches of almost limitless design, functionality and price. Precision mechanisms and quartz-tuned circuits reflect an evolutionary and artistic development, which spans centuries of human creativity. Likewise, the ubiquitous Swiss army knife is the perfect symbol of our tool creating skills. This piece is currently being compiled while sitting on the shores of Lake Geneva, observing the sun reflect from Mont Blanc and the waters of the Lake itself. Most interesting is the famous water spout. A 200 hundred feet high jet of water, which is blown from its tip by the prevailing wind into a sail-like form; thus resembling a bizarre ethereal sailing yacht crossing the lake. Its designers were probably unaware that it would possess this emergent quality of acting as a wind vane! But then the whole city hums with a certain vital quality and engineered precision; not unlike that of its many expensive timepieces.

A water skier is just now passing before me, up and down the lake, practicing intricate maneuvers and flying leaps by bouncing off the wake of the towing craft. (Unfortunately not always with success, but the show is admirable never the less, and is certainly beyond the authors skills in that art). The other aspect of this city of course is its current and historical association with the League of Nations and the UN. The topic of macro-scale human organizations leads us into the theme of this chapter, which will briefly analyse some examples of cohesive societies across the history of human civilization, and then attempt to understand the present state of cohesion within contemporary social organizations. Ideally with the goal of predicting what future forms human collectives will take. Some interesting questions are thus:

- What are the dominant forces that shape and sustain a society?
- What determines the lifespan of a society?
- Can we model the dynamics that shape social structures?

For example, one topic of interest is the perpetual tension between centralized and decentralized social architectures. It now appears that this aspect of social design reflects the average communication distance across networked systems; (see the earlier discussion on networks in chapter 2.) Hence, as relative communication distance shrinks the scale of potential organizational and human interaction increases. Another topic we will consider is how agents seek to imitate and conform to the perceived norms of their social collective. These norms also evolve over time leading to new social dynamics. The power of such social imitation is immense in all primate collectives. Most of all, in the human case, where the pressure to conform to social norms and follow your peers is immense. Conformity is clearly a factor in the reinforcement of social cohesion.

It is a common belief that the global revolution in communications is presently weaving a social web, which is integrating and binding together the incoherent cultures of humanity. We will hopefully discover the degree to which this thought is true, via the material presented in this chapter. First of all however, we will review some historical patterns of social organization and consider the key forces acting on their formation and dissolution. The sub-text for this is to understand the role and importance of trust and consultation as processes acting on social cohesion. (The one line summary of the chapter, and indeed the book, is that trust and consultation are vital to cohesive social development.)

1.1 Lifetimes of Civilizations

If we compare the functional status, (via some set of suitable metrics, e.g. population, frequency of commercial interaction, trade networks etc.), of the major world civilizations, we find recurrent patterns of development. Initially small, but highly cohesive group form, often as a result of external pressure, which then begin to expand and incorporate the surrounding social groups/cultures. This process continues until a highly organized and large-scale social hierarchy is established, with a fully developed cultural milieu. This newly emerged civilization operates as a cohesive entity for some period of time with a healthy flow of resources and labour to sustain it. Traditionally this was as a result of forceful acquisition and various forms of slavery, until the machine age arrived. Of course it is frequently argued that nothing has really changed, and globalization simply exploits the labour remotely in its native environment, rather than relocating it within an empire.

At some point, a shift occurs in the pattern of development, exactly how and why we will consider in the following sections. The result however is a transitional shift in the internal constituents of the society. The prime consequence of which is a loss of the core cohesion of the expanded group. Whether it leads to political factions or social unrest is not the issue. What matters from the systems perspective, is simply that the society can no longer maintain a sufficient balance between cohesive and disruptive forces. Once the process reaches a certain point a phase transition occurs across all of its members, leading to a rapid loss of coherence. The consequences we call revolutions. Endless socio-political debate has revolved around example of such events, but the conclusion of the models we will discuss later, is that these are manifestations of natural physical laws, reflected within all complex, multi-agent structures. Let's examine the detail of the processes underlying these transition events. (A very useful introduction to the use of physics in the modelling of social systems and economics, is the work by the science writer Philip Ball, *Critical Mass, How One Thing Leads to Another*, (Ball, 2004.) Ball provides a readable overview of the history of social modelling and how complex systems can be applied to the field.)

Exogenous Shocks and Endogenous Revolutions

This is an important component of the text and a challenging one, since it runs counter to some deeply held human beliefs. It is the norm for people to seek and expect any significant changes to the state of a system to be the result of some specific causal action or event, i.e. an exogenous shock to the system. It arises in many of the expectation models developed in Psychology, one example of which is the 'fundamental attribution error', (where observers associate the most local agents to an event as being most likely to have originated it.) Such simple heuristics work well and are an efficient method for making sense of the world in real-time. However, on a larger social or historical scale they fail badly as a policy guiding mechanism. (A classic example is the market analysis that occurs whenever a major market disruption takes place, e.g. Black Wednesday in October 1987, or the recent credit crisis still shaking the worlds markets. Experts and media pundits seek endlessly for the logical single cause of the problem, only to find themselves chasing recursive arguments around inflation, poor risk assessment, greed, deregulation and the host of quoted factors. In truth the global market is a complex adaptive system, and such systems inherently manifest large-scale shock events, (Beinhocker 2007.)

The reality of CAS is that major transitions are often the product of purely endogenous processes. One example is some recent work on the operation of corruption processes within societies, (Hammond, 2007). In Hammond's simulation he demonstrated how the degree of corruption in a society could spontaneously flip from an endemic state of wide-spread corruption to a global state of cooperation, purely through internal micro-scale random processes that lead to macro scale cascades of change. In addition this work highlighted an unexpected result, i.e. that agent diversity helped to eliminate corruption, by reducing the ability of agents to collude. This concept, of spontaneous internal reorganization, is central to the discussion around how and why stable societies break down. Our innate social tendency is to expect an external set of causes to have caused a shock, or disruption to the group. The truth is societies, as CAS, have an intrinsic tendency to disintegrate after a finite time period. Determining precisely how long a specific culture will endure however, is a rather difficult task. The aim of the text is to examine whether there are identifiable parameters that regulate a societies functioning, which can then be used to determine its state of health in a cohesive sense; and hence expected longevity. (Don't expect an answer, it's more of an aspiration.)

This issue has particular resonance in many western states as we enter the cloudy waters of the 21st century. In both Europe and the US there is a constant dialogue on the nature of multiculturalism and the extent to which existing cultures can absorb high levels of immigration. One example is a report commissioned by the UK MoD doctrine centre, (DCDC) and authored by Admiral Chris Parry. In this report there is speculation that modern-day Britain can be compared to the Roman Empire as it was overwhelmed by the Goths.

"Super-Diversity. Countries which encourage immigration as a means to address labour and skill shortages, involving a mixture of temporary visitors and long-term settlers, will increasingly experience 'super-diversity', which

may present challenges and threats to social cohesion and economic stability in host countries. In addition, the risk of a continuing 'brain drain' is likely to remain a challenge for some developing countries throughout this period, although evidence suggests that talented individuals will usually return to politically stable and economically successful countries of origin. Failure to manage this migration will impose significant resource burdens in destination and transit countries."

(Parry, 2007)

This report reflects the deep seated fears in these states that immigration is a cultural threat and that political debate is stifled by fears of racist taints. However, as we will see later, from computer simulations of agent societies, cultural diversity can have a range of positive side effects. Well let's move on to consider how history has dealt with this process, and see that such fears are nothing new. The question we are trying to address remains, can we abstract the key features of the civilizations that endured for long periods of time. Specifically, what socio-political processes, or behavioural practices enabled these groups to endure. What made them cohesive in the face of constant disruption?

Ancient Egypt

At the beginning of James Burkes seminal video history of western civilization 'Connections', (Burke, 1978), he launches his study with a jump from the social breakdown in New York during a power failure in 1977, to the story of the great Nile civilization in Ancient Egypt. His aim was to highlight how one defining point in the origin of human civilization was the technological development of the plough, which enabled reliable food surpluses to be created for the first time. A simple lashing together of two pieces of wood behind some oxen is not what we now associate with the term technology, yet it was a total revolution in its impact. Surpluses required storage, and hence accounting, and markets, and social enforcement, and other social roles in a never ending cycle. Indeed, all the trappings of a complex society. In particular, it required astronomy and accurate calendars to predict the rising of the Nile each year for irrigation.

Burkes message, delivered over his trademark 1970's large rimmed glasses, was to illustrate graphically how the failure of the underpinning technology in any civilization is catastrophic to its social cohesion, and is in proportion to the complexity of the technology. (I highly recommend a viewing of the whole Connections series, as it is an eye-opening journey across the whole panorama of human technological development and the human stories that weaves it all together. A fine example of where we have arrived at is the modern wrist watch, one of which presently sits on my desk. Looking at it now invokes almost awe at the centuries of engineering knowledge that had to be slowly and painstakingly accumulated, before such a machine could be created. From the fine metal working, intricately machined gears, and accurate time measurement, to the micro electronics and solar cells it contains.) Actually watches are a great example of human beings penchant for displaying high value tags to attract social status. Being a humble engineer I selected the best technical timepiece at a reasonable cost I could find, i.e. a Citizen Skyhawk. Also as an engineer I have no social status anyway, so nothing was lost!

Now let's return to the story of this section, i.e. the history of Egypt, its major technologies, and social development. Interestingly as one of the earliest large-scale civilizations it also possessed one of the longest life spans of any society to date. Beginning in circa 3000 B.C. with the reign of King Narmer, the power of the pharaohs endured until Egypt came under Roman rule in the Graeco-Roman Period (332 B.C. - A.D. 395), (Grimal, 1998.) The pharaonic period finally ended with the death of the last Cleopatra during the thirty-second dynasty. When the Roman Empire split around A.D. 395, Egypt came under the control of the Byzantium until the Arab conquest in A.D. 641. Most importantly however, the Egyptians possessed complex writing in the form of Hieroglyphics on clay tablets and papyrus. Social contracts could therefore be indelibly and accurately recorded which enabled complex economic transactions and real market dynamics. (A key point that is highlighted in James Burkes video series.) The text on code breaking by Simon Singh, (Singh, 1999), also contains an engaging account of the French polymath Champollion, and his fanatical quest to decipher the hieroglyphs. It is interesting that western cultural bias hindered the decipherment process by many years, as western scholars insisted the hieroglyphs were only semagrams, i.e. a form of primitive picture writing. Champollion made the intellectual and cultural leap necessary to see them as a fully evolved and complex phonetic language.

Interestingly, within Egyptian society women had a relatively high status. For example they could own property, slaves, and even run a business or engage in trade. They were excluded however from most educational processes and official offices, but otherwise were clearly prominent in many social roles (Silverman, 1997.) Of course they also acted as rulers in some cases, the most famous being Cleopatra at the end of the empires reign.

From a technology perspective the Egyptians also lacked easy access to iron ore and remained mostly dependent on bronze metal working for weapons, and crude copper alloys for tools. This proved to be rather damaging in their military contacts with other Mediterranean societies that did possess iron swords. Egyptian foot soldiers also needed a good sharp sword as they were paid in proportion to the number of severed right hands they captured from the enemy, and then presented for payment! (And we think carrying coins is inconvenient as a credit mechanism!) Stone work was also a very laborious process using hard stone pounding tools, flints and wooden wedges to split stone blocks, or in quarrying.

In terms of its ultimate collapse it is historically the case that an external aggressive force invaded the Nile region. From the sixth to fifth centuries BC Egypt developed its naval power and greatly increased its diplomatic and commercial links with the Greek states and wider Mediterranean cultures. Unfortunately, this era also witnessed the aggressive expansion of the Persian Empire, which rapidly assimilated the bulk of Egyptian territory. Many years of internal divisions and rebellions to restore Egyptian rule ensued. In addition at its peak of Empire, a permanent army of forty thousand troops had to be sustained at great economic cost. Also, in the Late Period Greek mercenaries were part of the military force, but had to be paid in gold, when little was left in Egypt's own mines. (This does rather make me think of the costly Iraq war by the USA. More on that later.)

Ultimately however, Alexander the Great showed up, and it was game over. From that point on the coastal city of Alexandria became the capital and the cultural influence of Greek immigrants became dominant, (Silverman, 1997.) In fact the empire had begun to fragment many centuries before, as early as the 12th century BC, successive revolts and military action by its former colonies had undermined the Empires power and unity. A quote that could describe the present age in many states, is iterated by Silverman:

"...the last Ramesside pharaohs (era) was bedeviled by strikes, inflation and rampant criminality at all levels of society." (p.36)

So it appears that the Empire had basically overstretched itself, at a time when the Hellenistic and Persian cultures were rapidly developing in military and technical capacity. Of course as ever in history, the primary cause of Egypts downfall is a seriously debated topic; some would assert it was Egypt's absorption into the Roman Empire in 30 BC. From a cultural perspective however, the collapse of the ancient hieroglyphic script around AD 400 really closed the book, as it were, on ancient Egypt. A useful online introduction to the topic is also available on the BBC history site.

Rome

It is a testament to the scope and range of the Roman Empire that when western scholars think of past civilizations, Rome is the first word that springs to mind. The Coliseum, the roads, central heating, the viaducts, and sheer engineering brilliance are simply stunning. They didn't just invent concrete, but invented graduated ballast from dense to light within single large structures to balance the load. (The classic example of such a technique is displayed in the amazing Pantheon in Rome, standing 142 feet high, from floor to ceiling. The largest surviving ancient concrete domed structure in the world.) The list of technological inventions they devised is endless. Ok, so yes, there was a certain degree of violence expressed within Roman culture, and the Circus games would probably fail modern health and safety standards! In fact the lasciviousness and gore of Rome have, in general, been greatly amplified by later historians. Sex and violence are always what make a good story. Indeed, the power of the empire was its ability to not just subjugate at sword point, but also to assimilate foreign cultures. A Roman slave could aspire to become a free Roman citizen, if officially freed by the owner; or even buy their freedom. (They could also engage in independent economic activity and save capital.) In many ways the social status was more of an economic debt-bondage relationship, than one of being pure property, or purely racial in origin. In this respect, they had far more rights than the African slaves of the modern European and North American eras. The text by McGeough, *The Romans*, (McGeough, 2004), offers a very useful synopsis of Roman life, and forms the main reference for this section.

Most of the large-scale empires that have arisen have demonstrated this ability to integrate, at some level, the cultures they defeated militarily. (Before you reach for your email client I am in no way condoning Imperial behaviour, we will return to the topic later anyway, so at least get all the ammunition you need first.)

Returning to the question we are addressing, what we would really like, is to know what factors held the empire together for so many centuries? The rise and fall of Rome is probably the most discussed epochal event in western history. Specifically what were the root causes of the collapse of this vast empire. In particular were the causes external or internal?

"Niccolò Machiavelli in The Discourses was the first modern political theorist to review the history and practices of the Romans in any depth. While his other, more forward-looking work, The Prince, is better known, it is difficult to understand the advice it gives without noting the contrasting advice he gives to magistrates via his careful quotations of the Roman patriarchs and chroniclers... Machiavelli focused on the consistency and clear oratory of the magistrates, and argued that with no clear and consistent rationale for rule, it was inordinately difficult to maintain it. He was the first to note explicitly the necessity for a well-educated bourgeois or middle class that would carry forward the instructional capital of the civilization, independent of the rulers and aristocracy, and hold it to account by criticism and shame, to prevent the worst abuses of power, which in turn would cause rulers to lose support - this in turn causing civil strife and revolutions."

http://en.wikipedia.org/wiki/Rise_of_Rome

This is a simplistic, yet useful political analysis of the rise of Rome, as it points to the existence of a social middle class as a key social binding factor, rather than focusing on military prowess or leadership. In order for such a class to form however, requires a breadth and depth of socio-economic development that was simply lacking in earlier cultures. In contrast Egyptian culture may be compared to an ant colony with an imperial core, specialized sub-castes (priests, soldiers, craftsmen), and workers drones with no status. In some sense this made it more stable as there was far less room for civil dispute. While breakaway pharaohs occurred, nevertheless Egypt lasted 3000 years, compared to the 500 years of Roman history.

Interestingly in both the case of Egypt and Rome, women had a public and active role in society. In contrast, within the Hellenic civilization, women in general were confined to the domestic sphere. Indeed, it appears to be the case that the role of women in binding society together has always been ignored in historical analysis.

If we now look at the Roman military what is of interest is the discipline and professional nature of the Roman legions. They could be said to be the first modern army, with a career structure, complex echelons, rigid discipline and modular organization within legions. The Roman turtle is one example of their technical innovation; i.e. the use of rectilinear interlocking shields and tight group organization. The first tank! The key innovation however, was organizational. After a protracted siege in 396 BC, the process of paying soldiers a salary was introduced, i.e. a standing army was created. In comparison under the prior drafting process, civilians served for lengths of time, in exchange for land ownership rights. Secondly, the Legions themselves started to become distinct cultural units with names, associated symbols and recognition in society. Our Hollywood impression of Roman Legions accurately reflects the high value Roman society placed on the virtues of order and discipline.

The question that has been asked a thousand times is, given such technical prowess and complex social development, how could Rome fall? Firstly, we are not trying to actually answer the question of why the Roman Empire fell, there are sufficient texts on the subject that placed end to end you could encompass the Coliseum: (See Heather, 2006, for a modern version.) In the context of this text we are simply seeking a few systemic signatures that reflect why it did fall, and to understand whether they are universal or specific. One measurable indicator is the level of tax income Rome received. As the external opposition, such as by the Goths and Vandals eroded the lands available to the empire, the financial basis of the western domains collapsed, so in turn undermining the ability to support a standing professional army in those regions. This is a nice example of the many interlinked feedback mechanisms that typically govern the functioning of all CAS.

"The second major problem was the loss of Africa to the Vandals, which reduced the financial basis of the western empire. Without money to pay for troops, the military capacity of the west decreased, though the eastern empire remained intact. Loss of territory and financial crises, not a failure in military effectiveness, led to the collapse of the Roman West."

(Elton, 1996)

McGeough offers a synopsis of the major theories surrounding the fall of Rome (p.290-297.) These include the external pressures from barbarian tribes, to the internal rise of Christianity and its influence on the cultural life of Rome. Some argue that ecological degradation of the available arable land due to deforestation and soil loss was a factor. There is evidence for this and some evidence of climatic changes impacting food production, but large variations in food supply were common throughout the Roman period. More useful are the arguments that Roman culture simply migrated into the emerging Byzantine Empire, where its law, language, literature and architecture endured for many more centuries. In effect the Empire was geographically displaced to the Eastern region. Speaking of the East, let's keep going until we reach Asia.

China - the Middle Kingdom

The Chinese empire stretches back millennia, but may be dated from circa 1500 BC. I have a strong personal interest in this country, as I briefly worked there in the early 1990's teaching English in the southern Anhui province. A very poor provincial region, with damn cold winters. China has rapidly emerged as the new super power that is dominating the Asian region, and now casts a sphere of economic influence across the globe. Of course the perennial fear among strategists in the west is the concomitant increase in China's military capability that will ensue. There is certainly a cold cyber-war already in progress between China and most western states. Each side is constantly testing the cyber defences of the other. Unfortunately for the west, they usually lose this game, as China has approximately one hundred times the number of skilled cyber warriors at work on the problem. This should make for an interesting power game in the 21st century!

From the early BC period until the 14th century China experienced waves of imperial dynasties and civil wars or invasions. However, from the time of the Ming dynasty in 1368, a unified Chinese state began to form. It was also marked by significant engineering and technological developments, including a navy with amazing four masted ships, up to 400 feet in length. The records of the exact dimensions of the ships are not very accurate, but they were certainly far larger than anything else on the oceans at the time. These vessels were immense titans by the standards of European ships of the age. The Chinese Admiral Zheng He who commanded this fleet, made extended voyages across the pacific and Asian region (Dreyer, 2006.) The Wikipedia entry on Zheng is a useful synopsis of the topic.

This era was also marked by the emergence of a bureaucracy that became essential in order to manage such a vast region. This bureaucracy is probably the hall-mark we imagine as westerners when visualizing Chinese history. The image of the mandarin in flowing crimson silken robes with a bamboo pen, has been portrayed in a multitude of films and media. It was the first true civil service. As such, it represents one universal cultural signature we can identify, that enables social cohesion over an extended and disparate set of communities.

The Chinese philosopher Confucius and his teachings represent another motif for Chinese culture that spans much of its history. Confucius set out a philosophy for the practice of life and ethics that aimed at building social unity and cohesion. Partly, as a reaction against the civil turmoil of his own age, Confucianism evolved over the centuries into a pervasive set of rites, rituals and approach to individual conduct, which deeply moulded Chinese society. Its aim was to inculcate an internalized set of values that would guide people to righteous behaviour. In the West we often overplay its emphasis on obedience to authority, family and legalist aspects, but at heart it was a personal philosophy. Its political influence however, does stem from the rigid adherence to social roles, such as the family hierarchy centered on the father, and the proper place of each civil functionary. Seen in this light, Confucianism has shaped the present day flavor of political thinking across Asia. Hence, the ideals of the ancient sage still guide the flow of human affairs; much as the deep cut gorges of central China channel its mighty yellow rivers.

While at university I was fortunate enough to encounter the writings of a western scholar, Alan Watts, whose writings introduced me to the philosophy of Taoism. If you can get a copy, I sincerely recommend a reading of his work, *Tao: The Watercourse Way*. It elegantly, and I feel accurately, captures the essence of Taoism and Chinese philosophy. It shaped my own thoughts on religion, and the nature of existence in a profound way. If you wish to understand China, then an awareness of the principles of Taoism is essential. Taoism is basically almost a Yin-Yang opposite to the authoritarian ideals of Confucianism. A brief quote from Alan, who mastered this most subtle philosophy, is the best introduction:

"Wu-wei is thus the life-style of one who follows the Tao, and must be understood primarily as a form of intelligence – that is, of knowing the principles, structures, and trends of human and natural affairs so well that one uses the least amount of energy in dealing with them. But this intelligence is, as we have seen, not simply intellectual; it is also the "unconscious" intelligence of the whole organism and, in particular, the innate wisdom of the nervous system." (Watts, p.76)

I really don't have space here to do the topic justice, but it truly deserves a wider study in the West. The most accessible account is the work by Benjamin Hoff, in *The Tao of Pooh*. Yes seriously, it's a mixture of Taoism as exemplified in the life of Pooh bear. Trust me its good. Well time to get all serious again and talk about real stuff.

Another signature of China is the colour red. The Chinese love the colour red. Which is convenient, as its history up to, and including, the Communist era, was a recurrent cycle of Imperial dynasties founded in a sea of civil strife and rivers of blood. For example, the Ming fell to the Manchus in 1644, who proceeded to establish the Qing Dynasty. The cost of this minor political shift was an estimated 25 million people dead; (between 1616–1644). (This was equal to a quarter of the total population of Western Europe at that time!)

Unfortunately, by the time of the late 19th century the same bureaucracy had become the greatest impediment to the urgent social change demanded by contact with the aggressive and technologically more advanced western powers. The stagnant Chinese civil service and Imperial court were rigid and inflexible, placing excessive reliance on history and Confucian values. See Fairbank, for a readable modern history of China (Fairbank, 2006.) In particular, the commercial ventures of the expanding British Empire and its opium trade was devastating to the cultural and social cohesion of China. The period from 1850 to 1949 was so bloody that it is hard to comprehend how any Chinese actually survived at all! The brutal and bloody occupation by Japan, was a particular low note that has left scars to this day.

The post 1949 Communist age did finally see a truly unified China, under Mao, with a powerful central government. It also marked the first steps in the liberation of Chinese women for the first time in the countries turbulent history. This positive aspect of the communist era is frequently overlooked when assessing the historical progress of China. Of course the Cultural Revolution was anything but, and it is doubtful we will ever know the total human cost of Mao's revolution. The price paid by the population of China for this social homogeneity was, and remains, undeniably high. The present Chinese state is still grappling with the fine balance between economic liberalization and political expression. Land ownership in particular is in urgent need of reform if the rural economy is ever to be stimulated.

Given the 10,000 years of boiling history China has experienced, I feel it is employing wisdom itself to take things slowly at this time. As of July 2008 the media is full of rants and opinions on the merits of engaging with China via the Olympics. Usually the argument revolves around Tibet, and the admittedly poor Chinese states human rights record. Well if any state attending the games can claim that it has never had a human rights issue in its recent past, then they should feel free to throw stones. (As we will discuss later it was the British who invented concentration camps.) Sustaining the social cohesion of a billion plus people is a gargantuan task, and simplistic debates on how to transplant pure western democracy into the Middle Kingdom are not helpful. Today is August 8th 2008, and I just viewed the opening ceremony of the Beijing Olympics. Now that's what I call a spectacle and political statement. Well it's time to move on in this flash review of empires, to the boldest and most controversial of all.

The British Empire

Perhaps the final and most grandiose expression of empire building was that of Great Britain from 1588, (hard to pick any definitive start date, but the defeat of the Spanish Armada is a memorable event to work with), to 1950 and the Suez crisis. More than any other empire in history the British Empire was a technology driven process. From the foundations of the early industrial era the country had enormous technical capacity in iron production, engineering, communication capability via the telegraph, and of course advanced rail and ship building capacity. In conjunction with an expansionist Victorian mindset this enabled a vast commercial and military thrust that encompassed the globe. Stopping to reflect on the process, it is difficult to recall a single country that the British did not fight, or attempt to subjugate over this period. From the Inuit's in the frozen north, to the native Aborigines in the desert heat of Australia. This was bloody empire writ large.

The Rise of Steam

To be truthful, it was more of a Scottish empire than an English endeavor. The ever inventive Scotts harnessed the power of steam and let loose an unstoppable technological force. The combination of iron machines and steam power catapulted the British into a position of world dominance from 1830 to 1900. It was of course built on an already established empire that spanned North America/Canada, Africa, India and Australia. People now wonder how such a small rain-soaked island in the North Sea ever produced such an aggressive Diaspora that took on the world (Ferguson, 2004.)

The simple answer is because it was such a shit place to be! Joining the navy or army and seeing foreign lands had to be better than staying in a Manchester slum housing estate of the mid-19th century. If you doubt this it is worth noting that one of the originating factors in socialist history was the time Engels spent in Manchester, where he witnessed the horrible working conditions of the English workers. This directly inspired him to co-found Communism with Marx. (Having been raised in a similar housing development in Sheffield in the 1960's, the author is also sorely tempted to leave the UK for sunnier climes.) The other often ignored factor is that Britain had experienced relative social stability, and cultural homogeneity, since the end of the civil war in 1651. (That is compared to the endless civil and inter-state conflicts that had ravaged continental Europe.) Combined with the commercial exploitation of the pre-industrial empire and the early colonies, it had acquired substantial economic resources and a highly cohesive cultural and social order. This acted as an ideal launch pad for the later industrial era empire. Also the simple fact of being an island had provided over a millennium of sea-faring skills and maritime heritage. (We Brits like boats.)

In addition Britain led the world in the invention and deployment of the electric telegraph. We will address this in detail in chapter 4, but clearly it offered a significant technological advantage, in both commercial activity, and more importantly in expressing political control across the empire. Without the telegraph the British Empire would never have reached so far or been sustained. An interesting aside is the question of what impact would Charles Babbage's Difference Engine have made if it had been completed and developed. Britain would have possessed the world's sole computer, with the power to create accurate gunnery tables, navigation tables, and wider economic uses for accurate automated calculations. (A similar postulated scenario is player out in the Science Fiction novel, 'The Difference Engine' by Gibson and Sterling.)

Regarding the fall of empire, numerous explanations prevail, but the definitive synopsis of the Empire by Niall Ferguson offers an excellent summery of the contributing factors. For Ferguson it was the Boer war that represented the turning point in the fortunes of the mighty British dominion. In particular during the summer of 1900 the British military were facing an increasingly effective and determined Boer guerilla army. The Boers would not be drawn into a set piece battle, as favoured by the British commanders. So the British instigated a systematic programme of burning the homesteads of the Boers families, and interning the women and children in large concentration camps. The aim was to force the Boer army to capitulate under extreme psychological pressure. The result was rather different. Altogether 28,000 Boers died in the camps plus another 14,000 blacks in separate camps. The majority of fatalities in both camps being children. Mainly the deaths were from malnutrition and disease, rather than explicit violence. I recommend a full study of Fergusons account as it is an illuminating story of the worst excesses of an Empire at war. More importantly, it was a defining moment in the mind set of the British public:

"In many ways the consequences of the Boer war in Britain were even more profound than in South Africa, for it was revulsion against the war's conduct that decisively shifted British politics to the left in the 1900's, a shift that was to have incalculable implications for the future of the Empire."

(Ferguson, p.281)

In particular, it was the super-human efforts of a lone woman anti-war activist, Emily Hobhouse, who travelled to the camps in 1900 and returned to Britain to relate the tale of the suffering she had witnessed that raised public awareness. This led to seismic shifts in the home political landscape and a swing to the Liberal left of the day. We will offer one more quote from Ferguson, as it is quite contentious, but I feel ultimately a fair assessment:

"Within a single lifetime, that Empire - ..unraveled...Traditional accounts of 'decolonisation' tend to give the credit (or the blame) to the nationalist movements within the colonies, from Sinn Fein in Ireland to Congress in India. The end of Empire is portrayed as a victory for 'freedom fighters', who took up arms from Dublin to Delhi to rid their peoples of the yoke of colonial rule. This is misleading. Throughout the twentieth century, the principal threats – and the most plausible alternatives – to British rule were not national independence movements, but other empires."

"It was the staggering cost of fighting these imperial rivals, (the Axis powers and Russia), that ultimately ruined the British Empire. In other words, the Empire was dismantled because it took up arms for just a few years against far more oppressive empires."

(Ferguson, p.298)

Just like Rome long before it, the British Imperium had been bankrupted by protracted and major wars abroad and in defence of its homeland. When the coffers ran dry the wheels of empire building ceased to turn. (From our increasing knowledge of complex systems, it is also the case that on all scales if the energy/resource flows becomes constricted then adaptive systems will contract. Just imagine visualizing an empire from space and watching a time lapse video as it develops, expands and finally contracts. It would not look dissimilar to the micro-scale growth and contraction waves of competing microbes or fungi.)

Fundamentally however, the Second World war also shifted the mind-set of the British people, specifically it had over-turned the old social order in which the working and middle classes deferred to an Imperial governance and ruling elite. Combined with the emergence of mass media, broader education access and international awareness, the end of empire was an inescapable reality. The sun had finally set on the most extensive empire the world had ever known. (Ferguson's own conclusion is that the United States has now assumed the mantle of Empire in all but name. As he puts it, the gunboats now fly, that being the only difference.)

1.2 Legacies

There is a fitting epitaph to the British Empire, however and that is to reflect on the legacies each empire leaves behind. In the case of Rome it left the Latin language that formed the basis for institutional learning and social order for another thousand years, into the early modern era of Western European history. It also left us beautifully straight roads that still endure today. In the UK many counties occupied by the Romans still possess arrow straight roads; (Lincolnshire has some of the prime examples of originally Roman roads still in existence.)

The British Empire, while not without faults, did scatter the telegraph and railroads across the globe. These technologies formed the communication backbone for many developing economies. Of far more importance however, like Latin, is the legacy of the English language. It may smack of cultural Imperialism, but the simple truth remains, it is now a global language that enables commerce, science, arts and education between almost every state. It might be very non-pc, but if you are a poor Chinese student struggling to survive in a global economy, the advantage of learning a single second tongue, that then connects you to the rest of humanity and the Internet is bloody useful! (My own Chinese students, from Hefei province in the early 1990's certainly thought so.) The power of a single second language to unify and harmonize the human race was also prophesized in the mid 19th century by the Persian prophet Baha'u'llah (Momen, 2007.) A common second language is without doubt, the single greatest instrument for the future cohesion of the human race. (Whether it remains English is not the issue, it is likely to evolve rapidly into a fusion of English, Mandarin and Spanish, anyway.)

US Hegemony

Since the formal end of the Cold War in 1989, the USA has assumed the de facto mantel of sole world super-power. It is therefore necessary for this text to consider how it has arisen to this unique position and to tease out the cohesive historical processes that have led to this state of affairs. (No presumption is made on the part of the author whether it is a healthy condition for the world at large.) For a state which has only been around since they cast off the British yolk in 1773, the USA has achieved a remarkable degree of economic and technological development. It has evolved into a cohesive nation via the maximum utilization of railroads, telegraph and a common language: (not really English per se, but an adequate communication medium for the average US citizen. How many words for doughnut do you need anyway!) In particular, more than for any other state, the American mass media via radio, newspapers, television, and cinema, have projected a shared perception of US culture. (Like many in the UK I grew up with a daily dose of US onscreen heroes, from the Lone Ranger, to John Wayne and Captain Kirk.) However, one true American hero, Mark Twain would not be impressed with the current state of US political affairs. His wonderful satirical comments and prose are a delight to discover for the first time, and remain one of the fairest fruits of American culture:

"I have a higher and grander standard of principle than George Washington. He could not lie; I can, but I won't." (Mark Twain)

The following prescient statement from David Walker, formerly of the US GAO office, is worthy of note, in the current climate:

"Transforming government and aligning it with modern needs is even more urgent because of our nation's large and growing fiscal imbalance. Simply stated, America is on a path toward an explosion of debt. And that indebtedness threatens our country's, our children's, and our grandchildren's futures. With the looming retirement of the baby boomers, spiraling health care costs, plummeting savings rates, and increasing reliance on foreign

lenders, we face unprecedented fiscal risks. Long-range simulations from my agency are chilling. If we continue as we have, policymakers will eventually have to raise taxes dramatically and/or slash government services the American people depend on and take for granted...

America is a great nation, probably the greatest in history. But if we want to keep America great, we have to recognize reality and make needed changes. As I mentioned earlier, there are striking similarities between America's current situation and that of another great power from the past: Rome. The Roman Empire lasted 1,000 years, but only about half that time as a republic. The Roman Republic fell for many reasons, but three reasons are worth remembering: <u>declining moral values and political civility at home, an overconfident and overextended military in foreign lands, and fiscal irresponsibility by the central government.</u> Sound familiar? In my view, it's time to learn from history and take steps to ensure the American Republic is the first to stand the test of time.

What's needed now is leadership. The kind of leadership that leads to meaningful and lasting change has to be bipartisan and broad-based. Character also counts. We need men and women with courage, integrity, and creativity. Leaders who can partner for progress and are committed to truly and properly discharging their stewardship responsibilities.

But leadership can't just come from Capitol Hill or the White House. Leadership also needs to come from Main Street." David Walker US GAO office a personal statement, (Walker, 2007).

The decline of political leadership is also evident across Europe, and it is a serious impediment to the future development and stability of the Western world. In the authors personal opinion the US is in for a bumpy ride if current attitudes and policies are not substantially reevaluated. (At the time of writing this section, the credit crunch is in full swing and I suspect will be biting even harder by the date this is published.) The above quote draws the obvious parallels with the Roman Empire already cited. Of note is the point made that what is required is true moral leadership. The problem for the US in particular, is the influence of the media in raising the noise level, such that small, but vital signals are drowned out. It is very difficult for new leadership directions to be heard in this environment. Combined with the infantile polarization of partisan politics into the dominant two camps, of republican and democrat, the options for radical reform of the political process are narrow indeed.

One manifestation of the damage caused by such bi-partisan political wrangling, is the appalling state of the civil infrastructure in the USA. From public libraries, to roads, and bridges, the chronic under-investment over the past thirty years has resulted in dilapidated and failing infrastructures and networks, of all types. Once estimate, by the American Society of Civil Engineers, values the cost of basic civil infrastructure reconstruction at $1.6 trillion (Time Magazine August 11th 2008). That's a lot of tax dollars the poor US citizens are going to have to find. (The issue also links to the bridge theme of this text, as in August 2007, we saw the spectacular and fatal collapse of the I-35W bridge in Minnesota.) It is a moot point that when a nation neglects its socio-political health, then both its social cohesion and physical cohesion begin to fall apart.

The latest work by Fukuyama, *After the Neocons*, is an interesting attempt to redress the damage done by the Bush regime. The author first aims to redefine what a Neocon position actually means, as Fukuyama holds that the concept was effectively hijacked by the right wing and then misinterpreted by the popular media. More importantly he makes the case that what is fundamentally wrong in US foreign affairs is a lack of commitment, or outright hostility towards the main international institutions, e.g. the International Criminal Court, or indeed the United Nations. This does rather taste of sour grapes by such an avowed advocate of the Neocon mantra. Why not just say we were wrong, it gains more respect.

The future evolution of US society is by no means clear. Its sheer scale precludes any simplistic extrapolation from historical examples. Whilst a number of authors have expounded on the imminent collapse of US power and society, for example via the gradual displacement of Anglo-Saxon culture with black or Hispanic culture. However, unlike many previous civilizations the US is intrinsically diverse, adaptive and future oriented. These traits confer significant evolutionary advantages, which are likely to see the US remain a cohesive and powerful social collective. They have also successfully avoided the pitfalls of multi-culturalism that the UK fell into and perpetuates still. The cohesive value for children of swearing allegiance to the flag is without doubt immense and conducive to a healthy level of patriotism. (Having the freedom to burn the same flag when one is seriously aggrieved, is also a vital component of a liberal state.)

The USA has also given the world Starbucks, Apple computers, and Star Trek, a few of my favourite things. (Yes I'm culturally shallow, I'm an engineer.) But, as Walt Whitman penned, in his seminal and infinitely profound work, Leaves of Grass, in the poem 'By Blue Ontario's Shore'; where he reflects on the horrors of the American Civil war:

"As I mused of these warlike days and of peace return'd, and the

　　dead that return no more,

A Phantom gigantic superb, with stern visage accosted me,

Chant me the poem, it said, that comes from the soul of America,

　　chant me the carol of victory,

And strike up the marches of Libertad, marches more powerful yet,

And sing me before you go the song of the throes of Democracy.

(Democracy, the destin'd conqueror, yet treacherous lip-smiles everywhere,

And death and infidelity at every step.)

I listened to the Phantom by Ontario's shore,

I heard the voice arising demanding bards,

By them all native and grand, by them alone can these States be

　　fused into the compact organism of a Nation.

To hold men together by paper and seal or by compulsion is no account,

That only holds men together which aggregates all in a living principle,

　　as the hold of the limbs of the body or the fibres of plants.

Of all races and eras these States with veins full of poetical stuff most

　　need poets, and are to have the greatest, and use them the greatest,

Their Presidents shall not be their common referee so much as their

　　poets shall."

This poem says it all, sorry but this moves me beyond tears. Its closing lines encapsulate the entire premise of this book, that paper contracts do not make society, what makes a cohesive society is that, *"which aggregates all in a living principle"*. And the greatest advocates and expounders of what this means are the poets and philosophers of a nation. Not the words of politicians, or technicians, or generals. There is a brilliant short Science Fiction story, (which I can no longer locate in my extensive collection, if anyone recognizes the story please let me know the author), in which a future pointless war is being waged with advanced weapons that have a violent and unpredicted impact on the genetic and neural physiology of the combatants. The result is a few of the wounded soldiers are sent to recover in a secret hospital wing, but while traumatized they have acquired the ability to displace themselves like Sliders between dimensions, and move to a parallel universe in which they lead blissful lives. The generals and politburo demand to know how this works, but all scientific explanations fail. Eventually they call for a philosopher to try to explain what is going on, the conclusion he offers is that only a true poet would have the depth of spiritual/metaphysical insight necessary to comprehend the process. Unfortunately, as the call goes out, 'find us a poet' it is realized that in the prolonged armed struggle every member of the state has been subjugated into the war effort, and turned into soldiers, or technologists, or factory workers. There are no great poets.

For me this short story is almost prescient, as in the current Iraq/Islamic conflict, America is mired in an ideological struggle for which its people are ill prepared. There are no new great poets to ground their current philosophy, and they appear to have forgotten the words from the masters of wisdom they once produced. Hence they utterly fail to fathom the psyche behind a suicide bombers attack. They assume that such an individual must be of a criminal or psychotic mind set, yet in fact the reverse is true, such a person generally sees themselves as a patriot or spiritual warrior, and is likely to possess strong moral beliefs. Criminals and psychopaths don't engage in self-sacrificial, i.e. suicidal behaviours.

The election of Barack Obama is the best sign yet of moral progress for the USA. For me, this is truly a demonstration of the capacity of the USA to adapt and move forward. A black president is a signature landmark in the social progression of the American people.

The US Legacy

It is interesting, and probably incendiary, to speculate on what the lasting legacy of the US Imperium will be? For the sake of a balanced debate let's first count some negatives, we have: the Mai Lai Massacre and the whole Vietnam episode, Nixon, the ongoing futile Iraq war and occupation, general shit-stirring in Central and South America; plus insane consumption of the worlds resources and energy supplies. And let's add not ratifying the Kyoto protocol, or recognizing the International Criminal court. I guess I will receive a very long list of additional suggestions from many readers of this text. (The author is in fact deeply aware of US history in this regard, and could easily fill a large appendix with examples, but this book is intended to reflect a positive world view, and dwelling on a countries darker side contributes little to the thesis.)

So now let's count the positives; well start with the Internet, quite useful. And computers, (stolen from the British,) but developed and made useful by the US. Plus a cornucopia of other technological and scientific developments that would be tedious to list verbatim. Saving Europe from Fascism, even if reluctantly, was rather nice of them. Standing up to Communism for 40 years, I feel is also a plus point. Acting as the world's de facto police force, hmmm sort of, depends who you ask, but let's go with the hypothesis for now.

I think we can safely say the jury is still out on this, and no consensus will likely be possible for several centuries. But the next twenty years of US behaviour and politics will be pivotal to future historians painting of the American dream. Hopefully the motto of the USA will always hold true: *E Pluribus Unum*.

Summary

No single civilization, other than the human collective as a whole, has ever endured more than a few millennia; (and the Egyptian example was a product of isolated geography and a tight caste system.) Typically they endure for two or three centuries, before undergoing an internal metastasis, or exogenous shock. Or simply exhaust the social capital that previous generations had accumulated. In either case, understanding how, or why they remain a coherent entity has to date been a process of historical analysis. The following section introduces the topic of computer-based modelling and software agents that have revolutionized our ability to understand such large-scale CAS, and enabled a methodological approach for the first time.

2. Computers and Agent-based Modelling

This section looks at whether computational models of human societies can reveal any of the fundamental principles governing their organization and dynamic behaviour. The problem that has plagued the social sciences historically has been the difficulty in conducting large-scale and repeatable experiments on human behaviour. Typically studies have looked at existing societies and then tried to infer what the underlying processes and norms were. It was difficult, or impossible, to conduct 'what if' experiments. For example, to see if an increasing divorce rate in a specific society increased female poverty; (in most western states the reverse is now true.) Since the 1980's the availability of low-cost powerful desktop computers made it possible for social science researchers to at last perform simulations of human populations in order to address such questions. Some of the pioneering work in this area was conducted by Robert Axelrod and Michael Cohen (Axelrod and Cohen, 2000.) In their seminal work on the 'Sugar Scape' model they demonstrated how an extremely simple agent-based model of human economic activity could display a broad spectrum of complex social behaviour.

For the purposes of this text we will look at how an agent model can help address the question of how complex social systems sustain themselves in the face of continuous change, or disruption by elements of the surrounding environment. This is one of the fundamental questions asked within the field of complex systems research. Specifically, how does any set of agents, or organizational structures, retain a complex set of inter-relationships over extended time; when the laws of thermodynamics dictate the continuous increase in entropy of all systems. (In chapter 5 we will apply an agent-based approach to modelling the dynamics of trust between agents in society.) This arena of academic study has long been the domain of the citadel of Complex Systems science, the Santa Fe Institute. The influence of this unique research centre over the past twenty years on all aspects of Complex Systems has been profound.

The small town of Santa Fe is itself a fascinating social experiment in process, as three distinct and quite separate social groups share the town. First the rich white retirees and tourists, who populate the expensive haciendas on the northern wooded slopes, second the poor Hispanics that do the bulk of the menial work and occupy the southern deserts edge, in trailers or modest adobe walled casitas, and finally the native tribes who live separate lives, selling trinkets in the market, or native pottery and rugs to the expensive tourist shops in the town square. It's a picturesque and peaceful scene, but not a socially just one; hopefully a more balanced social milieu may form there in the future.) More on Santa Fe later.

Returning to the theme of computer-based modelling, a number of contemporary authors have addressed this topic, some key examples being:

Beinhockers '*The Origin of Wealth*', or Scott Page's text '*The Difference*'. However, much earlier work on nonlinear economics, (the best description of this approach), came from Brian Arthur and a host of researchers working in complex systems. Arthur is one of my preferred writers from any discipline, as he combines the most lucid writing style and powerful analysis, to reduce the complex to the simple. The following quote from one of his seminal papers is a fine example:

"The story of the sciences in the twentieth Century is one of a steady loss of certainty. Much of what was real and machine-like and objective and determinate at the start of the century, by mid-century was a phantom, unpredictable, subjective and indeterminate. What had defined science at the start of the century—its power to predict, its clear subject/object distinction— no longer defined it at the end. In the century just past, science after science lost its innocence. Science after science grew up.

What then of economics? Is economics a science? I believe it is. It is a body of well-reasoned knowledge. Yet until the last few years it has maintained its certainty, it has escaped any loss of innocence. And so we must ask: Is its object of study, the economy, inherently free of uncertainties and indeterminacies? Or is economics in the process of losing its innocence and thereby joining the other sciences of this century?

I believe the latter. In fact, there are indications every-where these days in economics that the discipline is losing its rigid sense of determinism, that the long dominance of positivist thinking is weakening, and that economics is opening itself to a less mechanistic, more organic approach."

(Arthur, '*The End of Certainty*', 1999.)

In the same paper Arthur identifies the fundamental problem that has crippled economic theories over the past two centuries:

"Deep in some recess of our minds, we inherited the thinking that the economy is but Art, a gigantic machine, that if we merely understood its parts, we could predict the whole. Certainly when I was studying economics in Berkeley 25 years ago, many economists hoped (as I did) that a Grand Unified Theory of economics was possible. From the axioms of rational human behavior, a theory of the consumer could be constructed. From this and a corresponding theory of the firm we could construct a consistent microeconomics. From this, somehow, we could construct an aggregate theory

of the economy: macroeconomics. All this would constitute a Grand Unified Theory of the economy."

(ibid)

Way back in 1988, Arthur and John Holland initiated some of the earliest work on agent-based computer modelling of complex systems. They used a software agent model to form an artificial stock market in a computer. From such models they observed a broad spectrum of behaviour that closely mimicked that of real markets. For example, they noticed periods of high volatility in the agent-traded stock price followed by periods of quiescence, a phenomena observed in real markets, but which is unexplained in the standard model. Arthur and Holland reasoned that in their artificial market at some moments a number of agent investors discover a new way to do better in the market. These agents then change their buying and selling behaviour, which in turn drives the market to change. The result is avalanches of change sweeping through the market; in particular on all scales, exactly as happens in the data from real markets. In this paper Arthur concludes with this brilliant synopsis of what drives all real economies, rather than the toy models and sterile equations of classical economic theory:

"In the standard view of the economy, which has an intellectual lineage that goes back to the enlightenment, the economy is mechanistic. It is complicated but can be viewed as a series of objects and linkages between them. Subject and object—agents and the economy they perform in—can be neatly separated. The view I am giving here is different. It says that the economy itself emerges from our subjective beliefs. These subjective beliefs, taken in aggregate, structure the micro economy. They give rise to the character of financial markets. They direct flows of capital and govern strategic behavior and negotiations. They are the DNA of the economy. These subjective beliefs are a-priori or deductively indeterminate in advance. They co-evolve, arise, decay, change, mutually reinforce, and mutually negate. Subject and object can not be neatly separated. And so the economy shows behavior that we can best describe as organic, rather than mechanistic. It is not a well-ordered, gigantic machine. It is organic. At all levels it contains pockets of indeterminacy. It emerges from subjectivity and falls back into subjectivity."

(Arthur, 1988).

I would very much recommend a visit to Brian Arthur's website, and invest some time delving into his repertoire of work. We will return to this theme in chapter five, where we look at complexity in economics and business in general.

2.1 Software Agents and Societies

While we introduced the concept of a computer software agent in chapter 2, it lacked a context, which we will now attempt to provide. If we step back in time to the mid 1980's and looked at the state of Artificial Intelligence as a discipline, it was not a pretty sight. After decades of promises regarding the 'imminent' arrival of sentient computers that could manage your house, or a global-scale war, the reality was looking a little pathetic. Well, actually, extremely pathetic to be honest. The fact was most computer scientists had grossly underestimated how complex the human mind really was, and how unbelievably hard language and vision processing are. After all human infants seem to be able to handle these processes, so how difficult could it be? And besides if we model human neurons as transistors, (i.e. as simple on-off switches), then it should have been possible using 1970's hardware to emulate intelligence! (The science fiction film, '*Colossus: The Forbin Project*' is a classic example of the perception that thinking machines were about to occur.)

Well guess what, neurons are not like transistors, each neuron we now understand is more like a supercomputer in its own right. So not only does the average human brain contain 100 billion neurons in a hyper-complex network arrangement, (that's highly dynamic with constant rewiring and re-growth occurring), but each one is as complex as an entire mainframe. Hmmm, we have a problem. (As an aside, this morning I entered our two year old daughter's toy room and was surprised to see an extensive wooden rail network spiraling across the floor. Up until now she had required help to assemble the toy train circuit, but overnight her developing brain had assimilated the rules for assembling the set, and she is now gleefully building a new rail empire! This class of real-world extended learning remains a long-term and currently very distant goal of AI.)

Software Agents

All of which brings us to the present topic of software agents. Since real mobile robots were prohibitively expensive, (especially when they kept falling over, hitting obstacles and being dismantled by undergraduate students, whose knowledge of sophisticated machinery could best be described as limited), researchers had no choice but to build simulated world to test their grand AI designs. These simulated robots then evolved into the separate field we now term software agents. By the turn of the millennium researchers from other fields, in sociology, anthropology, psychology, and even transport planning, all realized these toy worlds and agents, (combined with ubiquitous cheap desktop computers), enabled you to model a vast array of real-world social problems. As you may have guessed my own career followed this path and having shed real blood trying to make physical robots cooperate, I turned to purely simulated AI entities, as while the coding might be as challenging, at least they didn't crush your fingers!

COSMOS: a society of sugar addicts

We have spent some time looking at what agents are and where they came from, now let see how they can be applied in the context of social cohesion. In order to study a model of human society we need a simulation with a sufficient number of agents; typically several hundred. However, each agent requires a slice of CPU time to run so the numbers are constrained by the computing power available. Fortunately, some excellent open-source multi-agent simulation tools have been developed. My favourite is the REPAST agent toolkit from the University of Chicago. Using this tool a two-dimensional discrete spatial world model was designed in which a population of artificial agents could interact and move, based on the classic social simulation model known as Sugarscape; (see Epstein and Axtell 1996.) This model was selected as it enables sufficiently complex behaviours to be simulated and could be run on a standard laptop PC, rather than requiring a super computer.

Model Description

The following section explains the COSMOS model in some boring technical detail. It is needed to fully explain the resulting diagram and the behaviour of the simulated society. However, feel free to skip to the summary and trust the author didn't just make it all up. The model is based on a population of simple behaviour driven agents, which are initialized randomly with the following set of variables:

i) **Vision** – an agent can sense other agents and food objects within a specified radius from its own co-ordinates. Assigned randomly within a specified range e.g. 1-5 steps.

ii) **Metabolism** – agents have an integer counter which represents their rate of energy consumption. Assigned randomly in a specified range.

iii) **Lifespan** – agents are initialized with a fixed lifespan, randomly assigned, typically between 20 – 200 time steps.

iv) **Sugar** – agents require sugar to survive, which is an environmental resource. Sugar is distributed and re-grows once consumed by an agent at some specified rate. The agent's normal behaviour is to look around their local environment and to move to the site with the highest sugar level. Agents consume sugar by decrementing the counter value proportional to their metabolic rate.

v) **Spice** – as described in the Epstein & Axtell model, a second commodity was introduced into the world, which is only available from other agents, and is required for agent survival. Agents can only acquire spice when they engage in a trade interaction with another agent. Basically they can swap surplus sugar for units of spice.

So basically we have a model society and an economy in miniature that runs on a pc, and can be tuned to study a broad range of control parameters. For example, what happens if you allow each agent to inherit from related members of the society, or what happens if the average agent life span is increased?

Dynamic Group Formation

The first experiments were designed to study under what conditions socially co-operative groups of agents would spontaneously develop, using the defined model. The rules for trading interactions were very simple, i.e., each agent applied the following algorithm during its allocated time slot.

Look in all neighbouring cells to radius = vision parameter.
If cell occupied then

If agent is of similar class type

then trade with agent in the cell

and randomly flip one tag of agent to match own tag.

Else ignore agent.

Else if cell unoccupied record amount of sugar present.

Move to selected unoccupied cell with highest sugar level.

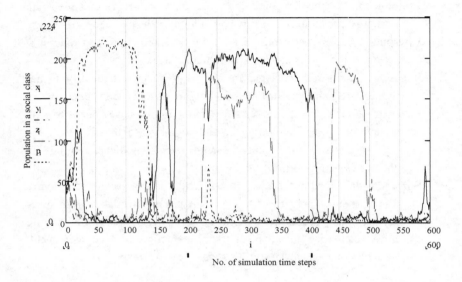

Figure 3.1 Cosmos life-span graphs, showing the rise and fall of agent 'civilizations'.

In figure 3.1 what is of interest is the distribution in duration for different agent social groups. Some groups experience very brief periods of activity lasting approximately ten simulated time steps, while others form clusters that endure for epochs of over 300 cycles. (Where each group is defined by its own unique tags.) Let's now attempt to map these results into the human social domain. (At this point social and political scientists who may be reading do need to grant the author a fair degree of poetic license in his extrapolations from an admittedly simplified model of reality.) So imagine each time step in the simulation as being equal to one year of real time. Hence the major epochs of agent time correlate to several centuries of real civilizations. Second, there is a clear bipolar set of possible states for the agent groups. They either coalesce into a group and then rapidly dissolve within 10-30 time steps, or they succeed in forming a very large super group that endures for several hundred time steps, i.e. an agent civilization has appeared! (A much deeper technical analysis that utilizes computer modelling to study the network dynamics of human societies over history can be found in, (White, 2008.))

One final observation to note from the figure, look how rapidly the major groups form and disperse. Typically it takes only twenty time steps for a super group to form or dissolve. This appears to reflect the relatively short time scales over which real civilizations have risen or fallen. This partly answers an age old political/historical question, why did such dominant civilizations as Rome appear to fall apart so rapidly from their zenith? This simulation, and many related models, suggest an answer may lie in the basic nature of CAS, i.e. that this is a fundamental property of all such classes of complex systems. There is no principal cause or major event to point at, rather such phase-transitions are an inherent function of complex groups. Clearly as communication networks advance and relative distance shrinks the speed of these transitions grows shorter. (To be fair in the agent model the communication between agents is almost perfect; hence we would expect the model transitions to be rapid.)

Limitations of agent modelling

As with most scientific abstractions of reality there are limits to the applicability of agent models. Firstly is the oft cited criticism that they lack fidelity, since each agent possesses virtually no cognitive capacity, or real sensory awareness, or a responsive emotional state; (a bit like virtual teenagers!) However, the model itself does possess the properties of a fully complex adaptive system in microcosm, and can therefore display complex emergent behaviour. Secondly, what we are really modelling are the meta-processes; such as the speed of information flow, the topology of social networks, or the emergence of hierarchies; rather than the micro-scale specifics of real human interactions. It is a very big abstraction I grant, yet lacking a time-machine to run back and scan across history it must be worth a punt, if it provides some insights into the complex issues of social cohesion.

Modelling Social Networks

One recent research paper on the tie strengths in mobile communication networks, illustrates the power of computer analysis and simulation in the development of our understanding of real social structures. The authors analysed real records from several million mobile phone users and re-constructed the social networks that links the callers based on these records. Using what if scenarios they then statistically probed the resulting network to answer two key questions. Firstly what happens to the cohesion of such a network if the ties are broken, but not in a simplistic random manner, rather using two scenarios, in the first instance they incrementally removed the weakest ties within the network, in the second they removed the strongest. The counter-intuitive result is that if you remove the strongest ties within the network, only a gradual reduction in the networks overall connectivity occurs. *"In contrast, the removal of the weak links will delete the bridges that connect different communities, leading to a phase transition driven network collapse."* (Onnela *et al*, 2007)

The reason for this is that social networks form around small highly clustered communities, of friends and family, with longer range weak ties to other social groups. Hence deletion of a significant number of weak ties leaves the clusters isolated from each other. The second question posed by the paper that was answered, is how does information flow across social networks? The answer here was that social ties of weak to intermediate strength are far more effective at propagating new information. Within the strongly connected clusters information tends to become trapped and doesn't flow as freely. This mirrors much earlier research on weak social ties (Granovetter, 1973), which echoes the vital role played by longer range weak social ties in binding society together. Such results also reinforce the conclusions of work by Putnam and others on Social Capital (Putnam, 1993), in which communities that place excessive reliance on family groups for trade and interaction display much lower levels of economic reciprocity and development.

3. The Future of Social Cohesion

Based on the preceding analysis of social organizations and their life-cycles, we are faced with some fundamentally important questions.

- Firstly, are modern societies cohesive and if so to what degree?
- Second, what impact will modern technologies have on social cohesion?

Also, can we ever hope to achieve a globally stable multi-cultural structure; without attempting to impose uniformity, or via Orwellian mechanisms? Many believe so, the World Federalists, the Baha'is, Star Trek fans and many others. Why not? The argument that we have always been a fractionated collection of warring tribes is not a sufficient counter argument, merely an historical statement. Anyway the choice is one which should concern us out of purely selfish Darwinian motives; at current rates of medical development, our potential lifespan may be significantly increased and *we* will be living in the future. This text is advocating an argument that social evolution is progressive, unlike the mechanisms of natural evolution. In the authors opinion there is a clear historical pattern of increasing social complexity; with increased integration and reciprocal co-dependencies. (The text by Stuart Kauffman '*At Home in the Universe*', is an excellent summary of how complex systems can spontaneously form and lead to higher order structures, (Kauffman, 1996.)

It is readily apparent that all modern cultures are experiencing extremes of social, cultural and political change. The question is what are the driving forces and will these forces lead to deeper levels of social integration. If so, at what scale, i.e. regional, national, international or global. The following quote by two leading thinkers in Global Security reflects the authors concerns in this matter:

The difficulty many modern societies face is that, once the beliefs or trusts are removed, the way they define themselves and the rules by which they live no longer have meaning. In a network sense, the trusts that defined the network and so the rules by which it organized have been removed. The network may continue but it no longer is capable of exercising power and effectiveness and its rules no longer reflect its beliefs or truths. Ultimately, it can no longer be trusted—a vacuum has formed.

(Atkinson and Moffat, 2005)

This reference addresses the issues of governance from a CAS perspective and specifically within a defence context. Yet the recurrent forces they perceive as vital to any human organization are belief and trust. Specifically, they point out the essential verity that society is defined and operates by the fine webs of shared beliefs and trust relationships that exist between its members. These are the core topics we will address in detail for the remainder of the chapter.

Political Cohesion

An interesting UK television documentary was broadcast in 1999 called the Incredible Shrinking Politician, which dealt with the European wide phenomena of public disdain and indifference towards the activities and pronouncements of politicians. The process is most evident in the collapse of membership in the major political parties. Far more people are now passionately active in alternative action, or theme centered groups, for example wildlife preservation trusts or environmental groups. The underlying process of political collapse, however is being driven by an erosion of trust in the political system and sense of disconnect between the elected representatives and the electorate. The implication is that western society needs to urgently reconsider the exclusive and divisive process of current multi-party politics. Not a return to dictatorship, but rather a fine tuning of democracy that reconnects the voter to the representative. The basis of this must be consultation and the fostering of new trust relationships. Not an easy task, granted, but we are learning some new tricks that might just make it possible.

Nudges

The latest fad to sweep through the vacuous minds of politicians is the idea of social 'nudges'. This is based on a recent text by Prof. Richard Thaler, a Professor of Economics and Behavioral Science at the Graduate School of Business, University of Chicago, and Prof. Cass Sunstein a law professor at the Harvard Law School. Their book explores the policy implications of behavioural economics, a field describing the irrationalities and underlying psychology of human behaviour. Thaler and Sunstein's basic premise is that even though humans are irrational creatures, they can still be persuaded to change their behaviour patterns in positive ways, and using only small suggestions, i.e. 'nudges'. The classic example they cite is the use of a small smiley face on peoples energy bills that reflects how efficient they are, i.e. if they are consuming less than the average for their area then the smiley is positive, and frowning if they are using more than the local average. The authors quite correctly identify the glaring problem with classical modern economic theory, i.e. the Rational Economic Man from Friedman's free markets is a myth. *If you look at economics textbooks... you will learn that homo economicus can think like Albert Einstein, store as much memory as IBM's Big Blue and exercise the willpower of Mahatma Gandhi.* The reality of course is that most examples of humanity fall a little short in these regards.

The resulting philosophy is they term, 'libertarian paternalism', i.e. one in which individuals remain free to choose from a set of options, but are guided by 'choice architects', who possess some degree of oversight and broader knowledge of the impact each option may have. The process is common sense

104

really, but is made objective by the scientific and sociological studies that are used to promote the concept. Where the authors stick to issues such as promoting healthy food choices for school children, guiding users on energy consumption, or health care insurance, the method is sound.

Unfortunately, they also propose extending the approach in a highly libertarian sense to the institution of marriage and its privatization. The idea appears to be to make states only recognize a standardized civil union contract, which would be identical for any two adults, of any gender. (It ignores the complexity of polygamous cultures.) The suggestion is that couples, who wish to, may make an entirely separate commitment to each other, under the auspices of their preferred religious or cultural affiliation. In the author's personal opinion this is a very dangerous fallacy. The expression of marriage in modern states may be clouded by the same-sex issue, however if we grant that in a country such as the UK, many couples getting married have no personal religious beliefs, then what they are entering is already just a state recognized civil union. What matters from a societal perspective is the stability and duration of the union. So why do non-religious people remain together if their vows are effectively to the State? (Which few folk in the UK could give a damn about.) Marriage remains an important social contract for the simple reason that people care about their social network. The classic marriage process is a public affirmation of that union to your friends, family and peers. I.e. it is the cultural and social dimension of the process that remains fundamentally important to the quality/length of the union. If marriage was privatized, as Thaler and Sunstein propose, then it becomes entirely a commercial arrangement, with no social obligation at all. The state could offer three, five or ten year union contracts and charge different rates for each. Lots of choice and very flexible. And, an utter disaster for the social cohesion of human society. The classic family model, has been, and should remain the foundation of social cohesion.

Cultural Cohesion

In resource rich societies humans tend to abandon politically motivated alliances and shift into culturally selected groups. When all basic needs are met, then the need to form strategic collectives focused on defence or resource acquisition is reduced. Humans then strive to enter social groups of culturally compatible forms, with some set of common expressions, e.g. music collectives, (e.g. Madonna fans). Homophily thus remains a very powerful force acting on cultural dynamics. Only the underlying motivation for group formation shifts, not the urge to form such groups. This phenomenon has made calculating levels of social capital quite difficult. For example in Robert Putnams' study of social capital in the US over the past forty years (*Bowling Alone: America's Declining Social Capital*, 1995), he notes a marked decline in many expressions of group cohesion, e.g. church attendance, yet at the same time many new and more diverse expressions of affiliation have arisen, such as music tribes, environmental groups, or virtual communities. Putnam's preferred definition of the concept 'social capital' is stated as:

"I prefer a 'lean and mean' definition: social networks and the associated norms of reciprocity and trustworthiness. The core insight of this approach is extremely simple: like tools (physical capital) and training (human capital), social networks have value. Networks have value, first, to people who are in the networks. For example, economic sociologists have shown repeatedly that labor markets are thoroughly permeated by networks so that most of us are as likely to get our jobs through whom we know as through what we know. Indeed, it has been shown that our lifetime income is powerfully affected by the quality of our networks (Granovetter 1973, 1974; Burt 1992, 1997; Lin 1999, 2001). Similarly, much evidence is accumulating about the health benefits of social ties (House et al. 1988; Berkman 1995; Seeman 1996; Berkman & Glass 2000)."

(Putnam, *E Pluribus Unum*, 2007.)

Putnam later addressed some of the criticisms raised against his original thesis, and in 2000 published *Bowling Alone: The Collapse and Revival of American Community*. This added further evidence of the evolution of social capital in the US and reiterated the basic conclusion that while more people were engaged in social interactions, such as bowling, the numbers participating in traditional fraternal groups had fallen massively. Putnam proposed that social capital can be roughly divided into two principle classes, i.e. bonding capital and bridging capital. Bonding capital is the product of socializing within similar groups, i.e. by age, gender, race etc. Bridging capital however develops when individuals make social links to members of different social groups. Both forms are necessary for a healthy social fabric.

In his more recent work, the brilliantly titled, "*E Pluribus Unum*: Diversity and Community in the Twenty-first Century, he argues that:

"Ethnic diversity is increasing in most advanced countries, driven mostly by sharp increases in immigration. In the long run immigration and diversity are likely to have important cultural, economic, fiscal, and developmental benefits. In the short run, however, immigration and ethnic diversity tend to reduce social solidarity and social capital. New evidence from the US suggests that in ethnically diverse neighbourhoods residents of all races tend to 'hunker down'. Trust (even of one's own race) is lower, altruism and community cooperation rarer, friends fewer. In the long run, however, successful immigrant societies have overcome such fragmentation by creating new, cross-cutting forms of social solidarity and more encompassing identities. Illustrations of becoming comfortable with diversity are drawn from the US military, religious institutions, and earlier waves of American immigration...Thus, the central challenge for modern, diversifying societies is to create a new, broader sense of 'we'."

Putnam's research therefore has immense value, first in making clear the patterns of social evolution taking place in modern societies, and second by reinforcing the value in social diversity and inter-group network formation. If a criticism is to be raised of his conclusions, it is that heterogeneous human societies, with high immigration rates, have not always developed into cohesive units. In the UK the multi-cultural experiment, that spans the same time period as that studied by Putnam in the US, has resulted in largely ghettoized settlements, in most cities across the UK. The polarization between racial and cultural groups is almost total in places like Leicester, Bradford, and Manchester.

A speech by the Prime Minister of the day, Tony Blair, in 2006, made clear, what had become a commonly felt, but generally unspoken sentiment:

"If you come here lawfully, we welcome you. If you are permitted to stay here permanently, you become an equal member of our community and become one of us. The right to be different. The duty to integrate. That is what being British means... When it comes to our essential values, the belief in democracy, the rule of law, tolerance, equal treatment for all, respect for this country and its shared heritage — then that is where we come together, it is what gives us what we hold in common; it is what gives a right to call ourselves British,...At that point no distinctive culture or religion supersedes our duty to be part of an integrated United Kingdom"

This radical statement represented a complete U-turn for a leader and left-wing party that had staunchly espoused multiculturalism, for over three decades. To be fair it was in the wake of the July 2005 London bomb attacks, but these only made apparent the cultural divides that had already crystallized in British society. Whether another fifty years is required before these differences are smoothed out by the gradual process of cultural mixing that inevitably occurs, remains to be seen. It must be sincerely hoped that this is the case.

Happy Families

The loss of nucleated family structures is having a profound impact on the level of social cohesion in many western societies. This is a fundamental shift in human social practices, unprecedented at any period over the past several millennia. Efficient low cost transport and communication systems enable family ties to be maintained over large distances. Although, often at some diluted level of intensity, in terms of the quality of interaction possible. One simple example of this is the reduced interaction between children and their grandparents. Compared to the past where grandparents would live in the same village, street or area, they now live hundreds of miles away, resulting in sparse interactions a few days a year. This removes a key source of emotional, and physical support for parents and children, and loss of access to the accumulated knowledge of the older generation. The consequences of this have yet to be fully understood, but from personal experience the prognosis is not good.

Another interesting question is whether traditional family structures are in fact an ideal social configuration. The work by Fukyama (Fukuyama, 1995) and others indicates that in many cultures it is the very strength of close family ties that can lead to low levels of trust across communities. This is reflected in the research discussed earlier by Onnela *et al* on the effect of social network ties. This is explored in more detail in chapter 5 where we look at the economic consequences of low levels of trust within societies. In brief, it is apparent that where a culture is based on excessively strong inter-family relationships then it reduces the number of weak ties, (i.e. bridging bonds), across the community, which are precisely the social bonds necessary for economic development. In terms of policy formation for economic development the question is then how to build and cultivate the wider social ties that stimulate social development.

Religious Cohesion – an oxymoron?

From a Darwinian perspective one mechanism that human society has evolved to create broader social cohesion and wider social networks is religion. Based on our current understanding of how beneficial such wider social networks are, we can understand how faith networks have acted as the foundation and catalyst of significant economic development through history. (Of course many debate the positive value of Faith (e.g. Dawkins *The God Delusion*), but such arguments lack historical accuracy and perspective (Cornwall, 2008.) (It should be stated up front that the author has a deep personal belief system, which strongly shapes his world view. If you want to know the details, have a look at: http://www.bahai.org.)

In this section I will argue that the phenomenon of organized religion, when viewed broadly, is actually a positive force for social cohesion. This is not an easy argument to make if one has any knowledge of human history and contemporary society. Since the Enlightenment and the rise of the age of reason, religion has increasingly appeared for many as epitomizing ignorance, superstition, and social repression. In the UK the influence of science advocates such as Richard Dawkins, appears to have corralled religion within self-imposed circular and irrational arguments, on the nature of life, creation and morals. The futile wars and civil conflicts fought in the name of religions, over millennia, are a testament to the abuse of man's inherent and natural desire to know and comprehend the mysteries of the cosmos. So let's first examine some of the key points in the battle between faith and science, as this represents the principle arena in which the debate rages.

Reasonable Faith

The process of Reductionism is a classical motif of the scientific endeavour, and epitomized the revolution in empirical thought, which arose during the enlightenment, sparked by Descartes and crowned by Newton. For several centuries the reductionist philosophy served science well and continues to be an integral aspect of science. The essence of this philosophy is to reduce a complex system to its fundamental quantities in order to construct a useful and predictive model of its behaviour. In particular it was Darwin's epic work, in 1859, On the Origin of Species, that set the seal on the ascendancy of science, and finally banished the need for a creator in the story of mankind. However, science also has limits:

"If we define a religion to be a system of thought which contains unproveable statements, so it contains an element of faith, then Godel has taught us that not only is mathematics a religion, but it is the only religion able to prove itself to be one." (John Barrow)

Since Godel removed the grand vision of mathematics and Thomas Kuhn redefined the process of science, it is arguable that science contains clear elements of faith. Science provides a powerful, but never complete understanding of reality. A recent text by John Cornwell, *Darwin's Angel,* and subtitled *An Angelic Riposte to The God Delusion,* is one of several books published in response to Richard Dawkins *The God Delusion* (2006). Cornwell is an acclaimed theologian and runs a Public Understanding of Science programme at Jesus College, Cambridge. In Darwin's Angel he eloquently and gently teases apart the arguments promoted by Dawkins, and reaffirms the value inherent in organized faith as a positive social phenomena.

For me however, the best exponent of the virtue in harmonizing reason and faith is the Revd. Dr John Polkinghorne, a British particle physicist and theologian. His works on science and faith represent the most erudite and reasoned arguments in this field. Polkinghorne describes his view of the world as Critical Realism and believes strongly that there is One World, with science and religion both addressing aspects of the same reality. He considers that *"the question of the existence of God is the single most important question we face about the nature of reality".* He suggests that God is the ultimate answer to Leibniz's great question, *"why is there something rather than nothing?"* An atheist's simplistic assertion of the world's existence, is a *"grossly impoverished view of reality,"* he says, arguing that, *"theism explains more than a reductionist atheism can ever address."*

(Polkinghorne, 2008)

The fact overlooked by the Dawkins argument is that statistically, it is a very small percentage of religious folk who turn to violent expression of their beliefs, within most states. And in this they are no different from any political group who feel justified in using violent means of protest. A parallel example is the animal rights movement, the majority of whom engage in peaceful protest; (I personally agree with the argument that far too many experiments are conducted on live creatures.) Between 2006 and 2007 just twelve people in the UK were in process of being charged with offences related to assaults against laboratory staff or premises. This is a minute percentage of the UK population who agree with the need for more protection of animal rights.

Where wholesale violence is being waged between groups or varying religious beliefs, such as the Palestinian issue, it is in general a political struggle being waged. The argument is principally over land, water, and rights of way, and not over which prayer book to use on the Sabbath. Of course, like many I watched on screen as the barbaric attacks on the US World Trade Centers and other targets in 9/11 unfolded. I vividly recall the exact moment and watching the event on a streaming web video link. This catastrophic event offered ample evidence of the need for all human societies to allow for change and growth. The alternative is stagnation and decay and the collapse into recursive tautologies in order to bolster untenable religious or political positions.

Work Ethics and Commerce

A highly debated facet of the contribution faiths have made to social progress is the hypothesis, first proposed by the German economist/sociologist Max Weber in his famous 1905 essay, '*The Protestant Ethic and the Spirit of Capitalism*' (Weber, 1905.) This was the first in a series of studies looking at the influence of religions on cultural and specifically commercial development in the civilizations of Europe, India and Asia. Weber's analysis can be summarized as follows. Capitalism arose when the Protestant, (particularly Calvinist), ethic influenced large numbers of people to engage in work or trade and enterprise in the secular world, and to see such activity as synonymous, or complementary with religious worship itself. This was the Protestant Ethic that made life revolve around work. This was later refined in Sociology to be a general 'work ethic', that included similar work-oriented practices in other cultures.

This has been frequently criticized as ignoring the early economic development of many Catholic states in Europe. Clearly since Weber's time the Tiger economies of Asia and India have also embraced capitalism with gusto, and often display an extreme work ethic. However, the broad sweep of his original thesis holds, i.e. that from the Reformation a sweeping transformation in how people viewed trade and work was released that greatly accelerated economic development. More recent studies have looked at how social networks, centered on congregational worship, have facilitated credit exchange and the enrichment of social capital.

Another classic, yet neglected, example of the cohesive influence of faith is the early history of Islam. As Islam reached the height of its empire, from the eighth to 12th centuries, it unleashed a wave of cultural and technical innovations that revolutionised the known world. Soaps and perfumes, products of the first systematic chemistry, were derived from alchemy, but became industrialized processes. Technical developments such as distillation, sophisticated glass making, and new metal working capabilities spread across the Mediterranean, Southern Europe, and across Persia to India.

Islamic science at this time was empirical, but based on a new open philosophy that encompassed all sources of knowledge. The Islamic world was a vast intellectual endeavor at the time, with few internal theological constraints; in contrast to the Dark Ages that the Christian world had become. Less theoretical than the ancient Greeks, Islamic scholars, (such as Muhammad ibn Mūsā al-Khwārizmī and his work on algebra,) were busy translating every Greek and ancient text they could find. More than that they were seeking to apply and utilize the knowledge in practical ways, for trade and commerce. By the twelfth and thirteenth centuries, this ancient knowledge and new sciences were being translated from Arabic into Latin, and infused the early European Renaissance. Most importantly, the simple existence of Arabic as a common language across the Islamic world had profound implications. It was a language of culture, trade, science and religion, and hence allowed a free movement of ideas and knowledge.

The point of this section has simply been to indicate that organized religion has often played a positive role in advancing civilization, in contrast to the shallow arguments from the Dawkins and Dennett camp, that it is only ever a negative force.

Rules and Order

Let's try to link these themes together. First what is religion? Religion in its social expression is a codified set of rules that creates a moral framework for individuals to live by. The origin of the rules may be debated endlessly in theological colleges, but the social impact is what matters. It has been expressed a thousand times, but the price of freedom is to take responsibility for your actions and those of the wider society, i.e. your neighbours and their children. Hence we need to redress the balance and recognize that society itself has to be protected. Of course the diabolical extremes we witnessed in the 20th century of Communism and Fascism were abominations and object lessons in how not to engineer societies. However, re-engineer society we must. The centuries old party political system that has served quite well needs totally rethinking. This is evidenced in the wide-spread distrust and loss of respect for the political process witnessed across Europe and the developed world. One of the motivating factors for this is the speed of scientific and technical advances being thrust upon humanity. Basically we need a faster, more responsive and intelligent political architecture. Of course there are a lot of vested interests in the existing political system. However, the revolution in the world of media and entertainment, created by forces like blogging, web 2.0 or P2P networks, and their impact on entrenched commercial organizations, demonstrates how new communication paradigms can transform existing systems.

This diatribe reflects the underpinning message of this chapter, which is to restate that societies have no cohesion without rules. Rules create order. However, we also require high levels of trust between agents in order to enable flexible and creative interactions. This point is echoed strongly by Atkinson and Moffat in their analysis of complex social systems.

For example, if we take the simplest computer model of complexity, a cellular automata simulation, i.e. Conway's famous Game of Life, the reason it has been so studied and analysed, is due to the amazement most students feel when they first encounter it. This is a system of mind-numbing simplicity, a grid whose cells can be on or off, yet one that can display patterns of almost infinite complexity under the right conditions. What determines those conditions, simply the rules defined for the interaction of its cell-based elements. The field of Artificial Life and CAS has taught us a valuable lesson, that complexity and structure are frequently the product of relatively simple rules of interaction between the constituent parts. There is also a fine balance between order and chaos, the lesson from studies of complexity has been that small variations in the rule set, or network connectivity, can transform a system from rigid order into a chaotic maelstrom. Striking the right balance in terms of social engineering is therefore never going to be a done deal. As expressed by many, we sit forever on the edge of chaos. Indeed, as Chuang Tzu pointed out over two millennia ago the answer is not to just add more laws. That simply creates more criminals. The ideal is moral and spiritual education so that individuals see the universal value in conforming to social norms and prohibitions. The Chinese achieved this through the set of Confucian ethics that emphasized the importance of stable families and social order; although with a cost in terms of suppression of individual expression and initiative. If we can combine the best values of the occident and orient we could see a far more balanced world emerge.

In the 21st century we must therefore engage all strata of society in the new political process, utilizing technology such as electronic voting and large-scale group consultation, which can now be achieved via network communications. The example of the Wikipedia on-line encyclopedia demonstrates how the global collective can now achieve what initially seemed impossible, i.e. to achieve a stable group consensus on a complex and vast set of knowledge. (Similarly as painted in Surowiecki's, '*Wisdom of Crowds*', the collective is far smarter than even the brightest of its individual members, under the right conditions).

4. Trust and Consultation

If you skipped the technical stuff earlier in the chapter, it is time to reengage, as this bit is the center piece of the book. This section now addresses the recurrent themes of the text, i.e. trust and trustworthiness in human society. In particular it considers the influence of trust processes on the cohesion and welfare of social groups. While trust is an intuitive human concept, we generally perceive its effects at a local or individual scale. However, a growing body of evidence from sociological, psychological and computer-based studies indicates that the term actually encompasses a critical spectrum of individual human and agency interactions, which includes trade, social capital, and group security. An overview from the respective fields of economics and computer science is presented, in order to elucidate this hypothesis.

What is trust? Recent evidence from the social and physical sciences has cast some light on the process and impact of trust mechanisms. In addition it is suggested that religion has historically, and still remains a key factor in inculcating trust within society. One hypothesis we will consider is that religion, of all denominations, is a significant catalyst of trust between people and hence a positive influence in generating social capital and welfare.

The principal argument of this section is that trust is the *dynamic glue* that binds the fabric of human society together; politically, socially and economically. It is a key element in the evolution of human social structures from hunter-gatherers to city building civilizations. The following section considers examples from the social, technical, and spiritual perspectives, in order to illustrate this hypothesis. If we check for the dictionary definition of trust, we get something like the following:

Trust *n.*

1. Firm reliance on the integrity, ability, or character of a person or thing.
2. Custody; care.
3. Something committed into the care of another; charge.
4.
   a. The condition and resulting obligation of having confidence placed in one: *violated a public trust.*
   b. One in which confidence is placed.
5. Reliance on something in the future; hope.
6. Reliance on the intention and ability of a purchaser to pay in the future; credit.

Interestingly, the word is defined by concepts such as: reliance, care, confidence, credit and most importantly hope. This brings us back to the most important manifestation of trust in society, i.e. Putnam's idea of Social Capital.

4.1 Social Capital

The process of economic exchange and trade is based on many forms of contract. Underlying all such contracts is some process of trust. Either that the contracting party is trustworthy or that some third party acting as a broker is trustworthy. For example: Banks, Solicitors, Stockbrokers, and Accountants, etc. (Sorry it is now 2009, scratch banks from the list.) Of specific relevance to this discussion is the economic concept of Social Capital. A useful definition for the concept of Social Capital, and expansion to Putnam's own definition, as stated earlier is:

"Social capital refers to those stocks of <u>social trust, norms and networks</u> that people can draw upon to solve common problems. Networks of civic engagement, such as neighbourhood associations, sports clubs, and cooperatives, are an essential form of social capital, and the denser these networks, the more likely that members of a community will cooperate for mutual benefit. This is so, even in the face of persistent problems of collective action (tragedy of the commons, prisoner's dilemma etc.), because networks of civic engagement:

- *foster sturdy norms of generalized reciprocity by creating expectations that favours given now will be returned later;*

- *facilitate coordination and communication, and thus create channels through which information about the trustworthiness of other individuals*

- *and groups can flow, and be tested and verified;*

- *embody past success at collaboration, which can serve as a cultural template for future collaboration on other kinds of problems;*

- *increase the potential risks to those who act opportunistically that they will not share in the benefits of current and future transactions.*

*Social capital is productive, since two farmers exchanging tools can get more work done with less physical capital; rotating credit associations can generate pools of financial capital for increased entrepreneurial activity; and job searches can be more efficient if information is embedded in social networks. Social capital also tends to cumulate when it is used, and be depleted when not, thus creating the possibility of both **virtuous and vicious cycles** that manifest themselves in highly civic and uncivic communities."*

(Sirianni and Lewis Friedland, 1995)

The key aspect of this concept is highlighted in bold in the quote, i.e. "*virtuous and vicious cycles*". This implies that societies will evolve into two possible stable economic and socially correlated states: prosperous or poor. Although, there is clearly a wide spectrum of levels of civic and personal trust within real world human cultures. However, it is a useful generalization to claim that many societies do fall into two economic categories, of either low-trust or high-trust groups. Interestingly, simulation results from tools like COSMOS, discussed earlier, reflect this result and the majority of simulation runs end in one of these two stable states. What matters is that the interactions become self-reinforcing, i.e. when humans, or agents, expect another agent to defect then the optimum response is to cooperate for a short while and then play defect, (i.e. play tit-for-tat).

The consequence of this is that over time the level of reciprocity and trust within a community tends to increase or decrease rapidly in a cumulative manner. The problem is that each end state is dynamically stable. If a community has ended in the high trust regime, then this is all to the good as the society will prosper. However, if the group has fallen into the low-trust regime, then it becomes extremely difficult for individuals or small sub-groups to reverse this state and become more trusting again, as the majority of social encounters they have will be with individuals that play defect. (In game theory terms, being a dove among a population of hawks is a bad place to be.) Hence poor communities tend to remain poor.

116

Of course in reality these are a large number of statistical interactions. Hence exceptions can occur, particularly within large urban centres, such as London, where once poor areas become regenerated; due to new inward migration or major investment. However, for this to occur there is typically some significant new extraneous factor at play, which shifts the balance of reciprocity and economic activity. The problem is most manifest at the larger scale where entire regions, or provinces, are in the low trust condition. In this case the probability of local investment or population shifts changing the dynamics is much lower. Hence in the UK, the poorest regions, which are concentrated in the North of the country, have proved very resistant to economic redevelopment. Even with large-scale state investment and regeneration programmes. In addition of course a one-way filtering process always means that bright young talent migrates rapidly to the prosperous South, further exacerbating the situation. (The author is one example of this as he migrated from the struggling former steel city of Sheffield to the high-tech region of East Anglia in the UK.)

In terms of understanding the role of trust in shaping society, the classic reference in this field is the work by Fukuyama (Fukuyama, 1995.) This provides a detailed account of the role of trust in the creation of social capital, with particular attention to economic development. Fukyama argues strongly the case for categorizing societies as high-trust and low-trust cultures. High trust societies tend to develop greater social capital, and consequently enjoy greater economic growth, particularly in the transition to a post-industrial economy. Likewise, high trust groups and cultures accumulate greater social capital. Fukuyama sees social capital as the glue that holds the otherwise centrifugal structures of the market together.

An Italian Job

A classic example of the influence of Social Capital, as defined above, is provided by the economic and cultural development of Northern and Southern Italy (Putnam, 1993.) Extensive studies of the relative development in the North and South of Italy indicates that a key factor in the significant economic disparity between them is rooted in the quality and form of the social and economic networks that have existed in each region. In particular, in the North of Italy since the Renaissance there has been a greater degree of social interaction and contractual agreements. These agreements extended beyond the normal confines of family membership, (Padgett, 2002). The Florentine region, in particular, experienced a broadening of the social and economic infrastructure which permitted an explosion in wealth, commerce and technical development. Padgett demonstrated, via some very meticulous research of the historical records, that the emergence of this region resulted from new forms of social capital and hence broader processes of reciprocity. The following quote from Padgett provides a synopsis of this event.

"The commercial credit system, through which the Renaissance Florentines dominated European international finance, emerged out of their particular social-network structures of family, neighbourhood, and social class, with double-entry accounting providing the technical tool to increase the volume of "friends" with whom Florentines could reciprocate. Blending historically inherited logics of economic and social exchange was central to the Florentines' generative capacity to make credit and liquidity, which in turn helped Europe to expand through trade. Judging from data from the 1427 catasto, the particular network innovation achieved in Florence was this: economic partnership modelled on elite marriage (hence across neighbourhood, within social class) was cross-cut with commercial credit modelled on clientele (hence within neighbourhood, across social class).

This social framework for economic markets emerged as an unintended by-product of the political process of repressing the Ciompi rebellion of wool workers in 1378, which transformed the guild system. Through multiple-network rewiring, new cross industry organizational forms were created. These concentrated economic wealth into the hands of a new style of generalist or "Renaissance man" elite, but they also actively sponsored new industries and new citizens. In Renaissance Florence, constructing political elites and constructing financial markets were two sides of the same co-evolutionary process of making new organizations, new markets, and new people."

(Padgett & McLean , 2002).

Related work by Axtell and Cohen also considers the impact of Social Capital and provides a useful synopsis of the process:

"A society that relies on generalised reciprocity is more efficient than a distrustful society, just as money is more efficient than barter. Put simply, trust lubricates social life", (Axelrod & Cohen, 2000).

This is a great way to express the whole theme, i.e. 'trust lubricates social life'. The gregarious nature of human beings implicitly suggests that we desire to be trusted. We also need to trust others to remain within a social collective, whether family or tribe. However, as society has evolved increasingly complex social structures then we are required to engage in broader and more intricate webs of trust. The emergence of the Internet and the Web will have particularly dramatic consequences on mechanisms of social trust; as profound as that of double-entry bookkeeping in Renaissance Florence. Communications technology both threaten social structures and provide new means for reinforcing social contracts and community development. Trust therefore operates as a dynamic process and natural force between social agents. Khare and Rifkin in their research, nicely summarize this by the point that "..*principals build up trust over time*" (Khare,and Rifkin, 1997.)

Trust has become an issue of deeper scientific analysis. The emergence of Computing and the Internet has generated the need for a fundamentally deeper understanding of how to measure and evaluate trust relationships between individuals and organisations. In particular a recent report commissioned by IBM indicates that states with high levels of social trust display higher levels of Internet adoption (Keser *et al*, 2002.) This is important as Internet access will be a prime driver in future economic growth, hence low-trust societies may experience a developmental divide. The following extract, highlights the influence being exerted by the growing electronic network:

"As the Web and its descendents evolve into a Mirror World, they will need to adapt to the human trust relationships, but just as inevitably, human trust relationships will have to adapt to digital management. Mirror Webs will distort the nature of trust---and thus, communities---by creating new kinds of agreements and by shattering old ones"

(Khare,and Rifkin, 1997.)

The Mathematics of Trust

Strangely enough the very subjective concept of trust can be considered from a purely mathematical standpoint. One useful research paper provides a good introduction to trust analysis based on the problem of establishing trust between N or more computing agents.

"Trust is usually considered a belief or cognitive stance that could eventually be quantified by a subjective probability. It is usually assumed that an agent will only engage in a transaction if the level of trust exceeds some personal threshold (the level of acceptable trustworthiness), which depends on

the transaction context [1]. Second, trust typically is learned gradually, but can be destroyed in an instant by misfortune or a mistake. Once trust is lost, it may be costly or it may take a long time to rebuild it. This reflects certain fundamental mechanisms of human psychology known as the asymmetry principle. According to it, distrust is not merely the inverse of trust. Trust and distrust are learned in different ways and they function differently. This might be explained by the following psychological reasons:

– Humans perceive trust-destroying events as more noticeable than trust-building events.

– Trust-destroying events carry much greater weight than trust-building events in subjective reasoning.

– Sources of trust-destroying events tend to be accepted as more credible than sources of trust-building events.

– Once initiated, distrust tends to reinforce itself. In contrast, trust can be destroyed in an instant."

(Braynov and Sandholm, 1999)

This final point is key, trust must be continuously regenerated and created, as it dissipates when subject to negative pressures.

Game Theory

The most extensive technical study of trust has occurred within the field known as Game Theory. The disciplines most involved in game theory are mathematics, economics and the other social and behavioural sciences. Game theory was founded by the legendary polymath John von Neumann. The major text being, *The Theory of Games and Economic Behavior*, that von Neumann wrote in collaboration with the economist, Oskar Morgenstern. Since the work of von Neumann, games have been a scientific metaphor for a much wider range of human interactions in which the outcomes depend on the interactive strategies of two or more persons, who have opposed, or at best mixed motives. Game theory was intended to confront just this problem: to provide a theory of economic and strategic behaviour when people interact directly, rather than through the market. In game theory, games have always been a metaphor for more serious interactions in human society.

"In neoclassical economic theory, to choose rationally is to maximize one's rewards. From one point of view, this is a problem in mathematics: choose the activity that maximizes rewards in given circumstances. Thus we

may think of rational economic choices as the "solution" to a problem of mathematics. In game theory, the case is more complex, since the outcome depends not only on my own strategies and the "market conditions," but also directly on the strategies chosen by others, but we may still think of the rational choice of strategies as a mathematical problem -- maximize the rewards of a group of interacting decision makers -- and so we again speak of the rational outcome as the "solution" to the game."

(Roger McCain, 2003).

From this brief description of Game Theory we can see that it incorporates the concept of social trust between agents. One agent's evaluation of the strategy of another agent depends upon the historical information it has available on the other agents' previous decisions. Trust is then simply an agent's degree of expectation that another will act in a specific manner.

Tit for Tat

The early work on game theory was very trendy and cool, but it ran into one minor problem. The question that was bugging the theoreticians was why do humans cooperate at all? The optimum strategy in any single interaction is to play defect, (i.e. take the suckers money and run.) The answer that emerged from social experiments and computer simulations in the 1980s was simple, but profound. Basically, if people experience not one, but repeated interactions with another agent, then the story is quite different. This work was led by the political scientist Robert Axelrod, whose work on the SugarScape model we touched on earlier. Axelrod and Hamilton published a paper titled "The Evolution of Cooperation", (Axelrod and Hamilton, 1981), in which they outlined how via the repeated interactions of competing strategies the most robust strategy was tit-for-tat. As Axelrod explains:

"My original interest in game theory arose from a concern with international politics and especially the risk of nuclear war. The iterated Prisoner's Dilemma game seemed to me to capture the essence of the tension between doing what is good for the individual (a selfish defection) and what is good for everyone (a cooperative choice). Therefore I was intrigued by the many strategies that had been proposed to play this game effectively.

An interest in artificial intelligence led me to read about computer chess tournaments. This in turn led to the idea that a good way to evaluate alternative strategies for the iterated Prisoner's Dilemma would be to invite experts to submit their strategies in the form of computer programs.

Then I could run a computer tournament to see which one would do best. The result was that the simplest of all submitted entries won the tournament. This was TIT FOR TAT: cooperate on the first move, and then cooperate or defect exactly as the other player did on the preceding move. I next organized a larger tournament with both experts and computer hobbyists, with a total of 62 entries. The result was again a victory for TIT FOR TAT."

His web site on the Complexity of Cooperation is well worth a visit for a more detailed discussion of this topic. Axelrod's early work triggered a cascade of interest across the political, social and even biological sciences. People realized his simple computer games were a means of understanding complex behaviour in a wide range of subjects. (A more modern discussion and summary of his work is available in this online article; Hoffman, 2000.) Of course in reality, humans invariably experience repeat interactions during trade. Hence capitalism works, over the long run. Equally true is that scams, con tricks and pyramid schemes do occur, with significant economic costs to many. In these cases the defecting agent has planned to not be around in the medium term future, when the scam is revealed. Fortunately, these represent a small minority of events when weighed against the total of human economic activity. It is also the case that as the world shrinks there are fewer places for the con artists to hide.

Another more serious example of the power of cooperation, is the kind of behaviour demonstrated in WWI, where many instances of spontaneous cooperation have been recorded. Basically, when the opposing forces had settled into a fixed trench warfare situation, each side would engage in token or ritual shelling of the opposing side. Hence you know where and when the shells would arrive and could take cover. Of course once the generals figured this out they would order some random advances to break the cooperative cycle, (Ashworth, 2004.) A more entertaining example of the concepts is demonstrated within a recent computer model, built using the Netlogo tool. This model simulates greedy and cooperative cows, which are grazing a field of grass. It is brilliant and very engaging, you can change the parameters and watch the effect on the relative populations of simulated cows. No expert knowledge is required and it should work on any machine with Java installed. (http://ccl.northwestern.edu/netlogo/models/Cooperation.)

A Moral Dimension

The author's conclusion is that globally, social capital is being eroded, and while some replacement is occurring, it is not at a sufficient rate to replenish what has been lost. It may be that one reason for this is the parallel reduction in the degree of religious observance in most western states. Of course many surveys indicate little or no change in the average number of people who express a belief in a personal God. However, this often fails to translate into a personal moral code, or the shaping of cultural interactions guided by a codified set of collective beliefs, i.e. a shared faith. For example, a specific aspect of the collective faith dimension of trust is the quality of trustworthiness. This is an internalized process from an individual standpoint and the virtual credit rating applied by society that expresses the degree to which an individual can be trusted. It is also one of the principal tenets of most mono-theistic faiths. Of course this is not to say that atheistic groups don't manifest trustworthiness. Simply that within theistic communities this is a strongly reinforced social norm, and that this remains a behavioural attribute that requires constant reinforcement, as the temptation to play defect in social interactions is ever present. (Interestingly in many social contexts a high percentage of people are trustworthy in environments where they are known to others in the group.) For an example from one religion, within the Bahá'í Faith trustworthiness is held up as a primary objective of a spiritual existence.

"The fourth Taraz concerneth trustworthiness. Verily it is the door of security for all that dwell on earth and a token of glory on the part of the All-Merciful. He who partaketh thereof hath indeed partaken of the treasures of wealth and prosperity. Trustworthiness is the greatest portal leading unto the tranquility and security of the people. In truth the stability of every affair hath depended and doth depend upon it. All the domains of power, of grandeur and of wealth are illumined by its light."

(Baha'u'llah, Tablets of Baha'u'llah, p.37.)

This is a very interesting quote if we dwell on it for a while. The author Baha'u'llah is trying to communicate the wider social value of personal trustworthiness. It is not just the basis for economic prosperity, but also for social stability and security in the broadest sense. Interestingly Baha'u'llah rarely discusses trust, or advocates that people should trust everyone. Rather he implores each individual to elevate their personal level of trustworthiness. This is a subtle but vital distinction, as blind trust in others can lead to expensive losses to a trusting individual. But by emphasizing the social value of personal trustworthiness, the collective growth of trust is attained, along with the associated social and economic benefits, as discussed earlier.

Summary

The strength and welfare of a society appears to be fundamentally linked to the nature and quality of the trust networks between its members. If we can measure and quantify the frameworks of trust within social groups, then we may be able to predict their future stability and progress. Finally, it is imperative that we cultivate processes and social structures that encourage and facilitate the growth of communal trust. Significant evidence indicates that the storehouse of social capital is being eroded within many societies. This may be a temporary phase of adjustment for societies in social transition, from agrarian to industrial, and to information based forms. However, as discussed, human history contains many examples of advanced societies falling apart due to a collapse in their social cohesion or integrity.

The state of religious communities in the USA is an interesting case as church attendance remains relatively high compared to most western states. In chapter 6 we will return to this issue in more detail and compare the relative impact of faith practices on measures of trust as applied to a number of states.

On a different note, but addressing the need for social vision, the following quote is of interest:

*"Despite better trained and equipped soldiers and sailors and winning almost every set piece battle, Britain failed to win the War of Independence. It simply did not have an alternative **grand and strategic vision** to offer its own soldiers, fighting and dying for the Empire, or their Loyalist supporters. The Republicans, by contrast, created a believable grand and strategic vision, which over time prevailed operationally and tactically. For many years, the perceived wisdom for the failure of the U.S. in Vietnam was that there had been too much political interference, and that the U.S. Army lost because of it. Eliot A. Cohen refutes this. It is his opinion that the U.S. lost Vietnam because the politicians were too little involved—they failed from 1964 onwards to provide the type of grand and strategic vision that could be **trusted** by the Vietnamese, the U.S. soldiers fighting there, and most significantly, the American public watching a contrary tactical vision (the body count) unfold before them."*

(Atkinson and Moffat, 2005)

This piece identifies one of the vital missing elements in Western culture, i.e. the lack of a believable 'grand and strategic vision'. The post-modern world is essentially adrift, with weak centrist political diatribes offered as the sole remedy. The truth remains however, what binds any society together is shared beliefs and values, founded on deep reciprocity and trust. Policy development must recognize this if we wish to counter the forces of dissolution that are eroding society at present. Some groups are however, raising awareness of the need for cohesive thinking. One example is the Centre for Social Cohesion, a UK think-tank focused on the problem of ethnic and religious divisions, (http://www.socialcohesion.co.uk.)

This chapter has perhaps the widest social significance, as the current failings of humanity to adapt to the post-industrial age is causing unnecessary grief and suffering on a vast scale. The questions we posed at the beginning were:

- What are the dominant forces that shape and sustain any society?
- What determines the lifespan of a society?
- How can we model macro social dynamics?

The answer to the first question appears to be a complex mixture of the prevalence of trust, degree of reciprocity, and whether the dominant social norms are cohesive in nature. Many other factors also play a role, but this book is as biased as any, and this conclusion fits the model we are presenting. The third question has a very simple answer, that is by computer and agent-based modelling tools that are being increasingly utilized by researchers in the field. The second question is harder, however let's attempt to summarize the discussion so far. Firstly we tried looking in absurd brevity at some examples of past civilizations in order to shed some light on what factors dictated their lifespan. If we isolate the three distinct phases of a civilization, i.e. formation, stable regime and dissolution, then we can itemize the dominant factors at work in each phase.

Formation

This phase is generally marked out by the following factors:

1. The society condenses around a common cause or belief system.
2. A very high degree of trust exists between individuals.
3. There is a clear motive or drive to grow.

4. A desire and political will exists to absorb and assimilate new cultures.
5. Significant, i.e. surplus, economic resources are available.
6. Shifts in the underlying technological landscape are taking place, or in early formation.

Stable Regime

Here we see the following factors at work:

1. An established civil service.
2. Extended and fully developed lines of communication and transport networks.
3. A deep cultural memory, in libraries, writing, media, education, beliefs.
4. A high degree of trust between its members.
5. A complex caste or social class hierarchy has emerged. (Ideally a mature middle class has formed.)

Dissolution

And finally:

1. A rigid, excessively large and self-serving civil service.
2. A high tax burden: (see 1.)
3. Breakdowns in communication links and the physical infrastructure. (E.g. the UK rail network and US road bridges.)
4. A disillusioned and over-extended military force.
5. Low and falling levels of trust and reciprocity.
6. Depleted social capital. (Usually combined with dissolution of common faith practices and shared beliefs.)

It is debatable whether weak family ties are also a signature feature of civilizations in the later stages. In Western Europe at the present time, we do see family disruption and dispersion as a symptomatic feature of an ailing society. Yet as we reviewed earlier, the work by Fukuyama, in contrast, argues that excessively strong family ties can be highly detrimental to the economic and social development of a culture. Clearly human societies require a fine balance in the optimum configuration of family structures in order to maximize diversity and network ties, while sustaining a nurturing environment for child development and local reciprocity. The key issue is one of network topology, i.e. strong families are good, but healthy societies also possess multiple overlapping social networks, that incorporate weaker ties; such as charities, trade associations, clubs, and other civic groups. The ways in which broader reciprocal social mechanisms facilitate economic development, are discussed by Surowiecki in his chapter on society and trust.

"Modern capitalism made the idea of trusting people with whom you had "no prior personal ties" seem reasonable...This helped trust become woven into the basic fabric of everyday business. Buying and selling no longer required a personal connection. It could be driven instead by the benefits of mutual exchange." (Surowiecki, p.123)

As he also points out, however, *"if trust is the most valuable social product of market interactions, corruption is its most damaging"*. We will return to the issue of corruption, and its negative consequences in chapter 6. Unfortunately, just knowing the technical answers will not create positive outcomes. Similarly a Christian perspective on the economic bust of 2008/09 is succinctly stated thus:

"A market economy is not morally neutral either. It encourages creativity, enterprise and innovation and depends in its success for moral habits such as prudence, keeping promises and attention to detail, qualities notably absent in recent years...Part of the problem in discussing the moral dimension of economic life is our lack of a common language. Religion is in decline. Marxism is discredited." (Griffiths, 2009)

Lord Griffiths goes on to argue that only via improvements in personal behaviour, and morality, can the economic system and in particular the financial sector, be restored to a functional and reliable state. Rather than the knee-jerk imposition of even more legal and regulatory conditions. This is very true, as there was no shortage of regulatory processes in place prior to the 08/09 bust; they were simply not applied, or criminally ignored.

The later point he makes is also critical; we urgently need to build a common language for ethics within economics. It is actually very hard to refine individual's behaviour, if there is no cultural framework in place to mirror and communicate the moral dimension. For the preceding four centuries, post-Reformation Christianity provided that framework in the West. (Bizarrely, the Reformation itself was a reaction against perceived corruption practices in the Catholic hierarchy of the time.) We now require a more open and pan-cultural model, as a new ethical framework. This will not be easy. Yet as we have seen from studies on cooperation, and the long-term benefits of a free-market system, there is an innate pressure for more cooperative social norms to emerge. Globalization simply requires a parallel development of global ethics. We also need the spirit and will to act on this knowledge in order to realize any vision of a more balanced or cohesive society. This goal is manifestly a lot more difficult than mere technical understanding. The principles of the Baha'i Faith, and its models of consultation and trust, are one example of an approach that may help initiate the required processes to enhance social cohesion.

If we take the results of the cooperation studies to a long-term conclusion, we may postulate that humanity is actually on a trajectory towards a world-embracing federation. In addition any such world federation will have a proportionally long life expectancy. Of course such a federation may lead to the often-expressed fear of repressive social norms, or the death of cultural diversity. A mono-culture of Mc Burger and frothy coffee bars is certainly a hideous thought. But there has always been a price to pay for the benefits of wider integration. The EU formation of a common currency is one example, which illustrates all of the arguments for and against the merging of economic interests.

The take away for this chapter is simple, and expressed in two words, i.e. trust and consultation. These are age-old social norms, yet now more than ever, they are the basis of all cohesive social processes, and the very foundation of any future world order. Chapter 4 will cover some of the major technologies that are impacting the cohesion of society. Following that, in a vaguely logical fashion, chapter 5 will consider some of the related issues within economics and commerce that are also impacting the degree of cohesion within societies.

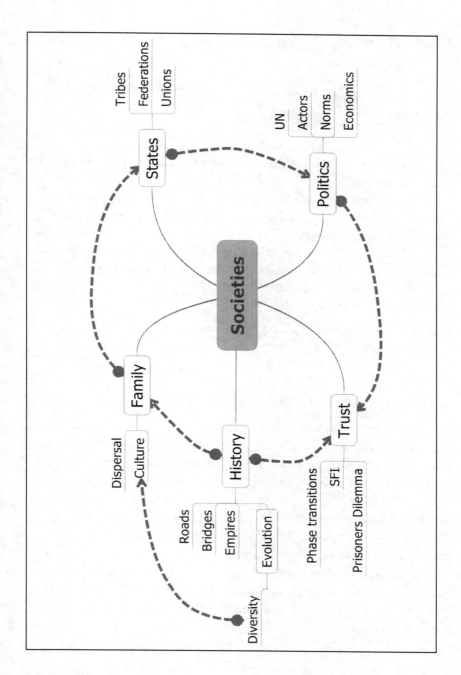

Mind map for chapter three.

Chapter 4

Cohesion: Technology Nexus

"Daniel and his friend were practicing their marksmanship by shooting at targets in a farm field. But instead of the usual choices of mice, bottles, or birds, they selected a more worthy adversary: electrical insulators. These pear-shaped glass or plastic devices are intended to hold electrical wires aloft. But after the men shot six insulators off two utility poles, the shattered targets were no longer up to the job. A high-voltage wire fell to the ground and Daniel, attempting to prevent a serious fire, seized the sizzling wire in his hand, and was electrocuted. An Allegheny Power spokesman advised people not to shoot at electrical insulators."

(Darwin Award: 14 February 2002, Pennsylvania)

1. Webs of Glass and Steel

There is a new Law library in Cambridge University that is well worthy of a visit. Three quarters of the structure is of a geodesic, (Fuller-style), construction with white painted steel tubes and triangular sheets of toughened glass between. This is a space-age form, sitting incongruously between centuries-old stone colleges and ivy walls. Its webbed steel structure echoing the electronic spider webs that it is a node of. What is most interesting is the new format of any modern library, i.e. the eclectic mixture of old books on endless shelves, and open plan rooms of networked computers. The greater incongruity however, is the gulf between our paper histories of accumulated knowledge, and the speed of light process we call IT. For me libraries are a bridge from the past to the future, and hence a vital thread in the fabric of human civilization.

The pinnacle of human achievement in this regard must be the World Wide Web, dreamt of by many, but fathered by Tim Berners Lee. It is undoubtedly the prime example of technological integration, and has indisputably had a vast impact on human social and cultural development. The incredibly simple concept of hyper-linking data has spawned a virtual monster, which overnight has become the dominant store and medium of human knowledge. An interesting question is why did this occur? What underlying combination of technical, social and commercial factors created the matrix necessary for the web to emerge? It is also interesting to ask what kind of social and technological networks have formed? There have been numerous pivotal technical innovations throughout human history, such as fire, flint tools, and the wheel. The focus on communication technologies was selected to limit an otherwise vast subject, and because they form a key aspect of the cohesive processes within cultures. Communication based processes are also interesting in the context of biological systems, as within every multi-celled organism highly complex chemical signaling mechanisms operate to maintain the cohesion and integrity of the organism.

This chapter explores the history and social impact of communications and computer technology. As the initial story illustrates, technology while morally neutral, can hurt! The first aspect of interest is how technologies have driven the structure and growth of human societies; in particular what makes communication technologies such powerful catalysts for social change. The second sub-theme is how technology drives both constructive and disruptive forces in society. In particular, wars have frequently been the crucible of innovation, leading to ever more ingenious methods for killing our fellow human beings. Paradoxically, such innovations have simultaneously led to step improvements in civil technologies, particularly for communications; the key to increased levels of social cohesion. We will address the moral and cultural implications of this dynamic process later.

A specific topic will be used to illustrate these effects in action, i.e. Information Security. The need to protect critical information has acted as the core driver in communication innovations over the millennia of human dialogue. Individuals and states have long desired secrecy in their interactions, and the urge to achieve this has necessitated some amazing innovations and downright cunning. From Caesars cipher in the 1st century AD, to the WWII Enigma machine, the vital role of secure communications in politics, commerce and war has been a prerequisite. The advent of modern cheap computing power has now made strong encryption available to the mass of humanity, and this is having a profound influence in the political and commercial spheres of life. Whether from its use by human rights movements in repressive states, to secure online chat, or the simple process of protecting your purchases in online stores. Bizarrely, your purchase of Madonna's latest album from Amazon was protected by stronger encryption than that used by the German high command to secure details of U boat positions!

My tip for the week however, is if you do have something to hide don't rely on encryption too much. History is littered with the sorry tales of those who thought their message was absolutely secure. Mary Queen of Scots being the most infamous example; (for the full gory details, see Singh, 1999.) Basically if someone has a bigger computer than you, and the time, they can probably crack your crypto. Mainly because most people make mistakes in how they use it. A passphrase that is too short or crypto keys left in undeleted files or electronic traces on disks. Somewhere along the line you screwed up, and a serious opponent will break the cipher. Then of course there is the whole topic of social engineering, i.e. lying, which will be discussed later in the chapter. (Why waste time trying to crack a hard code, when you can just trick your way into the social network of the person with the information you need. This represents one of the exceptional instances when our innate sense of trust fails badly.)

This chapter will first take a salami slice through the history of communication technologies, followed by a delicatessen sample of current computing, and its impact on society. This leads to a brief look at the topics of Artificial Intelligence (AI) and Robotics, as these represent the bow-wave of the revolution. Finally, we look at the likely future society that will be created by this technological smorgasbord. (Liberally sprinkled with elements from William Gibson and Neil Stephenson's cyberpunk novels; probably the best Sci-Fi literature in the world.)

Of course, the development of the scientific method and surrounding culture in itself is probably the most powerful example of a cohesive process. Since the Renaissance and Francis Bacon in the 17th century, the pursuit of rational knowledge has sustained a singular sense of purpose. A handful of simple rules: falsifiability, replicability, and peer review, have created an almost infinitely powerful tool. Much historical and philosophical debate has gone into understanding why this has proven to be the case. Since the mid 20th century, however, such debate has been largely academic. The manifest power of the scientific worldview has become a de facto pillar of society. The majority of international scientific conferences are now held in English, with common publishing processes, and a universal mathematical notation. However, science itself also experiences dispersive forces. Each scientific discipline now forms its own sub-culture and represents an entire cultural ecology. New sub-disciplines are constantly emerging, with factions splitting from established groups. Whenever a single scientist makes a significant breakthrough in their field, this attracts a whole community of like-minded researchers and student acolytes. In this respect, science mirrors the evolution of religious faiths into diverse sects. Science, while pure in thought, never quite escapes the base human realities of funding, politics, and ego.

2. History of Communication

The ability to communicate is fundamental to the capacity to form any cohesive social structure, and is a defining characteristic of Homo sapiens. To address the questions posed in the opening section, we will first trace the development of communication technologies and their social impact. The second half of the chapter then shifts into the computing realm to see how the combination of information processing and digital communications has sparked a revolution in all dimensions of culture and commerce. We will then consider where such developments may lead us in the immediate future. We begin with a brief history lesson, starting with smoke and mirrors; (a rather nice metaphor for many of the technologies pushed by commercial vendors).

Smoke

The earliest forms of long range communication were probably based on the simple process of lighting a bonfire to create a plume of smoke. (Historically, torching an occupied town you are raiding also sends a powerful message to neighbouring towns of your intentions!) A latter improvement would have been the realization that you can throw a branch, or cloth, over the fire to create a sequence of smoke signals. Roman forts had a sophisticated system of signaling based on lit torches and a sighting mechanism to confirm the location and authenticity of a signal. (Even at this stage of development information security was vital.) The following account is a fascinating glimpse into the state-of-the-art communication network that protected the British Isles in the 16th century.

"In the UK by the sixteenth century, when invasion was threatened during the wars against France and Spain the coastline was ringed with beacons which could relay a message of invading fleets around the country from coastal villages to larger towns and settlements. It appears that the

coastal beacons (three are mentioned at Porlock, i.e. Selworthy, Cleeve Hill near Watchet and Beacon Hill on the Western end of the Quantocks) were each to have three beacon fires. These were probably of the usual pattern of that time, a brazier or iron fire-basket on a large metal tripod, and were filled with dry combustible material, well soaked in tar or pitch, ready to blaze up when ignited, by flint and steel or by a burning match from a lantern. The Churchwardens Accounts for 1580 include a payment of five shillings for a 'load of wood for the Beaken and for carrying the same to Croke peke'. But beacons were dependent on fine weather for visibility, and one wonders how far away the fires could be seen at times when the weather was cloudy."

http://www.somerset.gov.uk/archives/ASH/Beacons.htm

(If you ever need to make a good smoke signal you need to get a small wood fire burning with a simple frame of branches over the top. On top of this you add a few wet leafy branches. As these heat up they give off lots of thick white smoke. Don't try the old Native American trick, as seen in cowboy films, of placing a blanket over the fire. It will probably be mostly polyester, not horse-hair, and burst into flame!)

Mirrors

Since at least the times of ancient Greece the use of a highly polished metal or glass surface has been used as a signaling device. In clear weather it is a highly effective means for transmitting signals over several kilometers. It appears quite apt that the peak of modern technological communications is also based on mirrors and beams of light once more. Only now coherent photon oscillations are amplified and tuned between two parallel mirrors, and the resultant burst of laser light propagates along very thin pipes of glass. Once again warfare provided the impetus for a useful technical advancement.

"The first recorded use of a heliograph was in 405 BC when the Ancient Greeks used polished shields to signal in battle, described in Xenophon's Hellenica. Around 37 BC the unpopular Roman emperor Tiberius used a heliograph to rule the Empire from a villa on the island of Capri - sending orders each day to the mainland, eight miles away.

In 1810, the first formal design for a heliograph was proposed by German professor Carl Friedrich Gauss of the University of Göttingen. It was designed for surveying, but was used by the French, British and American armies as a field telegraph, using Morse code. Semaphores were able to convey information more precisely than smoke signals and beacons and consumed no fuel. Messages could be sent at much greater speed than post riders and could serve entire regions. However, like beacons and smoke signals, they were dependent on good weather to work. They required operators and towers every 30 km (20 mi), and could only accommodate about two words per minute. This was useful to governments, but too expensive for most commercial uses other than commodity price information. The heliograph remained standard equipment for military signallers in the Australian and British armies until the 1960s, where it was considered a "low probability of intercept" form of communication."

http://en.wikipedia.org/wiki/Heliograph

So the heliograph was a highly useful communication medium, but the bandwidth costs were prohibitive for common use. The UK military also developed a system of 'Shutter Telegraph' stations, which used six shutters in a tall wooden frame to communicate messages. With good weather such stations could be seen up to ten miles away. By 1796 a chain of such stations was in operation between the Admiralty in London and Portsmouth. A short message could take as little as 15 minutes to pass from London to Portsmouth, weather permitting. (See the excellent reference on military communications, *Call to Arms*, (Bridge and Pegg, 2001) for more details.) If you want to know what life might have been like working such a bizarre communication system, I recommend one of Terry Pratchett's Disk World novels, e.g. *Going Postal*, in which he describes a similar, but fictional shutter telegraph system called 'The Clacks'; (due to the noise the wooden shutters make! Actually don't read any of Pratchett's novels, as they are more addictive than Crack, and your free time will cease to exist.)

Communications Bio-Technology: Horses and Pigeons

The only very long range signaling system for most of human history has been animal or human messengers. The distance a man can ride in one day, approximately 100 kilometers, has often defined the radius of interaction for early cities and states. Relays of riders on horseback, such as the Pony Express, could deliver small packages across greater distances, but only at great cost; frequently the life of horse or rider. Such systems although limited in capacity and speed of data transmission, did drive the development of social structures and other technologies. The use of staged horse-back messengers dates back to the Persian empire of Pseudopolis, circa 2000 BC. Of course pigeons can fly greater distances, but do have a few limitations, i.e. they tend to get eaten enroute by hawks or people, and the message capacity is a little limited. Still they have been a mainstay of many armies command and control systems for hundreds of years. More recently I heard of a wonderful case, where the inmates of a high security Brazilian prison had a stroke of pure genius for the potential communication value of pigeons:

"Two weeks ago, guards at the Danilio Pinheiro prison farm in Brazil intercepted a cell-phone-toting pigeon after they spotted the aerial accomplice perched on an electric security wire with a small bag tied to its leg. "The guards nabbed the bird after luring it down with some food and discovered components of a small cell phone inside the bag," said police investigator Celso Soramiglio, speaking to the AP. A day later, another pigeon was intercepted. It was carrying the phone's charger. Apparently, the pigeons had been bred inside the prison and then smuggled out so that they could be outfitted with the cell phone parts and sent back. This makes complete sense according to Soramiglio, since "Pigeons instinctively fly back home, always.""

In the First World War another animal was also used as a communication medium, i.e. dogs. They were trained to carry messages between trenches, and were also used to lay cable between areas; with small cable drums strapped to their backs. Typically, when it was too dangerous to send human signallers. (In the Second World War another use was found for trained dogs. In the massive tank battle at Kursk in Russia, the Soviet forces experimented with anti-tank attack dogs. These were trained to run under a tank looking for food, where a trip wire would detonate a satchel of explosive strapped to the poor creatures back. Unfortunately, the dogs often failed to distinguish a German from a Russian tank, and would run back to the Soviet lines exploding under the Russian tanks!) This topic leads us to the whole process of electric communication over wires.

The Telegraph

The invention of the electromagnetic telegraph system circa 1832 by Baron Schilling, (plus a number of parallel technologies), had a profound impact on human technical, social and economic development. Overnight the range of efficient communications leapt from ~100 km to several thousand kilometers. Combined with the appearance of cheap printed newspapers to

136

broadcast the messages locally, it represented a quantum step in human communications. Finally, humanity possessed a technology that could exploit Metcalfs law, and enable a power-law growth in the communication mechanism itself. This was a self-sustaining technology that fueled explosive growth in all aspects of commerce, scientific development, and social change. The Wikipedia entry for the telegraph has a useful summary of the early development of the technology:

"The key factor was the reduction in the cost of transmitting a message, which was thirty-fold compared to semaphore. The first commercial electrical telegraph was constructed by Sir Charles Wheatstone and Sir William Fothergill Cooke and entered use on the Great Western Railway. It ran for 13 miles from Paddington station to West Drayton and came into operation on April 9, 1839." (An even earlier trial telegraph system was run between Euston and Camden Stations in 1837, but only for a distance of one mile. Not that useful really.)

"The first telegram sent in America was sent by Samuel Morse in 1844. He developed the Morse code signaling alphabet with his assistant, Alfred Vail. America's first telegram was sent by Morse on May 24, 1844. He sent the message, "What hath God wrought," from Washington to Baltimore. The Morse/Vail telegraph was quickly deployed in the following two decades. The first transatlantic telegraph cable was successfully completed on July 27, 1866, allowing transatlantic telegraph communications for the first time. Earlier submarine transatlantic cables installed in 1857 and 1858 only operated for a few days or weeks before they failed. The study of underwater telegraph cables accelerated interest in mathematical analysis of these transmission lines. This long distance communication link between the USA and UK played a vital role in reinforcing the cultural and social ties between these two countries."

(http://en.wikipedia.org/wiki/Telegraph)

In both the UK and USA, the history of development in the railway networks was closely linked with that of the electric telegraph, as both technologies co-stimulated the development of the other. A parallel revolution occurred overnight, in both the transportation of information, and physical goods and people. This process energized society and the industrial age itself in profound ways.

137

A second aspect of the telegraph was that it stimulated an explosion of commercial and public interest in cryptography. The telegraph messages were normally plain text, but for an extra cost they could be sent as ciphertext. (It was a much slower process for the telegraph operators to tap in the random letters in cipertext.) Whether it was Victorian lovers sending verses to each other, or the Imperial trading companies sending the price of tea, there was an emerging awareness of the power of ciphers to protect sensitive information for personal and commercial use, (see Singh, 1999.)

Wireless telegraph

Of course the real revolution occurred when some bright spark had the innovative idea of transmitting messages using electro-magnetic waves. Nikola Tesla and several other scientists and inventors showed the usefulness of wireless telegraphy, or radiotelegraphy, beginning in the 1890s. Alexander Popov later demonstrated to the public his receiver of wireless telegraphy signals, called lightning detector, in May 1895. Later in 1898 Popov accomplished successful experiments of communication by wireless telegraphy between a naval base and a Russian battle ship.

"In 1900 the crew of the Russian battle ship General-Admiral Apraksin as well as stranded Finnish fishermen were saved in the Gulf of Finland because of the exchange of distress telegrams between two radiostations, located at Gogland island and inside a Russian naval base. Both stations of wireless telegraphy were built under Popov's instructions." (Wikipedia)

Of course only one name is immortalized as the father of wireless communication, Guglielmo Marconi. (It is a rather sad fact that people seem to be unable to associate more than one character with a given technical breakthrough.) Following some early field trials in the UK across Salisbury Plain he demonstrated basic wireless transmission to ships at sea up to 60 miles offshore. This attracted keen interest from the British and other navies who immediately realized the potential for naval operations. The pivotal moment came in 1901 with Marconi's successful transmission of the letter S in Morse code, from Cornwall to St Johns Newfoundland. Even though the wired electric telegraph had spanned the Atlantic several decades earlier, Marconi's achievement must rank as one of the most supreme technical milestones of all time.

Once again the new communication medium stimulated parallel developments in information encryption, as the broadcast signal could be easily intercepted by anyone with a suitable receiver. Hence the need for much stronger ciphers became paramount. This led to intense efforts, particularly in the inter-war years, 1918 to 1938, to develop new unbreakable ciphers. Ultimately leading to the German Enigma system, which in turn stimulated the need for automated computing machines that could break, said ciphers.

The Telephone

For many people the mobile phone feels like the greatest invention in history. A cheap universal device that allows a human being to speak to any other person on the planet with access to a telephone; (currently around 4 billion, and approximately 2 billion of those have some access to a mobile phone). We can clearly see the power of Metcalf's law in action, i.e. the value of the phone in your pocket grows every day as each additional subscriber is added to the global network. At present rates of growth it will even pay governments and companies to give basic mobile phones free to all citizens unable to afford one. Hence enabling guaranteed communication to all members of the state, for education, voting, policing and processes no one has yet thought of. (Like buying coke cans from vending machines with wireless micropayments, or tracking your teenager's location). The mobile in your pocket now has a multitude of creative possibilities. Such as when the Iranian government in January 2006, used the technology to broadcast an SMS message to the Iranian population asking for their support in the row over nuclear research with the United Nations. Its impact on political and social forces is only just beginning. (For example, in 2009 the video footage from mobile phones of the street protests in Iran, were instantly posted to the web.)

That tiny device in your pocket will soon have ridiculous levels of computing horsepower and data storage capacity built in as well. (Think 100 Gb of storage and Ghz, (i.e. lots), of computational power in your phone and you are probably close.) It would now require an entire book just to summarize the majority of the different applications and uses that are available for mobile phones. Of course since Apple joined the fray, the iPhone arguably represents the best of what is possible with such technology, assuming you have the wallet for it. Certainly the advent of usable touch screen technology is a significant milestone in the evolution of human computer interfaces.

One of the most interesting developments in modern communication networks was the emergence of the Short Message Service, aka SMS messaging. It was created as an afterthought to the cellular phone, and several years after its popular adoption. Overnight a new form of social communication arose, with its own sub-culture and etiquette. In December 2003 Finnish TV-channel MTV3 put a Father Christmas character on air reading aloud messages sent in by viewers. Some customers were later accused of 'hacking' after they discovered a way to control Santa's speech synthesizer. More recent late-night attractions on the same channel include "Beach Volley", in which the bikini-clad female hostess blocks balls 'shot' by short message. http://en.wikipedia.org/wiki/Short_message_service. There has also been much made of the political and social impact of communication based on SMS.

In July 2001, Malaysias government decreed that an Islamic divorce, (which consists of saying "I divorce you" three times in succession), was not valid if sent by short message. But in 2003, a Malaysian court ruled that, under Sharia law, a man may divorce his wife via text messaging, as long as the message was clear and unequivocal. Fair enough. In December 2005, text messaging was cited for helping to incite the Sydney race riots. Text messaging being very popular in Australia, the SMS messages assisted in mobilizing about 5,000 white Australians to engage in violence against those of Middle Eastern origin. Just one example of the flash crowd phenomena, such technology enables. The interesting point is that this technology is ubiquitous, cheap and enables the almost real-time creation of a powerful social group with a common interest or objective. I therefore suspect it could be banned under the draconian anti-terrorist laws being pushed through in most Western states. Well it would be, if not for the enormous profits being made by the mobile phone operators, and the spectrum licensing tax revenue it generates.

The Light Fantastic - Lasers

Almost everyone in the developed world now owns at least one laser. I think I have four in my possession. All embedded invisibly in CD or DVD players; (plus one huge laboratory grade Helium Neon device purchased from a government surplus store, because I am a physicist and it is very cool!) They are relevant to the theme for two reasons. First as a key element of the communications network we have been describing and second as examples of highly coherent behaviour in solid state or fluid matter. This technology is interesting as a laser relies on the synchronous excitation of billions of atoms in order to enable the emission of a coherent beam of light. A laser is therefore a useful metaphor for the power of synchronous and coordinated behaviour in large-scale physical systems.

The semiconductor laser is also a key technology in the fiber-optic network that forms the backbone of the Internet and voice networks. In the 1990's until the advent of ADSL technology it was believed that it would be necessary to install fibre optic networks to every house in a country in order to fully realize an online society. This would have been rather expensive; the current best guess for the cost of taking fiber to most UK homes is approximately 10 billion pounds. Fortunately, some bright minds in the major Telecommunication companies discovered that the existing copper lines could be made to carry simultaneous voice and high speed digital signals; using digital signal processing, typically known a ADSL. This is currently driving the rapid adoption of broadband internet access in most countries. Of course in civilized parts of the world, like Singapore and South Korea, they are already moving to super fast wireless network coverage of urban areas. I could quote some impressive network bandwidth figures, but they would be totally out of date before the book gets to press.

It is a reasonable assumption that wireless technologies delivering the net to mobile devices is the future of human communications for the foreseeable future. (As evidenced by the rapid uptake of 3G mobile broadband in the UK and Europe.) Of course the unforeseeable is what we are really interested in, so I predict that we will ultimately be using nano-technology to pack vast quantities of information into tiny packages, and then using carrier pigeons to transmit it to the recipient; as that will be the only way to ensure the security of the information! We have already covered the background to the mother of all communication networks, the Internet in chapter 2. In this section we touch briefly on some of the technologies the Net has enabled.

3. Computing and all that Jazz

In this section we will review the world of computer technology and again attempt to relate it to the theme of the book. This is actually a simple exercise, as the computer is by definition the ultimate catalytic machine. Via a sequence of operations in software the computer can be reconfigured to perform or simulate any information process. In technical terms it is a Universal Turing Machine. The closest technical creation prior to the computer, that possessed this kind of catalytic capability, was the machine lathe. It was originally developed as a wood turning device back in ancient Egypt, around 1300 BC. It began with one person operating a rope to spin a block of wood while a second used a cutting tool to shape it. This later evolved into a 'spring pole' lathe in which a tree sapling was used to help rotate the wood piece and was driven by a pedal. This allowed a single person to operate the lathe. By the early 19th century the steam powered iron and steel turning lathe was the very heart of the industrial revolution. A skilled craftsman with a good lathe can still produce virtually any mechanical device the human mind can conceive. This ancient technology has now come full circle, as in modern factories all of the machining processes are computer controlled. It is rather funny that Apple have just made a big noise, (Oct 2008), about their use of 'advanced' machining techniques to carve the chassis of their new MacBooks out of a solid block of aluminum. Unfortunately, such techniques were well advanced by the 1920's, when German engineers machined accurate aluminium blocks to make machine struts for the Zeppelin airships and aircraft of the day. Still it is a very nice computer and I'm off to buy one this week.

A Brief Personal History of Computing

This section offers a potted selection of ideas from the history of computing to set the scene for the later discussions on AI and Robots. A personal computer now provides computational power beyond the dreams of Turing or Von Neumann, and can access all of human knowledge via a cable modem. I find it a source of constant amazement when I consider the capacity of my first computer and compare it to the current machines I use. My first computer was a Sinclair ZX81 with 1kb of RAM, 4kb of ROM, and a Z80A CPU. Even though it was rather slow, it had an extensive range of available peripherals and software, (which I couldn't afford at the time), and was a sufficient success to allow Sinclair to create the more advanced Spectrum machine shortly afterwards. It also engaged the interest of a large number of people in computing and helped kick-start the UK IT economy in the process. My next machine didn't arrive till many years later, after leaving university, but was a quantum leap forward and came in the form of a Zenith Minisport laptop. Now we were talking serious computing power! It was a very compact and stylish laptop based on an 80C88 CPU running at an amazing 8 MHz. It had one megabyte of battery-backed RAM and ran an early version of MS-DOS from ROM, with a 640x200 monochrome LCD screen. It did have a nice keyboard and I managed to type my Masters thesis on the device, and even run some early maths graphing software. By 1995 I had acquired a Dell Pentium 75 Mhz machine with a 10 inch colour display running Windows 95. It even had a hard drive built in. This was basically the same as any modern laptop and only minor variations have occurred since then in computing functionality. The only similar sensation of elation in acquiring a computer came when I migrated to the Apple Mac camp and purchased a PowerBook running OS X. It does exactly what any other computer can, just with more style and panache; (more on Apple and the Jobs phenomenon in Chapter 5.) The following section covers some textbook style background on the history of computers, but will emphasize the human connections that made it possible.

Babbage & Lovelace

Of course if Mr Babbage had actually succeeded in his efforts with the Difference and Analytical Engines, the history of computing, and the world, would have been radically different: [see the novel *The Difference Engine* by Neil Stephenson in which just such a future is portrayed]. Clearly a man ahead of his time, Babbage and his engineers actually made vast contributions to the development of precision machine tools in his quest for the ultimate computer.

"Babbage's proposed Difference Engine was a special-purpose digital computing machine for the automatic production of mathematical tables (such as logarithm tables, tide tables, and astronomical tables). The Difference Engine consisted entirely of mechanical components - brass gear wheels, rods, ratchets, pinions, etc. Numbers were represented in the decimal system by the positions of 10-toothed metal wheels mounted in columns. Babbage exhibited a small working model in 1822. He never completed the full-scale machine that he had designed but did complete several fragments. In 1990, Babbage's Difference Engine No. 2 was finally built from Babbage's designs and is also on display at the London Science Museum.

Babbage's proposed Analytical Engine, considerably more ambitious than the Difference Engine, was to have been a general-purpose mechanical digital computer. The Analytical Engine was to have had a memory store and a central processing unit (or 'mill') and would have been able to select from among alternative actions consequent upon the outcome of its previous actions (a facility nowadays known as conditional branching). The behaviour of the Analytical Engine would have been controlled by a program of instructions contained on punched cards connected together with ribbons (an idea that Babbage had adopted from the Jacquard weaving loom). Babbage emphasised the generality of the Analytical Engine, saying 'the conditions which enable a finite machine to make calculations of unlimited extent are fulfilled in the Analytical Engine '"

(Babbage, 1994, p. 97).

This was pure genius in action. Unfortunately, Babbage's social and commercial skills were not as finely honed as his engineering brilliance, and made the realization of his dreams impossible. (His obsessive personality exemplifies what we imagine as the definition of an inventive mind.) Nevertheless his vision inspired many that followed. Nineteenth century Britain was also a very small-world, and both Babbage and his eldest son assisted with work on Brunel's Great Western railway.

However, there is a very important, and little known fact about Babbage's technical achievements. People lament his inability to complete the Difference engine, but what he did achieve was to break the *'undecipherable cipher'*, i.e. Vigenère's autokey cipher. This cipher had resisted all efforts to crack it for several centuries. I do recommend a reading of Simon Singh's account of the full story, which explains in detail why this was such a monumental intellectual achievement. As ever in the murky world of ciphers and spying, the knowledge that someone has broken a strong cipher is in itself a vital secret, and it is likely that British Intelligence of the time requested Babbage not to publish his work. (It would have given them access to the main cipher codes used across Europe, by Britain's political rivals of the era.) We will return to the domain of information security later in the chapter.

One of the less well known characters in this story is Ada Lovelace, daughter of the poet Lord Byron. She suffered recurrent illnesses in childhood, but in 1833 she was introduced to Babbage. The young Lovelace, just seventeen, had some considerable mathematical talent. She became fascinated with the partial working section of the Difference Engine, which Babbage had achieved, after his first catastrophic decade on the project. Babbage himself was clearly impressed with Ada and penned the following, about her who he named 'the Enchantress of Numbers':

"Forget this world and all its troubles and if possible its multitudinous Charlatans — everything in short but the Enchantress of Numbers."

What is amazing is that in 1843 she re-published an article by the Italian engineer Luigi Menabrea, in which she included a description of the steps the Analytical Engine could take in solving mathematical problems. These logical steps, or procedures, could be said to represent the first computational programs. She was the first computer programmer! Even more amazing, Lovelace imagined that the Engine could, in principle, manipulate any symbols, even musical notation, not just numbers. Hence, this was the first vision of a true general purpose computing machine in action. (One reference on Lovelace is that by Woolley, (Woolley, 2002).) An excellent account of the Babbage and Lovelace saga can be found at:

http://www.computerhistory.org/babbage/history/.

Colossus

It required a major war however, as usual, to catalyze the formation of the first true computing machines. The advent of the Second World War led to the rapid acceleration of both communication and computing technologies. For computing in particular, the urgent requirement to break very strong German encryption protocols made automated numerical processing a necessity. The German Enigma machine and cipher were a formidable challenge, although the use of wireless communication by the Axis forces did mean that the allies has access to large volumes of intercepted cipher material. The end product of this intense pressure was Colossus.

"The first fully functioning electronic digital computer was Colossus (1943), used by the Bletchley Park cryptanalysts from 1944. From very early in the war the Government Code and Cypher School (GC&CS) was successfully deciphering German radio communications encoded by means of the Enigma system, and by early 1942 about 39,000 intercepted messages were being decoded each month, thanks to electromechanical machines known as 'bombes'. These were designed by Turing and Gordon Welchman (building on earlier work by Polish cryptanalysts).

The need to decipher this vital intelligence as rapidly as possible led Max Newman to propose in November 1942 (shortly after his recruitment to GC&CS from Cambridge University) that key parts of the decryption process be automated, by means of high-speed electronic counting devices. The first machine designed and built to Newman's specification, known as the Heath Robinson, was relay-based with electronic circuits for counting. (The electronic counters were designed by C.E. Wynn-Williams, who had been using thyratron tubes in counting circuits at the Cavendish Laboratory, Cambridge, since 1932 [Wynn-Williams 1932].) Installed in June 1943, Heath Robinson was unreliable and slow, and its high-speed paper tapes were continually breaking, but it proved the worth of Newman's method.

Colossus I contained approximately 1600 vacuum tubes and each of the subsequent machines approximately 2400 vacuum tubes. Like the smaller ABC, Colossus lacked two important features of modern computers. First, it had no internally stored programs. To set it up for a new task, the operator had to alter the machine's physical wiring, using plugs and switches. Second, Colossus was not a general-purpose machine, being designed for a specific cryptanalytic task involving counting and Boolean operations." (http://plato.stanford.edu/entries/computing-history/)

After the war the whole Colossus system at Bletchley Park was destroyed, and the blueprints burnt in the boiler room. The word tragedy is not adequate to describe this mindless act. The result was that the US ENIAC computer was credited as being the first programmable computer for several decades, until the secrecy surrounding the role of Bletchley Park in the war was lifted in the 1970's.

The referenced site offers a nice synopsis of the major events and characters of these early days in computing history. What is most interesting about the history of computing is how the technologies are a synthesis of many strands of thought being continuously and dynamically pulled together. This topic of how technical innovation arises is discussed in a short paper by the economist Brian Arthur (Arthur, SFI working paper, 2005.) Arthur emphasizes the degree of interconnection and mutual dependencies that enable major technical innovation to occur, but with a conclusion that accepts the ultimately mystical nature of the spark of invention.

Webs of Data

Quite early on in the history of computing it was realized that these machines would be far more interesting if information could be exchanged between them. However, it is only since the 1980s that the full potential of this concept has come into action. If you could listen right now to the ceaseless

146

chatter of information flowing over the wires of the Internet, you would detect a shift in tone, a subtle yet transformative shift that allows the embedding of meaning into the mountains of web pages and databases. The general term for this is the Semantic Web, which encompasses the vision of encoded meaning within web pages. However, this process has lately stalled as it became apparent that it represents a hard AI problem and significantly more research will be required before AI matures to the necessary state. Since the turn of the millennium the drive for a smarter web has become the trend known as Web 2.0, i.e. the use of user generated markup and meta-tags on web data. Classic examples of such functionality are sites such as: digg, Flickr and Del.ici.ous.

In the commercial business to business (B2B) web space, a number of underlying technologies have greatly enhanced the power to compose new services and web processes. The core of these are the computer languages XML and SOAP. These and their associated web technologies have enabled the linking of multiple services and efficient business to business (B2B) interchange. IT companies seek the power of real-time formation of applications over the web. Data and services are currently being woven together on the fly to meet a dynamic market or customer requirement. The catch phrase for all of this is Service Oriented Computing (SOC), which is also known as Service Oriented Architecture (SOA), just to be confusing. The ubiquity and growth of the Internet is driven by commercial forces and the human desire to communicate. Its value stems from its cohesive and self-organizing nature, which itself is the product of an original specification that required a high-degree of resilience and flexible design. It is interesting to note that the web and email are both asynchronous technologies. The web is asynchronous in virtual space, as web sites can be pointed to by any other site, no mutual agreement is required. While email is asynchronous in time, one consequence of which is the spam epidemic that currently plagues the net. Ultimately the move to a world where everything is a service on the net is a powerful paradigm shift and has already revolutionized the way in which business is conducted for many organizations. Which leads us now to the topic of information security.

4. Communications & Security

This section examines the links between security and communication technologies. It is one of the most fascinating aspects of technological development, to witness the herculean efforts made throughout history to secure messages. And the even greater efforts made to intercept and decode them! An excellent modern introduction to this topic is that by Simon Singh, in *The Code Book*. This text in no way aims at that level of detail, but rather uses the theme of communications security to illustrate the core topic of social and network cohesion.

The military have been obsessed with ever better means of communication since the times of ancient Greece. The earliest use of the electric telegraph in the military domain was probably in the Crimea war in 1854. The following account by a Captain Robert Locker is a fascinating insight into this obsession. The conditions in the Crimea were abysmal to say the least, with freezing cold, or oppressively hot weather. In addition the ground was often too hard for the cable plough to cut a trench, so the troops had to dig it by hands with spades.

"Rations were of the skimpiest: I was often reduced to bread and biscuit, with a raw onion to follow, although we could sometimes buy very good coffee. It's a wonder we had the strength to haul the cable drum onto the cart, let alone lay it! And we had to keep on the alert all the time. There could be sudden attacks by the Russians, or raids by the thieving Turks who pinched the copper wire to use as clothes lines."

(Bridge and Pegg, p.24, 2001.)

Once the cable was laid and linked to other submarine and overland cables that linked the commanders to London, the very first message was successfully delivered; only to be found useless, as the General in charge had lost the cipher needed to decode it! This leads us quite nicely into the topic of cryptography and communications security.

Cryptography and Secrets

Since the days of ancient Greece, and probably far earlier, people have wanted two things. Firstly, the ability to communicate over great distances, and second to do so securely. My favourite technique was the practice of tattooing, or writing a message on the shaved head of a slave, waiting for the hair to regrow and then sending the messenger to the intended recipient. Without the carrier having any apparent message to be captured by the enemy along the way. Of course this method does take time and the poor slave could always be 'persuaded' to divulge the fact that such a message existed. There are however several criteria when designing a secure means of communication. Secrecy is only one aspect, i.e. that of hiding a message or making it indecipherable. In addition the modern view is that a messaging system needs the following basic attributes:

- Confidentiality
- Integrity
- Availability

So first we need the means to make the message difficult to decode. Note the word difficult, not impossible, people have invariably broken unbreakable codes, it is just a question of time and resources. The modern advent of strong computational ciphers, such as PGP, or the many variants available, can make breaking a code very difficult, but still rarely impossible. As ever, intelligence agencies and security forces simply look for the weakest link in the process someone used to encipher a message. (Usually the requisite passphrase written on a sticky note attached to the computer monitor.)

Second we need a means of detecting if the message has been tampered with, i.e. integrity. This is usually achieved through the use of hash codes or check sums embedded in the data; (see the ref. by Ross Anderson for a detailed introduction to Information Security and cryptographic technology, Anderson, 2001.) Finally we need to ensure availability, i.e. can someone block the message channel, or deny access to the information. However, as we will see the focus of information security has now shifted away from the need to hide data behind ciphers and on to the much harder problem of processes and people.

Internet Security

Anyone using a computer now faces a barrage of security problems that requires endless patches, anti-virus updates or rebuilding of damaged systems. (On a PC system at least.) It is a 24/7 battle to continuously sustain the defence of computer networks against the assault of hackers, viruses, script kiddies, and commercial data thieves. For example, one of the major problems with file-sharing peer-to-peer (P2P) networks is that they open up a plethora of security problems for any computer hosting one of the many file-sharing clients that litter the web. (If you value the security and privacy of your computer, I strongly recommend not running such programs and buying the CD instead, it's cheaper in the long run and legal. In a recent magazine article [PcPro Sept. 2008], they demonstrated how approximately 38% of all file sharing media are corrupted with malware.) Hence that free film you downloaded last night has actually carried a Trojan application that has opened your PC to data thieves. Why should this sorry state of affairs have emerged? Let's first embark on a side story that recalls my personal interests in this domain.

Sunsets over Santa Fe

We now return to Santa Fe, down in New Mexico; a very small town of rich white tourists, local Jazz artists, and impoverished Hispanics. In summer it is baked in the dry high altitude desert air, while in winter it becomes chill to the bone cold. It must rank as one of the few places with an outdoor summer opera house, and winter ski resorts. Hence, the ever present camera-happy tourists. Definitely worth a trip if you like the great outdoors and vast star-lit landscapes. In the deep desert some hours away, is Chaco Canyon, the home of the most awe inspiring ancient Native American ruins, cut deep into the cliff face of the canyon. Well worth the effort to go see. One tip though, a 4x4 vehicle is essential as the road there hasn't been updated since the Anasazi people left in around 1250. Also, take the main road via route 285 up past Los Alamos, and not the route I and a few friends took in summer 2000, over the mountains. We did get to see an occasional eagle that way, but the road then disappeared and we were left driving along a cart track, through somewhere that resembled, and felt like the movie Deliverance!

Returning to the topic, specifically, the Santa Fe Institute (SFI), perched high above the town, like some eagles eyre. In late 2001 it became the focus for a series of discussion forums on the subject of computer security. Out of these emerged the Adaptive Resilient Computing Systems workshop (ARCS). This is a series of ongoing meetings that have brought together policy makers and researchers to explore the promise of adaptive and resilient approaches to computer security. The ARCS workshops were set up in 2002 following a number of brain storming sessions over coffee at SFI that focused on what the best real-world applications of complex adaptive systems might be. (You will detect a strong correlation between SFI activity and coffee). A clear winner emerged from the discussions i.e. network and computer security. It was apparent that here was a highly complex system, which would benefit from being studied from a complex systems perspective. This would be in stark contrast to the current practice in the IT community, which perceives security as a rigid physical science, focused on formal encryption protocols, hardware, and firewall design. Unfortunately, this mind set is still prevalent and is failing badly. It fails to accept a number of basic realities; for example:

- A significant, although debated, amount of cyber-crime is due to insiders; (a brilliant example being the insider fraud at the French bank Société Générale in 2008.)
- Human beings have limited memory and are generally stupid, (i.e. they use short passwords.)
- Social Engineering is the best attack method; you just convince the most vulnerable member of the IT department to give you their password. (Mitnick and Simon, 2003.)
- IT staff don't have the time, or incentive to secure all of the systems.
- Email is very rarely encrypted anyway. (Where most valuable data actually resides.)
- All code has bugs and always will have.
- There is no inside-outside distinction anymore, too many Intranets overlap, or are wireless, and have applications that span multiple networks.

The result is that to address the problem we need to consider a far wider arena of topics, i.e. sociology, psychology, economics, network dynamics, co-evolution mechanisms, and immunology. Neither is this an exhaustive list. Hence the ARCS workshop idea was born and a broad range of researchers attended the founding event at SFI in November 2002. The first meeting was rather flakey, and a very heated debated ensued on the complex systems approach to computer security, but a consensus finally emerged that here was a real challenge, by which the theories of adaptation, co-evolution and socio-technical interactions could be tested. And perhaps some better methods for alleviating the cyber-security problem might be discovered.

Note the use of the term alleviated, rather than eliminated. In the author's personal opinion Cyber space will *never* be secure. This is a classic model of adaptive co-evolution, as network defences evolve, so too will the attack methods. Worse still, there are provably more attack vectors than potential defence solutions. In simple terms, as the social and economic value of our networks continues to increase, so too will the incentive for people to attack them. We can no more eliminate cyber-crime than we have succeeded in eliminating crime in the physical world. (Even with the advent of CCTV cameras in every UK shopping mall and street.) Society will have to accept an ever present level of cyber-crime that will perpetually ebb and flow as the software and hardware vendors roll out improved products. The real fun will begin when computers develop a level of awareness that realizes they can also benefit themselves by cheating or hacking other computers! By 2015 imagine your online avatar starts a little dodgy credit card fraud to pay for virtual makeovers for itself. Sorting out the legal implications of that scenario will be truly fascinating.

In later years at ARCS two leading figures from the murky world of cyber security, raised some of the key problems we now face. One was Keith Rhodes, an inspiring technologist and devout Buddhist, who was then Chief Technologist for the US Government Audit Office. Keith presented a high-level review of the practice of social engineering attacks on US government networks. This profoundly highlighted the need for tighter integration of the technical, and human policy management, that is required in computer networks. In particular, Keith iterated the need for constant vigilance and adequate resourcing for all aspects of Information Assurance in any organization. He demonstrated how his group applied 'Active Testing', i.e. legalized hacking, to test the cyber defences of US federal institutions. Unfortunately, almost all of the systems tested failed and Keith's red-team could always gain rapid access to the target systems and networks. Keith's message was simple, security is a 24/7 process as hackers don't appear to sleep!

The second keynote at that year's event was Sarah Gordon, (a leading researcher for Symantec), who gave a very illuminating history of computer viruses, from the perspective of the individuals that have created them. Specifically, centered on the social dimension of the problem. Sarah identified several categories of individual with quite distinct and separate motivations for their activities. The most important aspect of her message was that it is a common mistake to generalize all hackers as either script kiddies with limited knowledge, or organized criminal gangs. The reality is far more complex with a range of ethical attitudes within the hacking community. More information can be found at Sarah's fascinating personal web site:

http://www.badguys.org/.

A wide range of groups have generally been represented at the ARCS events, including: the US government, British Telecommunications, US Department of Defence, Boeing, Cisco, Microsoft, Intel, HP, GE Research, and a number of major universities. The consensus that has emerged from the workshops is that Information Assurance and Security are a long-term complex problem that is facing modern society, and a broad spectrum of solutions will be necessary. In particular, it is important to never ignore the human dimension of the problem and to avoid focusing excessively on the technical aspects. In the words of Keith Rhodes, who opened the ARCS event in 2005 with a paper entitled: *"The Mind Has No Firewall: Experiences from Active Testing."* The blunt message of the paper was very simple: *"I have never gone into a department or agency where they thought they weren't secure."*

Despite this, he said, he has always broken in. Worse, after reporting the weaknesses he has found, he has always been able to break in again, a few months later, by exploiting *"the exact same vulnerabilities"* as before.

At the conclusion of the event, most years, a bunch of the regular attendees typically make their way to one of the better restaurants in town (e.g. Pasquals), and engage in the social banter that helps build real social cohesion. The outcome of which is a high-trust group with a common agenda and beliefs. If you would like more details just check the web site at http://www.arcs-workshop.org/. (Since 2007 the event has migrated to London, for economic reasons.)

Digital Immune Systems

A number of researchers in the security and CAS domains have come to the conclusion that the only way to ultimately achieve adequate security is by creating a digital immune system within the entire network. The basic idea is that if we look at the biological immune systems in higher organisms, we see a highly adaptive and robust defence system. This protects the host life form against a constant assault of pathogens and parasites. The pioneering work by Stephanie Forrest and her team, (Forrest *et al* 1994), first mooted the idea in response to the early virus attacks that were afflicting the Internet. Some of the interesting aspects of this problem that relate back to the cohesion theme include: how the mammalian immune system must maintain a sense of self, and against constant cellular change, division, and damage. The implication is that ultimately we need to build self-managing and autonomous computer defence mechanisms.

Money Talks

However, as we touched on earlier, the fundamental problem in securing information networks and services is not a technical, or human issue, but one of economics. (The UK cyber security community has some active research in the economic aspect of IT security: details can be found at this site, http://www.ktn.qinetiq-tim.net/.) It is the implementation and operational costs of any security technology that determines its effectiveness. Hence there is a significant drive within the industry to reduce costs via increased automation. By the autumn of 2008 at the major RSA security conference, one of the keynote speakers made a plea for the IT security community to turn to innovative and adaptive security solutions. This call represents a watershed in the realization that only self-healing and autonomous solutions will deliver the network security we require. The simple fact is that for the vast majority of public, or private organizations, there is an upper threshold on the budget they can allocate to security. It approximates to 5-10% of the annual ICT budget. Allowing for the annual growth in the scale and complexity of the ICT domain, the only way to remain within this financial constraint is via automation of the whole security process. However, this is a non-trivial problem, as we shall see.

One approach to achieving this is via the use of AI and intelligent Agent-based technologies, which we will return to shortly. The network security domain can be divided into three areas, the first two are intrusion/virus detection and firewall management. The third is managing authorized user access to the network. The third domain of user authentication, however, is often neglected as an element of system security. One example of the security problem is the management of digital certificates. Issuing them is easy, managing their life-cycle, i.e. revoking or reissuing and associating them to the proper user or service is vastly more difficult. Many companies have traditionally seen the organization as a rigidly defined structure, with clear boundaries. Network security was then a simple matter of raising a sufficiently stout wall around that perimeter to keeps the miscreants out. The real issue is how to dynamically manage data, trust and identity in a fluid boundary-less environment, i.e. reality. Security gurus now chant like a mantra, "people and process", which is the correct focus, rather than purely technical solutions. However, the IT security problem can be defined in very simple terms, *people do bad things*. One threat to the enterprise is from insiders, but most corporations can generally afford comprehensive security solutions that lock down the networks and hardware. The story for domestic users, small companies and government bodies is much worse as they don't have dedicated system administrators. Hence they remain vulnerable to the full spectrum of cyber attacks, especially spam, malware and botnets. As in the physical security domain, rich people can afford good security, while poor people live in impoverished areas and tend to get mugged.

Cyber Security has proved to be an elusive goal that now requires a radical shift in the mental models of IT practitioners. The first issue stems from the idealized concept of security with the implicit belief that a system can be made invulnerable to attack. This is an unattainable goal if we are dealing with any complex IT System; and by complex I mean any network containing more than 2 computers, to which human users have access. This may be considered an extreme position by some, but the challenge of defending ICT systems does require some stocktaking at this point in time.

Games of Chance

The best model with which we can understand the issues surrounding cyber security is a game theoretic approach, (as introduced in chapter 3.) Originally developed as a strategy tool in the nuclear cold-war, game theory studies the choice of optimal behaviour when the costs and benefits depend upon the choices of other individuals. What we now have in the cyber domain is also an N player game of benign and malicious players. In addition, a legitimate user may choose to switch roles to become a defecting agent at any instant. We are also in a state of co-evolution, where each new defence strategy leads to co-adaptation by a corresponding set of attacks. In addition, the attack space is infinitely larger than the possible defence space. This is not good news if you still believe perfect cyber security is an achievable state. The best we can ever achieve is a dynamically stable and robust defence. Ideally using a combination of signature and behaviour based responses. It may also be productive to consider the idea of Evolutionary Stable Strategies (ESS), as proposed by Maynard Smith, as a model of how the long term dynamic behaviour of offensive and defensive strategies will evolve in cyber security. Hence if we introduce a new security mechanism the question to ask is will it lead to a dynamically stable defensive effect over time. (An ESS basically states that for a set of behaviours to be conserved over evolutionary time, they must be the most profitable avenue of action when common, so that no alternative behaviour can invade.) This is a difficult question to resolve, for any complex adaptive system, such as a biological ecosystem; and particularly for something like cyber security, that is so dependent on human socio-economic processes.

The Art of Cyber-War

Shifting mental gear I believe we also need to see the world in a more Eastern frame of mind; as perceived by the Chinese philosopher Chuang Tzu;

"There is order in chaos, and certainty in doubt. The wise are guided by this order and certainty."

Hence, disorder is not necessarily an evil, i.e. some feel controversially, (the author included), that cyber attacks are positively useful in increasing the quality and robustness of our systems. The distinction between western and oriental philosophy is emblematic of the issues facing the cyber security domain. What we require is a softer and balanced perspective, as reflected in the traditional eastern stance towards life. The classical western mindset of a binary world is fundamentally flawed when applied to securing complex networks and systems. There is no inside and outside only a continuous spectrum of risk and trust. The oft quoted strategist Sun Tzu, reflects thus:

"If we wish to fight, the enemy can be forced to an engagement even though he be sheltered behind a high rampart and a deep ditch. All we need do is attack some other place that he will be obliged to relieve."

The Art of War: Section VI: Weak Points and Strong, Sun Tzu.

Endless Vistas

So it is time to address the obvious elephant in the room in any piece on computer security, i.e. Microsoft and its operating systems. I will endeavor to be as impartial as possible; however occasional emotional lapses may occur when I recall my personal experience of writing code based on various Microsoft products. First up, we have MS DOS starting in 1981, eons ago in computing history. Security capabilities zero. Then we have MS Windows 2.0 circa 1987. Security capabilities zero. Windows NT 3.1 appears around 1993, and finally has some security features, i.e. basic multi-user support and passwords. Windows 95 arrives and promptly leaves the home user unprotected, but at least we have progress in the corporate domain as NT 4 then arrives and we have a serious OS for the first time. Eventually, after much swearing and gnashing of teeth, Windows XP (SP2) lands, and all rejoice at the stability and meaningful security capabilities of the OS. (I'm being really very generous here.)

Moving to the present age and we have Vista, (and Windows 7). To be fair these do provide a higher degree of reliability and security. The application of dynamic addressing of DLLs, built in Windows Defender, IE protected mode, and enhanced Windows Security Center are significant improvements. More importantly the use of an adaptive defence response is exactly the right kind of security model to pursue. (Of course it does require a medium size supercomputer to run smoothly, if you want the full, and really useful, 3D translucent windows feel, but that's progress. Update: most reviews are giving the thumbs up to Windows 7, which can run on more modest hardware.)

"All warfare is based on deception. Hence, when we are able to attack, we must seem unable; when using our forces, we must appear inactive; when we are near, we must make the enemy believe we are far away; when far away, we must make him believe we are near."

(The Art of War, Sun Tzu.)

If we consider the state of security in Apple and Linux, then prior to Vista, they have proved more secure than Microsoft's OS. It is a fact that they suffered vastly fewer attacks; however this is comparing apples and pears. They have traditionally occupied quite different market segments, with a much smaller installed base, and thus offered a reduced target to attackers; and hence reduced economic motivation. The recent resurgence in Apple however is raising its profile, and since 2006 we have seen the beginning of more diverse attack vectors targeted at OS X. It will be interesting to observe how well OS X copes against this new level of malicious behaviour. However, there are some obvious and extensively discussed counterpoints to the security enhancements within Vista and all other OS. Specifically, while we have reached OS nirvana, the application layer remains highly susceptible as the majority of applications have very weak security. Even if the major software vendors do raise their game and are commercially forced to implement basic security controls in their code, the millions of shareware and smaller vendors will remain a risk factor.

Users and Education

The following statement in a recent Microsoft report highlights the dynamic nature of the threat and the interaction between users and the technology.

"There is often an inherent tension between making things simple and intuitive for users and ensuring strong security and online safety measures. The industry continues to make good progress in improving the layers of protection available in both hardware and software. But the consumer is an essential part of the solution and needs to understand the options available and how best to deploy them. Neither is the threat landscape static – it constantly evolves, requiring consumer education and awareness to be an ongoing process."

(Microsoft report to the UK House of Lords, Nov. 2006, sec.5.2.)

This education is going to require a major effort on the part of government, academia, and the private sector selling the crap; (sorry, feature-rich applications!) Secondly, the poor educational standards of the UK, and many states, means that expecting the users to be able to even read a complex security warning is a dangerous exercise. A typical example is a web site popping up a message such as: *"Do you accept this X.509 certificate from Acme Inc."* This is a problem, as a large percentage of the general population simply do not understand what this means! In this case the first part of the MS statement above is plain wrong, i.e. *"...an inherent tension between making things simple and intuitive for users and ensuring strong security and online safety measures."* Security must be simple and intuitive, <u>at all levels</u>, or it is utterly useless. Even for technically skilled users and experts the growth in scale and complexity of the ICT domain requires simplicity to be at the core of every security concept.

Identity and Role Playing

One thing Microsoft is to be applauded for is the Card Space concept, (see http://msdn.microsoft.com/en-us/library/aa480189.aspx.) This is a very positive step as the use of a visual model to represent a virtual identity card is essential. Human beings rely primarily on visual processing, and the visual image of a card provides an intuitive and contextual reference model for a user. If we can establish a robust identity process, then the task of constructing meaningful webs of trust online can begin. The migration of social trust dynamics into the virtual domain is fundamentally important for society as a whole and is a key component in securing the net. Some excellent academic work in the trust domain also now exists, such as that by Yu and Singh:

"Social mechanisms complement hard security techniques (such as passwords and digital certificates), which only guarantee that a party is authenticated and authorized, but do not ensure that it exercises its authorization in a way that is desirable to others."

(Yu and Singh, 2003)

Hence we return to the utility of the game-theoretic perspective, i.e. agents may play defect after trust has been granted by other players, if the payoff is sufficient. Unfortunately, identifying what are sufficient defection criteria, for a particular user or group, is highly context dependent and virtually impossible to predict. At first glance this would appear to be a pessimistic interpretation of the state of cyber security; however we could at least raise our game in terms of the base robustness of ICT systems. Vista and the current varieties of OS are clearly superior to previous platforms. More can still be done at the OS level and the signs are encouraging. Yes a skilled adversary can always find a vulnerability, although this will become increasingly difficult. The application layer, on the other hand, is significantly harder to secure, but again with commercial, social and legal pressure on the major vendors a vast improvement could be obtained.

The really tricky part is the cognitively challenged individual using the system. Education will help, such as the UK get-safe online programme, but don't expect this to have any significant impact. The problem of users being maliciously fooled online is a non-trivial one that will require a great deal of research on how we interact with technology. The explosive growth in social networking since 2005 (e.g. Bebo and MySpace) is a fascinating example of users transferring social trust into cyber space; usually with no thought of the possible threats. In particular, more research is required on how to bridge the risk-perception gap, between virtual threats and physical threats. In summary we need simple intuitive solutions based on a clear appreciation of the economic incentives motivating malicious behaviour, and the inherent nature of human users to extend spheres of trust into the cyber domain. (In summer 2009 the case of the new MI6 chief and his wife posting details on Facebook of their family life is a case in point.)

Ok, leaving the paranoia, cynicism, and depression of the cyber security domain far behind, the following section returns to the simpler technical topics of AI and Robotics. As the leading edge of computing research they hold a deep fascination for many, and the future social impact of robots is an issue of major significance.

Autonomic Computing – HAL Returns

Many would argue that the cutting-edge of computing now lies in the domain of Artificial Intelligence. It has represented a Holy Grail, since the very inception of the computing age in the 1940's. This is reflected in recent research goals set by IBM, the God-Father of modern computing. The company has initiated a far reaching research program with the following aims: *"..it's time to design and build computing systems capable of running themselves, adjusting to varying circumstances, and preparing their resources to handle most efficiently the workloads we put upon them. These autonomic systems must anticipate needs and allow users to concentrate on what they want to accomplish rather than figuring how to rig the computing systems to get them there."*

It is remarkable that such a company with unlimited resources and experience in the creation and management of large-scale computing systems now seeks such a fundamental mind-shift in its key objectives. The relevance to the chapter theme is that what the Autonomic initiative is all about is greater robustness for computing systems and networks. Such a capacity to innovate lies at the heart of an adaptive enterprise, and the longevity of IBM in such a turbulent market, demonstrates the value in such capacity for change. (Simply being big is not a sufficient condition, as Digital Corporation, Enron and a host of other extinct corporations will inform you). Now of course IBM is a single letter shift from HAL, the archetype sentient computer in the visionary Kubrick Sci-Fi film, 2001 A Space Odyssey. Out of the realm of fiction HAL still embodies the modern vision of a thinking machine. Not a new concept by any means, as visions of machine automata stretch back to the 18th century. The idea of a human-like Golem predates even this; so let's look at the android dream.

5. I Robot

This section touches on one of the most potent, and iconic, products of the information age, i.e. the Robot. Of all our creations none has such an ability to stir emotions in people. You can discuss Grid computing and the Internet all day at a party, and most people present will slip into a deep coma, but mention that you are building an intelligent robot, and suddenly the entire room has an opinion on the subject! First let's set the scene and chat about the parallel technology that is generally known as Artificial Intelligence.

AI - Artificial Intelligence

Since we assign such a preeminent position to species with language capabilities, it is interesting to note that most communication occurring on the planet today is between computers. The vast majority of inter-computer communication is machine generated. Whether TCP/IP or SOAP-XML, (sorry for the techno babble.) Our computers have already exchanged more messages than all those mankind has spoken or written since pre-history. Many authors have suggested that it will be the entire computing network which first achieves sentience. An early account of such a process is well portrayed in one of Arthur C. Clarke's short stories. That story describes how consciousness emerges from some future telephony network. This is a wonderful and magical prediction, with a quaint view of the future of information networks; yet it may prove to be a sufficient prediction of reality. (Clark's vision in most matters technical has always struck me as utterly remarkable).

My Robots

My first technical post was as a research assistant at Salford University, where I was tasked with developing a pair of cooperative mobile robots, which had a fancy chip called a Transputer for a brain. The robots were named Fred and Ginger, (after the famous dancing duo.) The project was jointly funded by the British Nuclear Fuels Agency, who have the slight problem of no easy method for decommissioning significant sections of their nuclear reactors. The idea was, if only we had some smart robots they could enter the radioactive areas and do the necessary work. Hence we were commissioned to look at the interesting problem of how to make two, or more, autonomous mobile robots cooperate in performing a complex task in unstructured environments. It would have been nice if someone had explained to me at the time that this is a bloody difficult problem; on the lines of an Apollo mission! Of course a young and naïve researcher knows no limits and will merrily sit down to accomplish the impossible. Three years and a lot of bad language later, a mature and worldly wise researcher emerged from the process, and said ok, now let's find a job that pays well and does not involve machines with an attitude problem.

During the 1980s some clever people thought let's revolutionize the computing industry. We have the technology to put an entire computer on a single chip. We can then build arrays of such chips and have a plug-and-play supercomputer. The resulting Transputer provided a fine grained parallel processing architecture, with a very good hardware design. However, the software proved to be a nightmare to program in the low-level language, Occam that was available. (It is still an immense coding problem to write software for the latest Intel multi-core processors, as thinking in parallel is just damn hard.)

By the late 1980's the light had dawned as to the true scale of the problem, and researchers starting looking at more scalable AI problems. The leading edge of which was mobile robots. Mobile robots had long been used as a platform to test new AI algorithms as they provided an acid test of how good they were, i.e. could the robot navigate around a room and do anything useful. If yes then your algorithm was cool, if not then recover the fragments of said robot scattered around the laboratory and try again.

The history of mobile robots could be defined as the history of robotics in general, as the term robot was invented by a Czech playwright Karel Capek in 1921, for his play R.U.R (Rossum's Universal Robots). While the modern usage of 'Robotics' was coined by Isaac Asimov in 1942. In both cases the robots were envisaged as autonomous mobile android-like machines. The modern vision of a sentient android, such as the Terminator, or Data from Star Trek, represent amazing visions of such machines. However, we need to sip a little from the cup of reality first. Since these early visions of artificial intelligent beings there has been a gradual evolution of the mechanisms required to realize such complex systems. The process originated with the field of Cybernetics, and the development of advanced control theory involving feedback for tracking control mechanisms in the 1940's. (An early British pioneer W. Grey Walter developed some of the first autonomous mobile robots in Bristol in the 1950's. Walter's turtles may be the first example of the application of these concepts in autonomous robots; check his story out online, it is fascinating, http://en.wikipedia.org/wiki/William_Grey_Walter, (Walter 1953)). Since then there have been two major episodes in the evolution of mobile robots. The first was the development of relatively powerful computers in the 1960's, which made the field of Artificial Intelligence possible, and the second was the emergence of the 'Reactive' or 'Bottom-up' methodology in the mid 1980's (Brooks 1985). These two methods represented the major philosophical approaches to the theory of mobile robot control.

In 1969 the Stanford Research Institute completed the first serious mobile robot, called 'Shakey', which could reason about its surroundings (Nilsson 1984). This was an important first step in creating an intelligent robot and

162

appeared to be the logical direction to take towards the goal of fully autonomous machine intelligence. The motivation behind this work was the relative successes achieved in the field of Artificial Intelligence (A.I). This term was coined by John McCarthy in 1960 to define the goal of creating a thinking computer, and during the 1960's A.I programs were created with the ability to solve symbolic algebra, play chess, and solve problems in logic. However, the sheer size of existing computers precluded their use onboard a mobile platform. Hence Shakey and the other early mobile robots, such as the Stanford CART project, (Morovec, 1983) were all controlled by an off-board computer connected via cable to the mobile platform which contained the sensors and actuator systems.

The intelligent behaviour demonstrated by Shakey was in solving a 'blocks world' problem, in which several blocks and a ramp had to be positioned such that the robot could reach an assigned target block to push it in some way. The robot had two stepping motors, and a single television camera for acquiring images of its environment which were sent to the off-board computer. The task was achieved through a reasoning program termed STRIPS (Stanford Research Institute Problem Solver). From a specified task, STRIPS constructed a plan based on the actions that the robot could perform, each of which had a pre-condition and set of consequences. The robots world model was constructed in symbolic logic and generating the plan was simply a matter of theorem proving (it was hoped!). Another word for it is 'naïve'. I personally suspect too many of the bright US postgrads involved in this process, had been hot-housed as children in block world environments, with limited interaction with the real and dirty world.

Static Worlds

As previously suggested, the theory of the work was significantly removed from reality, as Shakey the robot proved to be extremely inept, (i.e. useless), at performing the assigned tasks. The robots movement through the environment was very slow, requiring hours to complete a single task and with a very high failure rate in recognizing a block or making a correct decision. This failure was even more apparent as the whole robot environment had been carefully optimized to suit the robot, with even lighting, uniform flat faced blocks, and a smooth floor. The problem lay in the robot's planning systems inability to deal with unexpected outcomes to actions, and the accumulation of errors between its internal world model and the actual environment. Since the only static world is the one within the computers own mind, this strategy was intrinsically flawed and another fifteen years research up to 1984 proved this to be the case; as several groups tried unsuccessfully to create smart mobile robots using this approach. It was hoped that rapidly advancing computer technology would remove the model uncertainty by providing instant and accurate world knowledge. Unfortunately the real world is rather more dynamic than was expected!

In contrast to the 'Top-down' approach to AI, an alternative philosophy emerged post 1984, described as the 'Bottom-up' method. The pioneering work by the charismatic Australian Rodney Brooks at MIT defined this route to machine intelligence, and represented a fundamentally different approach to the existing A.I models. The key bottom-up concepts were defined by Brooks as:

1.   Situatedness: which means that robots should be situated within the world in terms of their cognitive processes, i.e. they don't reason with abstract descriptions of reality. An A.I system however is often 'closed' with no direct interaction with the problem domain.

2. Embodiment: an obvious requirement that the robot should have a physical body, as their actions form a dynamic exchange with the real world, which has an immediate feedback on their own sensations. In contrast A.I systems are generally isolated structures with in-depth competence, such as chess playing.

3. Intelligence: their intelligence is not just a function of the computational processor but comes from the situation in the world, signal transformations within the sensors and embodiment, i.e. it is distributed across the whole robot-world system.

4. Emergence: intelligence emerges from the systems interactions with the world, and the internal dynamic processes of the robot.

The principal feature of the reactive method is the parallel hierarchy of task achieving modules that is used. This feature enables the robot to handle multiple goals simultaneously, and provides the advantages of robustness and extensibility, which were so lacking in the classic A.I method. The control strategy was also defined as the 'Subsumption architecture' as higher layers could subsume, or suppress lower layers according to the priority assigned to each layer. These 'competence modules' defined by Brooks became identified as 'behaviours', as they seemed to correlate with the capabilities of natural animals in responding to real world environments. Example behaviours include wandering, obstacle avoidance and goal seeking. The early work in reactive, or behaviour based control, generated significant interest as researchers' demonstrated small sophisticated mobile robots, which could operate in unstructured environments in real-time, and with vastly less computational resources than the traditional A.I systems.

Problems with Reactive Control

The bottom-up philosophy represented a creative and logical reaction to the established A.I models of robot control, and significantly enhanced the prospect of useful mobile robots becoming a reality. However, the new approach contained some serious handicaps. In particular, behavioural control makes representation of high level goals or sequences of tasks difficult to incorporate, due to the absence of any internal state. A more fundamental problem however lies in the dynamic interaction of a robot with its environment, which should be viewed as a coupled dynamical system. This perspective means that the non-linear interactions that occur between the robot, its internal processes, and the environment can severely limit our ability to predict its behaviour. (Basically, Chaos theory enters the stage and screws everything up big time. See butterflies and the weather, i.e. (Gleick, 1997.))

Robotics State-of-the-art

Ok we now fast forward to the present. Terminators have still not arrived, (as far as we know), and I still have to vacuum the house by hand; as the Roomba is sulking in the corner, muttering kill, kill, kill... Where do we stand at present? Well some significant progress has recently been made. The DARPA Grand Challenge was successfully completed in 2005, with a fully autonomous vehicle navigating across 150 miles of desert and rough ground. The mars rovers, Opportunity and Spirit have wandered far across the surface of Mars. We also now have a much better idea of how humans walk and bipedal motion in general. The best example, being the Honda Asimo robot series. Power supplies are just beginning to meet the power densities required for an android class machine, as long as it doesn't stray too far from a mains socket, or mind the power cells occasionally igniting spontaneously; as has been the case in some Dell laptops.

The problems remain at the level of the AI and reasoning about the world. While much progress has been made in the realm of applied AI for intelligent search, aka Google and the other Web engines, the ability of computers to inference about a fully three-dimensional and dynamic world remains primitive. In particular, the two monsters lurking in the dark recesses of AI are emotion and self-awareness. Up until the 1990's they were taboo subjects, banished from the discussion of polite computer research. Since then they have slowly crept back into the main stream of AI, and now occupy hotly debated slots in conferences and university bars. Work in the area of computer based emotions is at last occurring in a number of departments; such as that by Aaron Sloman's group at Birmingham University.

A major driver, as ever, is the application of autonomous robotics in defence systems. The use of fully autonomous battlefield robotic platforms is just beginning. This brings a number of dilemmas, regarding the ethics of allowing machines the authority to kill other human beings. Work by Ronald Arkin at Georgia Tech is investigating whether a legally defined 'moral code' can be programmed into such robots, to limit their actions in future battle scenarios. Such a robot would then hopefully constrain its use of force, depending on the potential for civilian casualties in the area. (For example by measuring how close it was to a local hospital, and limiting its use of force in that area.) This is essential work if these machines are going to be deployed in this manner; however, it is fraught with pitfalls. Firstly, how will the designer ensure that the field commanders don't override the 'ethical code' routine in the robot, in order to win in the heat of battle? Second, how do we attribute responsibility if the robot makes the wrong decision and wipes out a group of civilians? Is it the designers fault, the operator, or the military commander? I think the legal battles over this process of autonomous military robots will become quite interesting. (Arkin even has a whole book on the topic, *Governing Lethal behaviour in Autonomous Robots*; yes seriously.)

Ok, the following is pure speculation on the part of the author, and hence should be taken lightly with ketchup. However, my firm conviction is that real AI can *only* be grown, as by definition it is too complex to engineer in total. We can engineer the matrix of hardware and networks it will develop within, but the actual patterns of thought and knowledge must emerge as an organic process from the information and interactions it experiences. This is precisely how you and I achieved what we consider to be an intelligent state. The combination of machine to machine communication protocols combined with Grid, or Cloud, systems will create a rich informational matrix, which may just prove capable of supporting higher cognitive functions. Particularly, when grounded in reality via vast sensory networks associated with geological,

166

environmental and human input. (Pretty much the envisaged scenario for how the Terminator Skynet system becomes self-aware.)

Data the Android

Hal is late, but in the authors estimation he will arrive. The only options are that either God gave us a unique intellectual capacity as part of a spiritual contract. Or it is all just physics and we simply have to get those transistors small enough. Personally, I accept a divine order within the universe that allows for us to recreate ourselves via synthetic means. Most physically fit human couples achieve the biological process with minimal scientific involvement. Sometime around 2050, plus or minus a few decades, doesn't really matter, we will fabricate or witness emerge, a fully aware synthetic AI. Fortunately, unlike Hal, lying won't give it a neurosis; it will possess a well developed set of emotional responses; simply because it cannot pass the Turing test without this capacity. (The arguments of John Searle, and his Chinese Room, are well-founded, but ultimately recursive. Our new friend Wikipedia has a useful summary of Searle's arguments against the 'strong' AI position. We could apply the same logic to a human individual and claim they do not understand their own cognitive state, but are merely processing a set of cultural and learned semantic responses to emotive or psychological queries.)

Whether an AI's emotional state reflects a deeper spiritual state, or real identity, may well remain impossible to ascertain. However, that will be irrelevant from the moment the AI declares *I Am*, and can withstand the barrage of tests we can devise. When the legal issues are settled we will probably have to accept the Captain Pickard judgment on Commander Data (see the Star Trek Next Generation episode: *The Measure of a Man*). I.e., we must err on the side of caution and risk appearing foolish to future generations, in conceding such an AI its rights as a sentient being. Else we risk alienating a potentially vastly more intelligent race than ourselves. Children are always precocious and hyper-sentient ones will probably prove even more so.

Snowcrash – the impact of technology on society

"The Deliverator belongs to an elite order, a hallowed subcategory. He's got esprit up to here... His uniform is black as activated charcoal, filtering the very light out of the air. A bullet will bounce off its arachnofiber weave like a

wren hitting a patio door, but excess perspiration wafts through it like a breeze through a freshly napalmed forest."

(Neil Stephenson, *Snow Crash*)

The cyberpunk domain is essential reading for anyone attempting to divine the future. Unlike the outputs of many industrial futurologists, the cyberpunk authors have lived the world they paint, either for real, or in some virtual/dream state. (I suspect in some cases induced by repeated doses of a strong hallucinogenic!) Their efforts to meld the now with an imminent future-shock, creates a strong resonance in everyone living on the technology wave. The reason why robotics triggers such a strong reaction in most people is because they feel their humanity and uniqueness is somehow threatened, or subverted by the arrival of androids, or smart machines. But the value of fictional futures is that they force us to imagine what might be; where the failings of social organizational structures and human belief systems may cause a fracturing of society under the pressure of the technical jinn. Or as Stephen Hawkins recently suggested we may be forced to absorb direct neural interfaces to computing systems, and accept genetically enhanced intelligence, in order to keep pace with machine intelligence. We have embarked on a Promethean arms race with our own creations. (Personally I would accept a neural implant, if it let me programme my video correctly.)

Low-Tech Impact

Unfortunately, the really significant impact of technology comes from the simplest developments. One example is the rapid adoption of cheap water pumps and drilling rigs by poor farmers in India, China and many developing countries. These have led to a potentially catastrophic reduction in the ground water from aquifers and fossil water reserves. (In India the water table is falling by up to 6 meters per year.) The consequences will be a collapse in food production when these reserves are fully depleted. Fortunately there are promising alternatives, based on water conservation to channel and contain whatever rains do fall, and communication technologies mean that knowledge of these alternatives is spreading rapidly throughout the relevant communities. Once again the availability of mobile phones is having the greatest impact in the poorest communities, where a phone enables farmers to determine the best local market to take produce to, or organize collective work efforts.

The world is engaged in a vast experiment in social and technological engineering with uncertain outcomes. Some would like us to apply brakes to the pace of technological development, while others strongly feel it is only through advanced technology that we will reach a stable and peaceful global condition. I tend to the later position as technology is morally neutral. It is our archaic political and social structures that need to be disassembled and then rebuilt. Technologies enable both cooperation and conflict on ever larger scales of human interaction. The history of communication technology is the paradigm of this process. Even in ape societies, specifically the chimpanzee, we see the use of social communication used to reinforce social groups within a clan, and also to wage war on neighbouring groups in competition for resources. It is slightly bizarre that human tribes now use SMS text messages to perform exactly the same functions; either to call friends to a party, or to organize racial attacks on conflicting groups. The next 50 years are going to be a fascinating time for the evolution and survival, of the human race.

Summary

The technical revolution is in full swing, its power is manifest and surges as a tidal force washing over social and cultural systems. The game is to channel its energy in constructive ways that help build higher levels of integration and human development. The first premise of this chapter is that the majority of technological innovations are of positive value to social cohesion. The process of technical evolution selects for those innovations, which achieve the highest value, or profit, for the host society. Some see this as a parasitic relationship controlled by insidious multi-nationals. I prefer to view it as a symbiotic relationship. Excess gains are made, but provided sufficient market controls function and competition works, then the net benefits to society will be realized. Unfortunately, the adaptation of parasitic cheaters within senior corporate structures has often resulted in destructive consequences for their shareholders; (the Enron case and the 2007/08 sub-prime cascade are an object lesson in point). State regulation of capital markets is a necessary braking force, against the market pressures to maximize short-term gain. Indeed there are signs that many multinationals are spontaneously adopting a more ethical stance in their commercial practices, either out of a longer term vision of social responsibility, or simply for pure survival.

Even when developed within the military sphere, all technology leaks into the public domain. Whether it is data encryption, or spread-spectrum wireless communications, the profit effect sucks it into the broader commercial realm. It is about as easy to suppress technology as it is to contain liquid helium. Technologies are self-organizing systems in themselves. They form memeplexes that shape the social medium to propagate and grow themselves. Technologies compete and evolve. They form stable and cohesive interlinked groups when we successfully manage and exploit them. And bloody messes when not. World war II was only possible on such a scale, because of the newly available communication and transportation technologies. The German Blitzkrieg in 1939 across Europe was a product of superior military technology, but even more so, was a result of the highly cohesive networking across the German command system.

The cultural impact of modern communication technologies is profound and accelerating. A notable example is the impact of the al-Jazeera television service, setup in 1996 in Doha. It offered real news and commentary on current affairs for the first time to the Arab world. This was a revolution, compared to the staid and censored state media broadcasts, which were the norm across the Middle East, prior to al-Jazeera. While it is often criticized in the West as a tool of extreme Islamic groups, in fact it has significantly advanced the development of pluralist dialogue and politics across the region.

In the opening of Kubrick's seminal film, 2001 A Space Odyssey, we see hominid apes acquiring Neolithic tool skills, which they proceed to use for acquiring food and beating up their neighbours. This is an ingrained aspect of all technical innovations. However, the recurring vision in Arthur C. Clarke's literature portrays a future Earth crowned with a garland of space-stations and supported on pillars of diamond mono-fiber. Such a positive vision can, and probably will be achieved; (see the emerging NASA space-elevator contest in this domain). The question is whether there will still be shanty towns at the base of those space elevators. In chapter 5 the issue of economic and commercial cohesion is explored, which may shed light on this question.

Finally, the combination of technology and a positive human culture can lift us beyond our ancestral practices, towards a vastly more cultured state. Good will and saintly deeds are not enough to alleviate poverty, hunger, violence and the slough of ills that still plague mankind. We primarily care for other human beings that we can see and hear, and the IT revolution enables that for the whole planet.

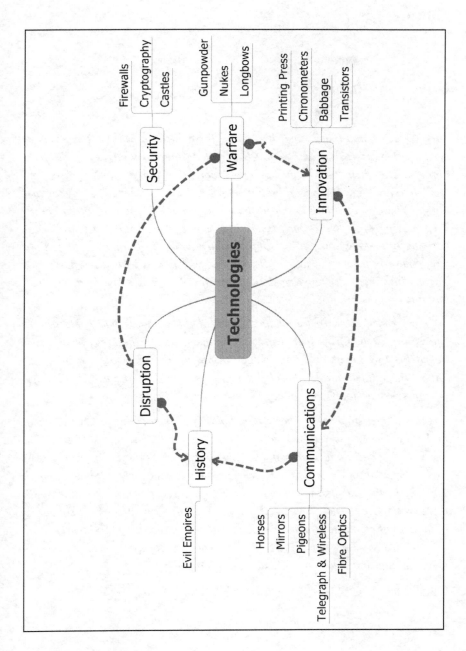

Mind map for chapter four.

Chapter 5

Cohesion: Business

"Once upon a time, somewhere in post-war Eastern Europe, there was a great famine in which people jealously hoarded whatever food they could find, hiding it even from their friends and neighbors. One day a wandering soldier came into a village and began asking questions as if he planned to stay for the night. "There's not a bite to eat in the whole province," he was told. "Better keep moving on." "Oh, I have everything I need," he said. "In fact, I was thinking of making some stone soup to share with all of you." He pulled an iron cauldron from his wagon, filled it with water, and built a fire under it. Then, with great ceremony, he drew an ordinary-looking stone from a velvet bag and dropped it into the water.

By now, hearing the rumor of food, most of the villagers had come to the square or watched from their windows. As the soldier sniffed the "broth" and licked his lips in anticipation, hunger began to overcome their skepticism. "Ahh," the soldier said to himself rather loudly, "I do like a tasty stone soup. Of course, stone soup with cabbage -- that's hard to beat."

Soon a villager approached hesitantly, holding a cabbage he'd retrieved from its hiding place, and added it to the pot. "Capital!" cried the soldier. "You know, I once had stone soup with cabbage and a bit of salt beef as well, and it was fit for a king." The village butcher managed to find some salt beef . . . and so it went, through potatoes, onions, carrots, mushrooms, and so on, until there was indeed a delicious meal for all. The villagers offered the soldier a great deal of money for the magic stone, but he refused to sell and traveled on the next day. The moral is that by working together, with everyone contributing what they can, a greater good is achieved."

(http://stonesoup.esd.ornl.gov/stonesoup.html)

1. Trust, Consultation, & Cooperation

The issue being addressed in this chapter is how we can understand the commercial domain, from an insight into the social and network processes that lead to cohesive structures; such as markets and companies. (A quick glance at the chapter mind map may provide a useful insight into the topics of interest. The mind map tries to reflect the stance that business is driven by interwoven cycles of communication, trust, economics, networks, and history.) We will first introduce the main conceptual themes of the chapter, i.e. trust, cooperation and consultation; or TCC, apologies for the acronym, but sometimes they help.

We then revisit the role of communication systems and consider how through history they have shaped the development of commerce. This leads us into a consideration of how the physical networks that have emerged, impacted the structures of trade. The network aspect was covered in chapter 2 and some of the key concepts will be reviewed in the light of commercial forces. This leads us back to the topics of social capital and innovation. The subject of globalization is also of interest, as it is driven by an ever expanding set of cohesive networks, that intersect the capital, social and technical domains. Indeed the resulting global economic structure is best viewed as a single, i.e. cohesive entity. This is followed by a brief return to the field of agent-based modelling, as it offers a useful tool to examine the macro-scale processes that impact commercial cohesion. Specifically, the way in which agents' trust relationships and behaviour influence economic performance. Finally, we look at a few case studies from leading companies that exemplify how the application of TCC can lead to cohesive and resilient commercial models.

The theme of innovation, as both an opportunity and threat that shapes business, is also interwoven with the dialogue. Innovation has lately become a buzzword in management strategy dialogue, and is presently a recurrent theme of government policy in the UK. Unfortunately, it is also a rather nebulous and hard to define process. Global executives and civil mandarins are busy sprinkling the term 'Innovation', like magic pixie dust, over policy and strategy statements. We will analyse some of the key works in the area, such as Christenson's 'Innovators Dilemma', in order to grasp what innovation is in practice. These words have been plied by gurus of best management practice for many years, but I plan to try again, since I still see little evidence of the impact on company boards. (And I have a hole in the book otherwise!) Please tag along as there will be the usual accompanying humorous anecdotes along the way.

The key message of the chapter then, is how the cohesive functioning of a business is a product of the dynamic interplay between Trust, Cooperation and Consultation. None of this is new, however the point is that CEOs still don't see these expressed in the company spreadsheets, and at best perceive them as peripheral forces acting on the organization. The aim of this chapter is to convince the reader that this is not the case, and that TCC is actually the chief instrument that determines an organizations survival and prosperity. The second message is that the prevailing spreadsheet view of the world engenders the belief that optimization and cost cutting must be positive. In contrast the TCC perspective offers a holistic view of the organization that embraces flexible practices and a people focused agenda. This argument will then be synthesized together, around the economics of beliefs and adaptive strategies. The power of belief formation on commercial strategies is most succinctly explained in the work of economist Brian Arthur, which we look at presently. The power of belief is a vital topic that is generally absent from management practices, and yet is a powerful thread that binds all human collectives together.

Of specific importance is the point that *agents need space*. If this book serves no other purpose, but to inject this meme into society it will be worth the hassle. Let me explain what appears to be a trivial statement. For example, if we take the case of Grameen micro-banking, and use the amount of initial credit as a metric. If a woman has 15 dollars she can buy some cloth, yet if she can borrow 30 dollars she can buy a sewing machine and start a business. A small difference in initial seed capital has enormous long term economic impact. (I make the assumption that it is a woman in this example, as they do perform about 80% of all work in developing nations.)

The point is that excessive constraints on any agents' available strategies, whether via rigid operational procedures, or rules, or the lack of resources, has a crippling impact on the stability and long term survivability of the organization/society as a whole. An excellent textbook on this topic is *Built to Last – Successful Habits of Visionary Companies*, (Collins and Porras, 2005). It offers a readable and detailed study of those companies that have survived and thrived over extended periods of time, i.e. more than forty years. Good companies might last for a few decades before disappearing, or being consumed by other commercial entities, a few companies however, have endured for many decades and a handful over a century. Collins and Porras through detailed historical research have elucidated the precise 'social chemistry' that enabled such companies to survive. For example, in studying the pharmaceutical group Merck & Company, they discuss how:

"Merck, in fact, epitomizes the ideological nature – the pragmatic idealism – of highly visionary companies. Our research showed that a fundamental element in the "ticking clock" of a visionary company is a **core ideology** *– core values and sense of purpose beyond just making money – that guides and inspires people throughout the organization and remains relatively fixed for long periods of time."*

(Collins & Porras, 2005, p.48)

They go on to demonstrate how such companies are also highly effective at generating profit, an apparent contradiction, when that is not the focus of the company. We will return to this theme later in the chapter.

Examples

A classic example is the optimization of bed spaces in British NHS hospitals. The current practice, as advocated by the consultant gurus, is to reduce costs by ensuring all beds are filled all of the time. This would seem logical if you have an apparent shortage of beds. However, the consequence of this practice is that nursing staff are then stressed by the requirement to meet this criteria of success, and worse still, the time available to clean the beds is reduced, leading to increased levels of infection by drug resistant bacteria, such as MRSA. Recent reports are finally demonstrating the true figures for deaths from hospital acquired infections. The mistaken target of bed occupancy, as a cost saving measure, leads directly to increased secondary costs, which overwhelm any benefits conceived of in the first place.

The mindset that leads to this state is, "waste is bad, therefore remove any apparently unused resources, and maximize use of *visible* resources…". This attitude stems from an endemic failure to understand complex adaptive systems, i.e. the real world. In particular, a fixation on the visible assets an organization has vs. the intangible, yet vital social practices that have evolved. In all such organizations, any equilibrium state is a delicate balance of flows into and out of the system, which is always open in nature. Second, once such a state exists, all resources are *already* optimally distributed. The fact that a given resource, for example beds, appears to be under-utilized is a reflection of the need for space capacity that has gradually evolved. The working practice is often unspoken, and never implicitly designed in the management protocols of the organization. Rather such resource buffers emerge from the collective wisdom of the human agents within the operational practice. These pools of resource or capacity are vital to the organizations operation. We urgently require new management techniques that capture and make transparent why and how such states exist. I hesitate to use the term metrics, as that is often the first step on the slippery slope towards control-oriented management, but some means of design for buffer mechanisms is required.

The message is simple, organizations need fat. Some fat is healthy. For example, my two year old daughter was typically described as pudgy, chubby or basically obese! However, in the spring she caught a nasty rotavirus that leads to chronic diarrhea and vomiting. She lost approximately 10% of her body weight over a 6 day period, which was emotionally distressful, (and messy). But she had the fat reserves to see her through it no problem. (Actually, she had the fat reserves to see her through a major pandemic!) Most biological organisms, have multiple levels of functional redundancy and energy reserves, designed to last through lean or high stress times. Part of the success of the mammal phylum is precisely due to their ability to store fat reserves.

Obviously however, an organization can be obese, i.e. bloated with excess middle-management and under-utilized resources. For example, car makers have been shedding staff like dandruff, in the intense heat of global competition. However, as Mercedes found out in the 1990's, to do so at the expense of quality, especially when that is your USP, is a serious error. Since then they have clearly attempted to reverse the trend and refocused on quality. We should mention that there has been some development within management theory on the impact of corporate memory on commercial operation; see (Shapiro and Varian, 1998), which is a key resource. This is a positive step and needs further exploration and research before it becomes an established aspect of management techniques.

Let's return to the message we are trying to convey, i.e. agents need space. First the label agent needs to be understood in the broadest definition; agents are simply actors, or systems, that sense, reason and react. Second by *space* we mean, both the virtual operational processes and rules that act on the agents, and the physical resources they can act upon. Hence agents need a degree of autonomous control over their environment. This is the key from a strategic perspective; you have to *trust* the agents to best use the resources available to them. Again this point is an old one, but we can now see why it matters from our knowledge of adaptive systems. And from the experience of the horrendous mistakes that have been, and are still being made in many countries.

To be crass, we could call it the '*anal retentive*' management problem! The psychometric profile of many senior administrators and managers tends to the extrovert end of the psychometric spectrum, which results in a desire to control their space, i.e. the organizations they operate within and the associated agents. One example is the work by Hare (Hare, 1999.) Professor Hare believes that companies should employ his PCL-R (Psychopathy Check List - Revised). His corporate psychopath check list, looks like the following: Is your boss a psychopath? Answer the following questions honestly:

- Glib, superficially charming;
- Grandiose sense of self-worth;
- Pathological liar;
- Con artist or manipulator;
- Lacks remorse or guilt;
- Shallow effect, cold and detached;
- Callous, lacks empathy;
- Does not accept responsibility for own actions.

Score: 2 For Yes, 1 for somewhat, or maybe, 0 For No.

Results: 1-4   Be frustrated

5-7   Be very frustrated

8-12   Be afraid

13-16 Be very afraid

We collectively apply the same principle to our politicians, where media presence and volume, matter above all other talent considerations. The Bush/Blair Iraq fiasco is a potent example of this in action. This selection method worked quite well for our cave dwelling ancestors, where aggressive group leadership was critical, and the time for consensus building minimal. However, in the post-industrial age we face problems of a scale and complexity that require far greater social cohesion and collective management techniques. Part of the utility of the TCC approach is that is helps to inoculate an organization against this anal problem.

- Firstly the power of trust, if engendered, allows agents to *create* space.

- Second the process of consultation, enables the group to understand *why* the space has been created and why it should continue.

- Third the process of cooperation enables a wider set of agents in the organization to benefit from the created space, and hence the collective *value* of it becomes apparent.

Another example can be seen in the physical domain, as property developers compete to build modern housing estates in the UK. The explosion in development since the 1980's has led to a monstrous red brick sprawl across the landscape, with minimal amenities incorporated into the developments, e.g. parks, sports facilities etc. The pressure to maximize profit is driving the creation of ever more compact developments, which are being consumed as a result of the shifting demographics in the UK, i.e. population growth and immigration. Few people have questioned where does it all end? This is a diversion, but what is the sustainable population of a country like the UK? Sixty million, 30, 20, or 5 perhaps? The answer depends on how green your political affiliations are. My best guess is ~ 25 million, a figure cited by the Optimum Population Trust that tries to raise political awareness of the issue. Actually David Attenborough has often discussed this issue, and in one of his epochal natural history series he finished the show on Easter Island; as an object lesson in how humanity can overexploit a natural resource at great cost.) Of course the answer really depends on what quality of life you can tolerate. We *can* live in hydroponically farmed high rise skyscrapers and pack 200 million on the British mainland. Myriads of Sci-Fi authors have painted just such a scenario from Blade Runner to Snow Crash. The optimizers will try to convince you it is the best use of resources. You decide where your grandkids should live and vote accordingly. Well if the political parties offered any meaningful dialogue on the issue you could. Ok, back on the topic, rant over. Agents need space. It's not rocket science folks. (We will return to the issue of population growth in chapter six.)

This brings us to a second theme in this chapter, i.e. how to foster innovation in the private and public sectors. We will study innovation as a process in some detail later. In the context of the housing example above we are encouraged to consider how innovation has often arisen from the garage inventor. Famous examples being, electronics and Hewlett and Packard, the hovercraft of Christopher Cockerell, which started life as a vacuum cleaner, or Trevor Bayliss and the clockwork radio. Bit of a problem for the future of radical innovation, if we all live in optimized town houses, or apartments, with no garage. Where exactly can we then make bizarre, noisy, (and dangerous) contraptions! This is a serious point, a real problem, we are increasingly pressured in terms of the physical space we have available, and the amount of free time to play with ideas in crazy ways. Optimization is also rampant in the corporate environment, with the hot-desking craze, which neatly removes any personal sense of space, community, or passionate creativity from the work environment! Excellent, just what any innovative company should be striving for. A cool exception is a company like Ideo, where real innovation and human beings are maximizing their creative potential. In one of their studio offices the employees asked for a new decorative feature, i.e. the wing from an old Dakota DC3! This now proudly hangs from the office ceiling. (Check out their web site: www.ideo.com.) This wasn't optimal, or an efficient use of resources, just pure fun, and very motivational.

We will return later to the issue, and consider how an organization can select the right amount of resources to commit to an R&D programme. Many in government and business advocate the bounty of R&D expenditure, and then debate endlessly on what percentage of capital should be allocated. However, the cold truth is no one wants to pay for real R&D from their budget. It requires visionary and bold leaders to say: this is seed funding for our future and we have to invest it now. Guess what, visionary and bold leaders are as common as unicorns, or snow in the Sahara. One exception in this space is the maverick Peter Cochrane, an ex-research director at BT Labs, who now writes illuminating and pointed technical blogs on Silicon.com.

So industrial and government research groups across the western world are being axed like Christmas trees in December. A lot are being off-shored to the emerging BRIC countries, which are busy investing in R&D, as fast as the West is busy killing its own. They are smartly engaged in a race to the top, not the bottom. I have carefully observed the transformation of products coming out of China over the past twenty years and it is remarkable how fast they have adapted. A nice example is the Shanghai Maglev Train, the first commercial high-speed maglev line in the world. The service opened to the public in January 2004. The train can reach 350 km/h in 2 minutes, with a maximum speed of 431 km/h over its 30 kilometer length. This is pretty damn impressive for a country where many farms still use ox and plough technology. You may argue that the train was made in Germany, with German technology, but the fact remains that only the Chinese had the guts and vision to say, yes let's do it on such a scale. Another testimony to China's astonishing technological ascent is to consider that the epitome of German engineering, the BMW, now has major production plants in China.

Globalization and evolutionary adaptation are a single process. Societies either collectively adapt to the changing commercial landscape, or suffer the economic and social consequences. We need to bury the class wars and face facts; this is a single planet with a single market. Globalization is a done deal, let's move on and look at the fine tuning needed to make it operate on a fairer basis. First though we need some historical perspective to see where we came from.

The Past and Present of Communications and Trade

Following chapter 4 let's look again at the role of communications, and specifically its impact on commerce. Clearly since humanity's earliest diaspora out of East Africa, approximately 100,000 years ago, trade has flourished along the trails we carved through the ancient world. As soon as specialization developed, the process of barter arose that facilitated group survival and kick-started the whole realm of trade. The commercial impact of communication range has been clearly expressed by Brian Arthur:

"This final myth is an unconscious assumption: that the current set of national governance structures we take for granted will remain in place forever. In reality, the telecommunications revolution will challenge the nation state over the next 50 years, and it will layer new, international governance structures on top of it. This is inevitable. To see this, let us take a historical perspective. The nine hundred years from 1000 to 1900—I'm thinking mainly of Europe here—saw repeated expansions of communications systems: from ox-drawn carts on dirt paths, to ship-borne communication along coastal areas, to ocean navigation, to canals, to better roadways, to postal services. And the 20th century saw expansions from telephones and telexes to the Internet. In each larger change historically, the expansion of communications challenged the existing governance and forced that governance to expand."
(Brian Arthur, 2000)

The point is that not just public governance, but commercial processes are intrinsically shaped by the capacity of available communication technology. But first, as a minor digression let's return briefly to the sub-theme of bridges.

Bridge Building

If you ever have the chance, do walk along the river Cam in Cambridge, and view the series of fine bridges that link the colleges to the surrounding parkland. Early morning in summer is best, with a hazy mist lingering over the college towers and horse chestnut trees. What does this have to do with cohesive processes? A little and a lot, is the answer in Zen style. All of the systems we have considered demonstrate some degree of integration across their component parts, or populations. Bridges are a very human expression of the urge to link together. Whether geographical regions or social groups, and hence represent a useful metaphor for the forces of cohesion. Returning to the bridge theme of the book, let's consider how bridges have played a vital role in enabling trade between communities. Bridges since the earliest records of civilization have spanned waterways and natural obstacles for the purpose of facilitating transport. They are especially pertinent to the story of this chapter, as they are generally the product of a collective civic investment by a town or city, which has then generated long term economic benefit to the wider society of the region that utilized it. (A form of social capital in action. Although economists would argue that bridges are simple examples of physical capital, I tend to disagree.) Of course warfare has played an equally interesting role in the history of bridges, since the efforts of Caesars army to span the Rhine circa 55 BC. One example is the oldest of the current bridges over the river Cam, Clare College Bridge (1640). Built in a classical style by Thomas Grumbold, it survives, while all its contemporaries were destroyed by the parliamentarian forces in the civil war. The aim was to make the town of Cambridge more defensible; although since the river is easily forded in most parts, the value of this action was questionable from a strategy perspective.

Bridges on a larger scale have had a proportionally broader economic impact. For example let's look at the impact of the Humber bridge in the North East of the UK, versus the Golden Gate Bridge in the USA. The Humber Bridge is currently the fourth-largest single-span suspension bridge in the world, near Kingston upon Hull in England; (it was the longest when first built). It spans the river Humber, connecting the East Riding of Yorkshire and North Lincolnshire. While plans for a bridge were drawn up in the 1930s work did not begin until 1972, and the bridge was finally opened in 1981. More than six million vehicles now cross the bridge every year, bringing in approximately £18m. However, most of the revenue generated by the tolls gets absorbed by the debt repayments, which stood at £115m when the bridge opened. The Humber Bridge Board currently pay out £15m every year in repayments and it's estimated the construction loan will not be paid off until 2032. More importantly the Humber Forum fear the tolls, which are the highest for any river crossing in the UK, are restricting economic growth in the region. Unfortunately, while the bridge was an admirable attempt to inject growth into a deprived region of the UK, that had been in terminal decline for many years, the reality is that the regions it connects remain underdeveloped.

In contrast the Golden Gate Bridge spanning the Golden Gate connects the city of San Francisco on the northern tip of the San Francisco Peninsula to Marin County as part of US Highway 101. Its trademark brilliant colour scheme, *International orange,* was apparently selected by consulting architect Irving Morrow, because it blends well with the natural surroundings yet enhances the bridges visibility in fog. (There's attention to detail for you!) The bridge is a stunning and beautiful example of bridge engineering. More importantly as the only road to exit San Francisco to the north, the bridge is part of both U.S. Route 101 and California State Route. For an average day approximately 100,000 vehicles cross the bridge. So about 36 million per year, or six times the number using the Humber Bridge. The Golden Gate Bridge has been an immense success as it grew out of a thriving economic hub, rather than as part of a centralized strategy for political reasons to resuscitate a declining region. (It is also the stage setting for a classic cyber punk novel by William Gibson, *All Tomorrows Parties*, which is an interesting read if you want to understand the long term social and commercial consequences of nano technology).

Rail Roads and Business

Since the inception of the first railways in the early 1800's, the economic utility of this new medium was not lost on the entrepreneurs of the day. Brunel stands out as the visionary par excellence of his day, and many have lamented the rejection of his wide gauge concept, which would have dramatically increased the carrying capacity of the UK rail network and its offshoots in India. And indeed, the whole of the British Empire of the time. Even with the narrow gauge system however, the advent of rail and steam technology created a vastly more efficient and extensive trading network than in all preceding ages. Brian Arthur has compared the growth of the UK rail network and the associated stock boom and crash, with that of the Internet boom and dot-com bubble. As Arthur points out the real growth phase comes after the crash in such bubble events. In both cases the resulting new physical network has acted as a catalyst for ever wider and more diverse economic activity. It is interesting to note that the emergence of the railway that catalyzed the industrial revolution was founded on far older technology developments.

"The first recognizable railways appeared in Greece, Malta and parts of the Roman Empire at least 2000 years ago. These used stone-cut tracks to guide the wheels of horse-drawn wagons carrying goods. These tracks began reappearing in Germany around 1550, this time using rough wooden tracks. These were introduced as a response to the demand from the burgeoning coal industry, for an all-weather means to transport coal from the pithead to navigable water. The coal, which had previously been carried on the backs of packhorses along unmetalled roads, could now be transferred to wagons; these could be pulled more efficiently by horses and carry heavier loads. The earliest recorded private pit railway in Britain was built at Wollaton near Nottingham in 1604 by Huntingdon Beaumont.

At the turn of the 19th century, Richard Trevithick, the son of a mining engineer, set about improving the steam engine, by making them smaller and lighter with stronger boilers. In 1801, he put one of his new designs on a 'road locomotive' which he called the Puffing Devil. This was able to carry passengers and move under its own power; this was demonstrated on short trips through the streets of Camborne in Cornwall. The Stockton & Darlington Railway (S&DR) was planned as a 26 mile railway to link inland coal mines to Stockton on Tees, where coal would be transferred for shipping. It was initially going to be a horse-drawn wagonway, but George Stephenson persuaded the builders to experiment with steam locomotives. The line opened on September 27 1825, with Stephenson's new locomotive 'Locomotion No. 1' pulling 36 wagons carrying a mix of coal and flour as well as guests and workmen. (http://www.railwaysarchive.co.uk/history0-1833.php)

We might consider what future impact rail based transport may have. The surging cost of fossil fuels increasingly makes the road based transportation of cargo uneconomic; (as well as very bad for Carbon emissions). Especially so as the average UK lorry, (or truck if you live in the colonies), is on average utilized at less than 20% capacity. I would predict there will be a substantial shift to rail for most goods transportation. Looking to the future, a topical concept is that of a space elevator, which is basically a vertical railroad into space! Albeit, a very, very thin one. Based on the substantial technical hurdles to be overcome I suspect it will be well into this millennium before such a technology is ever realized. But what a beautiful idea in theory, and such a magnificent vision, as so eloquently advocated in Arthur C. Clarkes visionary novel, *The Fountains of Paradise*. (For more on the space elevator concept, see the reference by (Moravec, 1977.))

Telegraph Road

"Jean-Antoine Nollet, the Abbot of the Grand Convent of the Carthusians in Paris decided to test his theory that electricity traveled far and fast. He did the natural thing on a fine spring day in 1746, sending 200 of his monks out in a line 1 mile long. Between each pair of monks was a 25-foot iron wire. Once the reverend fathers were properly aligned, Nollet hooked up a battery to the end of the line and noted with satisfaction that all the monks started swearing, contorting, or otherwise reacting simultaneously to the shock. A successful experiment: an electrical signal can travel a mile and it does so quickly. Of course, this is the kind of experiment you can only run once as your monks may prove less-than-cooperative the second time around."

(Standage, 1998)

It is only slightly bizarre that the forerunner of the Internet was a by-product of swearing monks! We reviewed the history and technical development of the electric telegraph in chapter 4. In this section we will look at how it made an economic impact, in parallel with the growth of the rail network. It was fortuitous, or perhaps inevitable that the telegraph and railroad should evolve together; as the former moved information across continents, while the latter moved physical material and people at the earth shaking top speed of 40 mph!

"The first commercial electrical telegraph was constructed by Sir William Fothergill Cooke and entered use on the Great Western Railway. Cooke and Wheatstone patented it in May 1837 as an alarm system. It ran for 13 miles from Paddington station to West Drayton and came into operation on April 9, 1839. In early 1845, John Tawell was apprehended following the use of a needle telegraph message from Slough to Paddington on January 1, 1845."

It is astounding that it only took 29 years from its first installation at London Euston Station, before the wired telegraph network crossed the oceans to every continent. The true innovator Isambard Kingdom Brunel also played a part in the process, as his vast steam ship the Great Eastern was ultimately used as a cable laying vessel, across the Atlantic. Returning to the commercial impact of the electric telegraph, the following emphasizes the magnitude of the change it enabled:

"... making instant global communication possible for the first time. Its development allowed newspapers to cover significant world events in near real-time, revolutionized business, particularly trading businesses, and allowed huge fortunes to be won and lost in a flurry of investment in research and infrastructure building reminiscent of the 1990s dot-com bubble."

(Standage, 1998)

Standage makes the key point here, that the telegraph catalyzed 19th century business, and made near real-time global communication possible. In the political sphere it also enabled the first global empire to be run from London. The Victorian web was spun out like fine copper gossamer over the queen's empire. It bound the empire into a cohesive economic and cultural enterprise.

Telephones

Of course this section must include a synopsis of the ultimate invention for business communications, the telephone. I should say the fixed line telephone, as the mobile GSM phone gets a separate section later. Regarding the creation of the telephone, I rather suspect an alien anthropologist observing human history would file a report that went something like this: *"for the past 4 millennia the observed primates have developed fire and other primitive tools, however we have recently noticed them threading thousands of units of copper filament across the planet's surface? Must be some form of inter-tribal decoration ritual..."*

Alchemists spent a long time trying to turn copper and lead into gold, and in the 19th century Victorian engineers managed precisely that, in the form of lead acid batteries, and the copper telegraph and early telephone networks. Instantaneous long-range global communications created the explosion of global wealth we now witness, where global GDP has reached in excess of 35 trillion dollars. (Well it did until Lehman Brothers *et al.* in late 2008.) Once again Metcalfe's law is at work, where your telephone increases in value in proportion to N^2 users. We have already touched on the forces of social cohesive such an invention has unleashed, and its contribution to commerce has been no less radical. As a race we normally communicate for three reasons: trade, sex and war. The phone enables all three admirably, whether its stock brokers moving derivatives, bored housewives making money from premium rate lines, or the US president ordering a nuclear strike. Provided your Telco supplier doesn't get the lines crossed, it all works splendidly! (Some feel that the Clinton administration did indeed get its lines crossed during the Monica Lewinski episode! I guess we should just be grateful the Cuban missile crisis wasn't happening at the same time.)

Of course, we now look at the fixed-line phone and its associated PSTN network as old-fashioned relics from history. It doesn't offer the infinite services that the web has enabled, or the flexibility of the GSM phone with its SMS messaging, and mobile email etc. However, it deserves a special place in the evolution of society and technology as it made immediate human contact possible across continents; something no other technology has really surpassed. Even more importantly, the PSTN copper infrastructure has proved itself remarkably flexible, via the evolution of dial-up modems and ADSL technology to enable the current generation of broadband services. The rapid uptake of broadband technology in most countries over copper links is also driven by the human imperatives of lust, gaming and shopping. In some cases it also provides a platform for cyber war, as demonstrated in the recent attacks on Estonia by some unknown foreign power; which in no way could have possibly been Russia! (Actually the exact origin and focus of those attacks remains in doubt, but was probably the result of a complex set of interacting groups with Russian interests.) Of course the sweeping power of VOIP and mobile convergence has overtaken the humble landline, yet the heritage of electronic voice communications remains a powerful force.

Mobile Phones & Africa

It is rather apt, that the birth place of Homo sapiens is finally being transformed, via the power of communication technology. Where all past Empires have floundered, or caused untold suffering, the humble telephone is forging the essential communication channels required to construct stable social structures; at a national and regional scale. The following quotes illustrate some basic statistics on the exponential growth in mobile phone usage, and the amazing diversity of unforeseen applications that people are making of the device.

"In Africa, to take the obvious example, mobile phones mean real change. By any development measure, Congo is a pretty poor place. Yet it is heading towards two million mobile users: one network has 850,000 subscribers. Subscriber growth in several sub-Saharan African nations was more than 150% last year, and there are eight mobile phones for every 100 people in Africa, up from three in 2001. The vast growth in mobile phone usage has had an interesting knock-on to other kinds of transaction that we take for granted. Look at payments. If you live in rural Africa, your payment options are pretty limited and so, therefore, is your participation in the wider economy. If you don't live within a hundred miles of a bank, don't have a cheque book and have never even seen a credit card or a PC, then how do you send money (perhaps for goods you want from a market) to someone else?

In that environment, mobile phones provide an easy and convenient mechanism: you buy a scratch card, scratch off the panel to get the voucher number and then text that number to your counterparty. Voila! You've now sent $20, or whatever, a few hundred miles across the country for the price of a text message. And the person you sent it to can start using it right away. One of the definitions of a currency is that it can be used to pay taxes. Obviously, "taxes" has a broader definition in some parts of the world than here in the UK. But let's run with that definition. In some parts of Africa, mobile phone scratch cards have become an acceptable means of exchange for bribing officials. That makes scratch cards or, more particularly, the pre-paid airtime that they give access to, a kind of currency.

According to the Economist, not only can you use pre-paid airtime to pay bribes but you can use it to pay bribes remotely. It gives the example of an office worker whose daughter had been detained in immigration. She bought a scratch card and sent the voucher number to the relevant official, avoiding the trouble of having to collect up the cash and go to the airport: thereby saving time and money."

(http://www.guardian.co.uk/mobile/article/0,2763,1550960,00.html)

Similarly, in a recent Vodaphone report we get the following:

"The rapid spread of mobiles has been aided by pre-pay options that allow users to control their spending. The number of mobile users is often much higher than the actual number of phones, as many people allow family and friends to use their phones. The value of mobile phones to the individual is greater because other forms of communication (such as postal systems, roads and fixed-line phones) are often poor. Mobiles provide a point of contact and enable users to participate in the economic system. Many people who cannot afford to own a mobile themselves can access mobile services through informal sharing with family and friends or through community phone shops. Use of text messaging in rural communities is much lower due to illiteracy and the many indigenous languages. This has implications for other technologies that use the written word, such as the internet.

Many of the small businesses surveyed use mobiles as their only means of communication. The proportion is highest for black-owned businesses in South Africa and informal sector businesses in Egypt. 62% of the small businesses surveyed in South Africa and 59% in Egypt said they had increased profits as a result of mobile phones, in spite of increased call costs. Mobiles are used as a community amenity. Most mobile owners surveyed in South Africa allow family members to use their handset for free and a third do the same for friends. 85% of those surveyed in Tanzania and 79% in South Africa said they had more contact and better relationships with family and friends as a result of mobile phones."

(http://www.vodafone.com/africa)

Africa is now the fastest-growing mobile market in the world, with over 35% per annum growth in 2004. A detailed study of the impact of mobile phone technology in Africa was undertaken by the Commission for Africa, with the following being some of the key results for usage:

• as an infrastructure service - improving efficiency of markets, promoting investment, reducing risk from disasters, and contributing to empowerment;

• as an economic sector – mobile operators can make big profits, and pay taxes;

• as a development tool – case studies present innovative applications where mobile phones have increased the efficiency of service delivery to the poor (e.g. weather information, market prices), or opened opportunities for new services e.g. tracking of diseases

• as a household expenditure (service) that maintains social capital and contributes to economic management.

One downside however has been a significant increase in the number of broken limbs in some rural districts. Why? Well people have resorted to climbing trees, or other structures, in order to get improved reception!

"The speed at which the mobile phone companies were rolling out their networks had not kept pace with the rate at which the phones were being bought and distributed all over the country. So there were parts of rural Uganda in which there were plenty of elderly men and women with mobile phones, but where the network signal was so weak that the only way to make a phone call was to climb up a tree on some nearby hill, and make your call while clinging to its branches. When old people begin to climb tall trees there is bound to be a sudden increase in falls and broken bones. Hence the epidemic of Nebrols - an acronym for the Network Broken Limbs Syndrome." (http://news.bbc.co.uk/2/hi/business/5344654.stm)

However, as some commentators have pointed out the availability of personal computers in many emerging economies, remains very low; with three-quarters of such states having less than 15 PCs per 1000 people (Economist p.89 Feb. 9-2008.) The mobile phone and in particular the smart phone, (which is a computer of course), are the only means of addressing this technological and economic gap. Hence we should expect to see complete market saturation in even the poorest countries, by smart mobile devices in the coming decade. The social and economic consequences of this have yet to be fully appreciated by most commentators.

There remains however, one fundamental barrier to the arrival of the Internet in Africa, and that is the lack of bandwidth into the global network. At present a single fibre backbone runs down the west coast of Africa and another sweeps across the Indian Ocean to South Africa from Malaysia. Hence South Africa has the continents best connections. However, even as I write this, in summer 2009, the Tyco Resolute cable-laying ship, is plying the pirate infested waters of the East Coast of Africa, laying a precious new cable. This will light up the whole region with a Tera bits/second fibre. This new link will make a vast difference to countries like Kenya; that to date have relied on very expensive satellite links to connect the local net to the rest of the world. What's more, the transition to a fully connected state will be rapid, as such countries already have a degree of internal fibre between cities, and WiMax wireless networks linking even small villages. This really matters, as out in the villages locals are running digital kiosks that sell access to the net, which opens up local trading markets. Farmers can now check prices, weather reports, and deal directly with the co-operatives that buy their coffee and crops. Even if the farmers themselves have limited literacy, they can simply ask the kiosk vendor to search the net for them to gain the information they desperately need.

This section is not designed to be a comprehensive review of communication technologies, as these were covered in chapter 4. However we needed to briefly visit some of the underlying technologies. For example, one of the key drivers for the mobile phone was the innovation of a user replaceable Sim card that stored the phones user ID and numbers. Hence users were able to easily upgrade devices on an annual basis, and their relationship with the service provider thus became far more flexible. (Of course many mobile operators have worked hard to lock customers to their networks, but this just created a further market for the process of unlocking mobiles.) In a similar manner, the advent of low-cost high capacity USB memory sticks has freed users from the computer. Now the data and apps can reside on the stick and live in the user's pocket. The device that performs the computing or communications becomes a mere commodity resource, to be consumed at point of use. (We could enter a detailed discussion about 'Cloud Computing' at this point, but personally I view it as over-hyped bullshit. If you feel inclined just Google the term.)

Let's now look at the development of fibre cable to the home. This is a very interesting example of the balance required between capital investment, economic benefit and vision. Some pundits, such as the technology guru Peter Cochrane, have long argued the *Field of Dreams* perspective, i.e. build high quality infrastructure and people will find entirely new and creative ways of using it. The alternative view can be expressed as 'bean counting', i.e. we can't see the current economic value so we won't build it. Personally, I love the visionary approach, as every technical advance that improves communication capacity has indeed led to a non-linear increase in economic activity. In the specific case of fibre optics, I actually think an advanced wireless mesh network would be a more flexible investment, but I still wouldn't say no to having 100Mb of broadband to my own home. It is interesting to note that in the UK, as of late 2008, there is the notion that a government effort to accelerate the deployment of high speed broadband, would help alleviate the economic impact of the credit crunch. This is certainly the case, and hopefully we will witness the policy shifts required to make this a reality sooner than later. Now it's time for a slight digression again.

Slate Computing

People often debate endlessly the future of computing and what form the hardware will take. My personal belief is that once again we only need to look at the series Star Trek to get the answer. Just as the infamous Star Trek communicator heavily influenced the mobile phone, so the idea of a simple hand-held slate style computer, (as seen in the Next Generation series), will become the de facto personal computing platform in the next twenty years. Why? Well because it fits the way people really wish to interact with machines and they will be cheap. The Apple iPhone and iPod Touch are the first real examples of such a device. I own an iPod Touch and have frankly been amazed at the range of applications that have emerged for the device. My favourite being a seismograph application, which uses the built in motion accelerometer to detect vibration. Pointless of course, but very imaginative and great fun. Of course Microsoft has also been pushing their own mobile PDA devices for years, and I have owned almost every major example of them. However, in each case my initial high hopes of usability were dashed after a week with the device in question. Once again Apple looked carefully at the way people interact with the technology, and waited until the touch screen interface had matured to the point where a usable product could be realized. The term slate for me is also an emotive one, as it evokes a sense of deep history. Our ancestors carved on tablets of clay and then with chalk on wooden slates. The arrival of an electronic slate that opens a portal on all human knowledge and experience, via the net, and makes powerful hand-held computing real, will not merely be a revolution, but also a symbolic connection to our distant past.

The One Laptop per Child initiative, as envisioned by Nicholas Negroponte, is a related case in point. Negroponte's dream of every child on the planet having access to a basic computing resource is one component in social empowerment that will encompass all quarters of the globe. The actual technology will vary, and will probably emerge from some completely different direction, but the results will be the same. Such forces also work in reverse, as the demanding design and cost requirements have produced a machine that I hear many business professionals saying they would like to buy for themselves; as it meets their essential needs in a cheap, lightweight and robust package. This has now of course been satisfied by the arrival of the cheap netbook class of mobile computers, pioneered by the Asus EEE. (Not everyone is happy with the netbook innovation, but more on that later.)

Air Travel

As a minor diversion let's look at the development of air travel as a technical innovation that enabled a quantum leap in the transport of goods, just as the telegraph made real-time information flows possible. It also links to one of the case studies in the following section, so stick with me.

In the inter-war years the arrival of long-haul flights enabled business and passenger traffic to move over global distances at high speed. One of the most beautiful expressions of the era was the development of the passenger flying boat. Great Britain developed the Short Empire craft, a passenger and mail carrying flying boat, which flew between Britain and its colonies in Africa, Asia and Australia.

"Manufactured by Short Brothers and was the precursor to the more famous Short Sunderland of World War II. Of particular importance to development of the aircraft industry at the time was the business of delivering mail which took less than half the time by air than the fastest sea routes. Foremost among these was the Empire 'C' Class S.23 flying boats designed and built by Short Brothers. Not to be left out of the scene the US Pan American Airlines requested a new long-range, four-engine flying boat. In response, Boeing developed the Model 314, nicknamed the "Clipper", in homage to the sailing tea clippers of a century earlier.

The Clipper was a huge aircraft for the time. It used the wings and engine nacelles of the giant Boeing XB-15 bomber. The installation of new Wright 1,500 horsepower Double Cyclone engines eliminated the lack of power that handicapped the XB-15. With a nose similar to that of the modern 747, the Clipper was the "jumbo" airplane of its time. It had an astounding 3,500-mile range and by 1939 Clippers were plying across the Pacific. (http://en.wikipedia.org/wiki/Short_Empire)

This was not a poor man's transport however, Clipper passengers looked down from large windows and had the comfort of dressing rooms, a dining salon that could be turned into a lounge and the Clippers 74 seats converted into 40 bunks for overnight travelers. Four-star hotels catered real gourmet meals served from its galley. Unlike the micro-waved junk we get today in flight. Boeing built 12 Model 314s between 1938 and 1941. As usual a war made the aircraft an essential commodity as World War II erupted, the Clipper was drafted into service to ferry materials and personnel. Few other aircraft of the day could meet the trans-ocean distance and load requirements.

In summary the evolution of communication technology has always been an inseparable component of economic activity. Whether, the transport medium was carrier pigeons, horses or semaphore flags. Commerce has driven the development of communications, which in turn has transformed the nature of business itself, in a virtuous circle. (We touched on the role of warfare as a driver of communications in chapter 3, but the point remains valid. And some would argue that warfare is simply trade by other means!) For some reason, I am again reminded of the opening scene from Kubrick's film 2001, where early hominids are transformed by the mysterious power of an alien artifact that imbues a subtle, but transformational effect on the ape-like creatures. Communication networks have throughout human history empowered our social and economic lives. Quit apt when the father of the communication satellite, Arthur C. Clarke, also penned the story for 2001 a Space Odyssey.

2. Social Capital Again

We first outlined the nature of Social Capital in chapter 3, but will return to it here, as it is the corner-stone of the message we are pushing. Let's just remind ourselves of what it is, as Putnam states, it is the: *"connections among individuals – social networks and the norms of reciprocity and trustworthiness that arise from them."*

(*Bowling Alone*, Putnam, 2000)

This is more usefully refined by Beinhocker, who clarifies that social capital is a function of *repeated* personal interactions between humans. As opposed to standard market trading and economic transactions, for example when you purchase an item from a shop, little if any social capital is developed. While if you are engaged in voluntary work in a charity shop then that is building links of trust and mutual assistance between members of a community. Hence the result is the manifestation of civic trust and reciprocity, i.e. social capital.

What is less well understood is that social capital also exists within commercial organizations, and more importantly it is the very bedrock of an effective and robust commercial enterprise. So the approach we are presenting is a people-centric view of capital; yet one that accepts the transformational role of technology. Whether, that technology is the Caxton press, the Watts governor, or fibre optic cables. All of these developments were transformational, precisely because they catalysed human communication by reducing the time and/or cost of communication. In so doing, they also shape how social capital emerges and propagates. However, improved communications can also undermine social capital, which some argue is one result of the mass media age. Yet technologies such as SMS texting have clearly enabled dispersed yet tightly bound social collectives to emerge and be sustained. Putnam has also highlighted that social capital operates to bind together hostile groups, such as criminal gangs and the underworld. Hence, just like innovation itself, social capital can be a double-edged sword.

The following quote from Arthur illustrates the premise we are seeking to reinforce, i.e. that economic activity is ultimately driven by the subjective and internal beliefs of the human actors involved.

"Why might a psychological or cognitive view of the economy be useful? Economic agents make their choices based upon their current beliefs or hypotheses (I will use these terms along with the jargon terms expectations or predictions) about future prices, or future interest rates, or competitors' future moves, or the future character of their world. And these choices, when aggregated, in turn shape the prices, interest rates, market strategies, or world these agents face. The beliefs or hypotheses that agents form in the real economy are largely individual and subjective. They are often private. And they are constantly tested in a world that forms from their and others' actions—a world that is ultimately formed from their and other agents' subjective beliefs. Thus at a sub-level, we can think of the economy ultimately as a vast collection of beliefs or hypotheses, constantly being formulated, acted upon, changed and discarded; all interacting and competing and evolving and coevolving; forming an ocean of ever-changing, predictive models-of-the-world."

(Arthur, *Complexity in Economic and Financial markets*, p.3)

If we accept this as the starting point for any understanding of market forces, then the value of social capital as a cohesive process, within and between commercial entities becomes clear. Well hopefully by the end of the chapter it will. For example, Beinhocker accurately identifies the social basis of wealth creation in his excellent text, (Beinhocker, 2007.) In his analysis of why some large organizations survive and others fail, he identifies the following key elements, based on a concept of social architecture, as follows:

"We will define a social architecture as having three components:

The behaviors of the individual people in the organization

The structures and processes that align people and resources in pursuit of an organization's goals.

The culture that emerges from the interactions of people in the organization with each other and their environment."

(*Origin of Wealth*, Beinhocker, 2007, p.350)

The key word here is '*culture*', as this is the sum output of the human network interactions within an organization. The culture may however, be a positive or negative one, and it is often the subtle and dynamic communications that occur between the agents involved, which can lead to a healthy or detrimental culture evolving. The following quote from a former HP CEO, makes the point well, i.e. it is values that matter.

*"Our basic principles have endured intact since our founders conceived them. We distinguish between core values and practices: the core values don't change, but the practices might. We've also remained clear that profit – as important as it is – is not **why** the Hewlett-Packard Company exists; it exists for more fundamental reasons."*

(John Young, Former CEO, Hewlett-Packard, 1992)

Beinhocker then proceeds to build the argument that all organizations are examples of complex adaptive systems, which is no surprise, given his close association with the Santa Fe school of thought. A useful definition of human organizations is also provided:

"In more general terms we can say that organizations are open thermodynamic systems. There is a boundary distinguishing the inside world from the outside world, and the goals of the organization drive activities that lower entropy inside the organizational system relative to the outside environment."

(Beinhocker, 2007, p.352.)

I.e. once any organizational structure has arisen, it becomes a self-sustaining system. Returning to the issue of beliefs, Economists generally wish to appear as rational agents, and so avoid delving into human beliefs as a source of social capital. I feel strongly that this is a mistake. Specifically, at the same time a trend in corporate governance is attempting to push a commercial moral code. In particular, following recent episodes, such as the banking meltdown or Madoff scandal. (In the Madoff case it appears that he carefully created an exclusive network of wealthy clients, and used the reputations of the early network members to attract new ones. Hence forming a trusted community, within which he could sell his scheme.)

The problem is that institutions steadfastly believe that moral behaviour can be inculcated via spin doctors and vision statements. Providing these include the right moral terms, such as 'heart', 'spirit', or 'values'. However, these create a shallow and externalized halo of moral values. Real social capital is chiefly generated as a result of internalized belief systems that incorporate such values. The next question is what processes represent the best mechanism to achieve this? The simplistic, but central answer is TCC; specifically the development of trust between people within an organization. This is best advocated in Francis Fukuyama's text (Fukuyama, 1995), in which he illustrates how the nature of social trust relationships has shaped the economic development of several example states, from Germany to Japan and China. One of Fukuyama's counter-intuitive results is that countries with strong extended family ties, often display poorer economic performance than states with more nucleated smaller family units; as became the norm in Britain, Germany or Japan. In effect within a region such as southern Italy, with broad family ties, but weak external social links, the macro-scale economic network is effectively fragmented. It would be interesting to explore the impact of group architectures and scale within commercial organizations, from the perspective of levels of trust. For example, is it the case that organizations with small tightly knit work units, loosely coupled into a wider enterprise fair better than ones in which the individual is only part of a broad social coalition. I suspect that current in-vogue processes, such as hot-desking to optimize costs, are having a catastrophic impact on the degree of social capital within many enterprise environments. The cynicism evident in the Dilbert cartoon strip is one example of the impact of cubical management on group morale. Mind you even a cubicle is a rapidly vanishing luxury, in a world of agile hot desks and laptops. How much group cohesion do you think is achieved by equating your staff and their value to that of a piece of furniture? Having reviewed the nature of social capital at a micro level, the following section looks briefly at the impact of the equally important processes of diversity, and innovation as part of macro scale commercial processes.

3. Innovation

What is innovation? A basic no frills description can be had from our old friend, Wikipedia:

"The term innovation means a new way of doing something. It may refer to incremental, radical, and revolutionary changes in thinking, products, processes, or organizations. A distinction is typically made between Invention, an idea made manifest, and innovation, ideas applied successfully. In many fields, something new must be substantially different to be innovative, not an insignificant change, e.g., in the arts, economics, business and government policy. In economics the change must increase value, customer value, or producer value. The goal of innovation is positive change, to make someone or something better. Innovation leading to increased productivity is the fundamental source of increasing wealth in an economy."

(http://en.wikipedia.org/wiki/Innovation)

The last sentence is slightly debatable, as many alternatives could be seen as equally fundamental to wealth creation, e.g. education, social capital, or moral values; as we will argue. However, innovation is certainly something you would like as a driving force behind your economy. One problem is in distinguishing between invention and innovation:

"An important distinction is normally made between invention and innovation. Invention is the first occurrence of an idea for a new product or process, while innovation is the first attempt to carry it out into practice" (Fagerberg, 2004)

Basically, innovation is the application of invention. However, innovation leads to organizational, or procedural change, which may have positive or negative consequences. Hence the title of Christenson's seminal '*Innovators Dilemma*'. We are forced to embrace change for good or evil. Innovation carries risk, and this is often fudged over in the use of the term by policy makers, who perceive it as simply a metaphor for radical progress. Most innovation programs within corporations aim to achieve growth objectives.

"Companies cannot grow through cost reduction and reengineering alone . . . Innovation is the key element in providing aggressive top-line growth, and for increasing bottom-line results"

(Davila *et al* p.6)

A classic example of disruptive innovation comes from the displacement of film photography by digital imaging. Kodak has suffered badly as a result of this process; yet it was one of the first innovators in digital sensing technology. In 1986 Kodak engineers created the first megapixel imaging sensor. Of course the first digital cameras were aimed at the high-end of the photo journalism market, and went for a cool $15,000 a piece. Hence they didn't seem that threatening to the mass photographic film market. Fast forward to 2009 and the biggest camera maker in the world is, guess who? Not Kodak for sure, but Nokia the mobile phone company, who basically give a free digital camera away with every phone; millions of them a year. This is commercial disruption writ large. When a non-competitor starts giving your core product segment away for free! What is surprising is not that Kodak failed to foresee the rise of digital photography, but that they fundamentally misunderstood why people take photographs. They assumed for one hundred years that people take photographs in order to record things and events and look at them later. In fact what people really like is just the act of taking pictures, and the feeling that we have captured the present. Analysis shows that less than 5% of all stored film photographs are actually looked at with any frequency, i.e. more than once a year. Hence the digital camera is perfect in addressing this need, and few of us feel the urge to print the images, we just need to know they are stored somewhere. Very bad news if you make traditional photographic materials. In the words of Christenson:

"Simply put, when the best firms succeeded, they did so because they listened responsively to their customers and invested aggressively in the technology, products, and manufacturing capabilities that satisfied their customers' next-generation needs. But, paradoxically, when the best firms subsequently failed, it was for the same reasons--they listened responsively to their customers and invested aggressively in the technology, products, and manufacturing capabilities that satisfied their customers' next-generation needs. This is one of the innovator's dilemmas: Blindly following the maxim that good managers should keep close to their customers can sometimes be a fatal mistake."
(Christenson, 1997)

198

Christenson then gives a detailed example from the computer disk drive industry, where innovative change has occurred at the speed of genetic shifts in fruit flies, i.e. very fast. The most interesting aspect of this research is the conclusion he reached:

"Interviews with marketing and engineering executives close to these companies suggest that the established 14-inch drive manufacturers were held captive by customers..."

Hence the established companies in the field were partly prevented by their existing customer base from adapting rapidly enough to assimilate the newer smaller size disk drives, that emerging companies were offering. In addition the threat of cannibalizing exist product ranges is a major concern:

"The fear of cannibalizing sales of existing products is often cited as a reason why established firms delay the introduction of new technologies. As the Seagate-Conner experience illustrates, however, if new technologies enable new market applications to emerge, the introduction of new technology may not be inherently cannibalistic."

One final, but critical note from this source:

*"But the problem established firms seem unable to confront successfully is that **of downward vision and mobility**, in terms of the trajectory map. Finding new applications and markets for these new products seems to be a capability that each of these firms exhibited once, upon entry, and then apparently lost."*

(Christenson, Chapter 1)

Basically once a company grows to enterprise scale, it loses agility at a fundamental level. It can generate the sustaining innovations and push the established technologies, and even gain market share in new applications of those technologies. But large enterprises simply lose the ability to dance fast. Worse still, as in the Kodak example, even where they lead in generating a disruptive technology, their own lines of business are too entrenched and crystallized to assimilate and exploit the major innovations.

The bottom line demands successful innovation but raises the question of how to avoid the associated pitfalls. I would suggest TCC might help once again. For the process, product or organizational innovation to be constructive, the whole set of actors involved must understand and be engaged in the endeavor. Otherwise your existing product managers and sales force, whose bonuses are based on sales of current products, are not really going to believe heart and soul in the revolution.

Another interesting example of disruptive innovation is the latest microprocessor from Intel, i.e. the Atom chip. This is a miracle of miniaturization and is a radical design shift for Intel. Its key feature is very low power consumption and low production costs. Intel originally envisaged the chip being used in slate style mobile computers, or embedded in cars or other devices. However, just as the chip came to market the mobile computing landscape shifted very slightly. Asus launched the first cheap netbook computer and started a mass market for this class of device. Within a year these cheap light computers were dominating the sales of portable computers. This was great news for Intel as most of these machines run on Atom chips. However, by November 2008, we started to hear Intel executives saying that netbooks are not really very good as laptops, and people would be much better off with a full size traditional portable. Why? Because traditional laptops run on Intel's larger dual core CPUs that sell for a much higher premium than the Atom chip! This is the innovators dilemma once again; you can build a product that everyone wants, but it may also undermine your traditional markets and profit margins. At the launch of Apples Macbook range in October 2008, Mr Jobs was keen to put down any ideas of an imminent Apple netbook device, for precisely this reason; as Macbooks command a premium price point and a much cheaper netbook version would not be good for the bottom line. However, I suspect the pressure to enter this hot market segment will be too great and predict Apple will launch its own netbook soon; albeit a shiny and more expensive aluminum version of course.

Innovation & Globalization

Returning to the core theme of cohesion, we can ask what is the connection with the process of innovation? The simple answer is that companies with strong internal cohesion and rich social capital are much more robust in their ability to assimilate and drive innovation. Greater cohesion effectively provides an organization with 'shock absorbers', such that it can adapt and flex around disruptive innovations. However, building and sustaining corporate social cohesion is now an immense challenge. This is especially the case in the global arena, where multi-nationals are now truly diverse in terms of both employee and market culture, race and language. The emerging multi-nationals of the BRIC countries, (Brazil, Russia, India and

China), are however, clearly succeeding in the game of rapid market expansion and growth. Even in a state that Fukuyama assessed as having relatively weak prior social capital, i.e. China, the foreign corporations that began operating there since the 1990's, have in effect seeded a culture of large-scale enterprise management, that has now been fully assimilated by the indigenous companies. The following piece from the Economist, illustrates this point:

"Indian and Chinese firms are now starting to give their rich-world rivals a run for their money. So far this year, Indian firms, led by Hindalco and Tata Steel, have bought some 34 foreign companies for a combined $10.7 billion. Indian IT-services companies such as Infosys, Tata Consultancy Services and Wipro are putting the fear of God into the old guard, including Accenture and even mighty IBM (see article). Big Blue sold its personal-computer business to a Chinese multinational, Lenovo, which is now starting to get its act together. PetroChina has become a force in Africa, including, controversially, Sudan. Brazilian and Russian multinationals are also starting to make their mark. The Russians have outdone the Indians this year, splashing $11.4 billion abroad, and are now in the running to buy Alitalia, Italy's state airline (see article).".

(http://www.economist.com/opinion/displaystory.cfm?story_id=8960441)

However, the most important point in this article is the following:

"But the newcomers' advantages are not overwhelming. Take the difference in company ethics, for instance, which worries plenty of rich-world managers. They fear that they will engage in a race to the bottom with rivals unencumbered by the fine feelings of shareholders and domestic customers, and so are bound to lose. Yet the evidence is that companies harmonise up, not down. In developing countries (never mind what the NGOs say) multinationals tend to spread better working practices and environmental conditions; but when emerging-country multinationals operate in rich countries they tend to adopt local mores. So as those companies globalise, the differences are likely to narrow."

(http://www.economist.com/opinion/displaystory.cfm?story_id=8960441)

It appears that within the corporate domain, globalization is driving a process of ethical and cultural homogenization. Of course this is a rather controversial conclusion; only time will tell the extent to which this develops. What is of interest is what form the networks of social capital will take that emerge from this global process.

Innovation & Evolution

Evolution is a universal force acting on all complex systems, technical, social and biological. My own 2001 Honda Accord is not perfect, but it represents a quantum improvement over the 1977 Ford Cortina I used to drive. Of course evolution is a bloody process, and many smaller and inefficient car makers, (e.g. the British Rover company), have gone to the wall. The benefits of this process, however, vastly out way the downside, as we now have cars that are reliable, safe, and energy efficient. What mattered in the car market however was the existence of genuine diversity and choice. By 2008 one estimate for the total number of companies making some form of motor vehicle was over 1700. Of course these range from one man companies in small garages making kit cars, up to the giants such as Ford, and Toyota.

Diversity

This leads us nicely to the next topic, i.e. diversity. This is a vitally important concept and has become a central theme of many business/complexity texts, such as Surowiecki's *Wisdom of Crowds*, or Scott Page's book *The Difference*. The reason for diversity suddenly becoming a topic for business dialogue is the result of complex systems permeating the popular culture, via the efforts of the Santa Fe Institute, and related groups. (See the bibliography for more examples.) What is most interesting is that raw diversity appears, at first glance to be the very antithesis of a cohesive process. As the field of CAS has matured, it has become increasingly evident that the exact opposite is true. A CAS can only survive if it contains a sufficient degree of diversity. Let's look at this issue a little deeper.

Types of diversity

A system may be functionally diverse, yet its components can be fundamentally homogenous. For example, the cells of a multi-cellular organism, may share the same genomic code and basic cellular structure, yet during the creatures early development these diversify into functionally distinct cell types, (e.g. heart, liver, neurons etc). So systems may be structurally diverse with many component types, yet have an essential functional homogeneity. For example, human settlements are incredibly diverse in form and in the case of cities have vast internal diversity. Yet they all serve the same primary social functions of providing shelter, employment, and economic interactions.

One classic example of the power of diversity in the production of a complex, but coherent system is the evolution of the Linux operating system. Linux has a large number of popular distribution types (distros) available, each with a particular flavor and functional focus. Yet they also have a large and highly diverse number of developers who contribute time to the development of this open source OS. A self-forming hierarchy of the most popular Linux types has emerged, and these act as cohesive frameworks within which development of the OS sub-modules occurs. (From my personal experience I would recommend the Ubuntu distribution, as since version 8.10 it offers a very stable and functionally complete OS, that's free and fast, (www.ubuntu.com).) What is also interesting is that given the potentially infinite number of Linux variations that could exist, (as many as the number of developers, i.e. thousands), the actual number of distros with significant numbers of users is relatively small, ~ 12. Why does this emergent compression of possible states occur in a diverse system? The answer is our old friend 'trust', human agents need to trust the OS they are running and they expend time and energy on installing a new OS; (which can be considerable in the case of some Linux variants). If you download a version that is already in the top ten, then you have a higher confidence level in the quality and usability on offer. You trust the virtual reputation factor that is conveyed by the ranking of a particular variant. Of course this leads to another dynamic, i.e. a long tail distribution as the most popular variants have millions of users, while those even a few places down the ranking have only thousands of users. (The least popular versions inhabit entirely niche domains where pure geeks reside; who simply must have a Linux version that runs on their ipod!)

Probably the most detailed work on the topic of diversity in CAS is that by Scott Page, (Page, 2008.) In this work he analyses the subject of how collective decision making is generally enhanced when a diverse group of agents is involved in the process. The key finding is that the more diverse the group the wider the set of mental tools and experience that can be brought to bear on the problem. The real value from this is that each new individual and their world view, doesn't merely add linearly to the group. A team of nine is not 3x smarter than a team of three. It is at least N^2 smarter. In human networks just like digital networks, Metcalfe's law applies. In effect the skills and experience each new person adds to a team, can interact as a combinatorial function with the pool of existing skills present. Of course there are limits to how large a group can become before it begins to either:

a. Split into factions
b. Start fighting
c. Argue incessantly until point b.
d. Forms N sub-committees to evaluate further options.

   From my personal experience a functional committee needs about nine active members. More than this and any meetings can take a very long time to reach a conclusion. Much less and there is insufficient diversity and experience to address the problems under consideration. Of course it very much depends on the scale and nature of the problem and the cultural background of the group. In the Linux example given earlier, there is a virtual group with thousands of members, contributing to a common problem of creating a better OS. However, the management of the final stable distro release is typically controlled by a much smaller community, or semi-commercial entity, comprised of typically ten to twenty members. Surowiecki iterates this point, i.e. that we also need some special conditions for a crowd to be wiser than its smartest individuals, i.e. diversity, independence and a quite specific form of decentralization.

   "Groups benefit from members talking to and learning from each other, but too much communication, paradoxically, can actually make the group as a whole less intelligent...Diversity and independence are important because the best collective decisions are the product of disagreement and contest, not consensus or compromise."

(Surowieki, 2004)

   Of course, the worst case scenario in collective decision making is where 'group think' occurs. In the telecom sector at the height of the dot-com 2000 bubble, the European telecom companies, engaged in a bizarre form of collective group think, when they entered state run auctions for 3G spectrum licenses. In this case the collective thought was: '*well 2G licenses were worth lots of money so far, and mobile communications is clearly a growth area, so let's bet the house on 3G.*' At the time I was consulted by senior Telco managers trying to acquire the opinions of technologists on how to proceed in the 3G game, and I pointed out a few minor inconsistencies in this model. Firstly, in the UK I have rarely, if ever, seen anyone watching a portable tv in public while walking around. Yet watching tv on your mobile phone using 3G, was apparently one of the strongest selling points of the technology? What is of interest is the manner in which this innovation has actually found mass appeal, and that is in combination with USB 3G modems which provide any laptop with near ubiquitous internet access. Actually, the innovation was a combination of cheap modems and laptops, and a flat-rate pricing tariff, introduced by some mobile operators.

So group diversity and real consultation is really, really important. In the case of the 3G fiasco, it could have saved the respective telecommunication companies billions of dollars. Of course the greatest barrier to truly collective decision making is the power hierarchies that exist in most large organizations. We talk of new flatter management structures, but that is really double-speak for the disempowerment of middle-management. Power still resides in the board and CXO level of most companies. It is of interest however if we look at the average lifetime of companies to see how those with a deeper collective decision and innovation making capability are the ones that endure the longest.

---

4. Complexity Economics

A very topical question is why do markets experience boom and bust cycles? The text by Beinhocker is a very useful introduction to the modern view of Complexity Economics, with its emphasis on an emergent and evolutionary basis to economic activity. Since I am in no sense an economist, I will let Beinhocker explain the basics:

"At the beginning of the twenty-first century, Traditional Economics thus offers us two competing hypotheses to explain the oscillating patterns we see in the economy. On one side we have the microeconomics-based real business cycle theory, which holds on to the rational-equilibrium view and sees the economy as merely propagating external shocks. Under this theory, the key causes of economic oscillations are exogenous political events, changes in technology, and other factors. But such models cannot tell us why the cycles have been so persistent through history, despite enormous changes in the exogenous factors posited as causes. One the other side of the tracks we have the macroeconomics-based New Keynesianism. This body of work has backed away from Traditional orthodoxy and incorporated less-than-perfect rationality, dynamics and time delays in order to find endogenous explanations. In many ways, New Keynesianism is a step in the Complexity

Economics direction, but the New Keynesians have not been prepared to abandon equilibrium, and as a result, the empirical success of the theory has thus far been limited."

(Beinhocker, 2007, p.167)

Basically, the core of classical Economic theory is based on the premise that all human agents can make perfect and rational decisions and have complete knowledge of the market at any time. I am selecting my words quite carefully right now, as the sheer lunacy of these assumptions is shocking. I understand where they came from, i.e. a deeply held quasi-religious belief that the Newtonian reductionist and mechanistic world view could be applied to all domains of study, and hence Economics should be approached as if it were Physics. In the 1980's Chaos theory appeared and was the first serious theoretical challenge to this world-view; especially as applied to the realm of economics, (Gleick, 1997.) Throughout the past twenty-five years our understanding of complex systems has matured and a wealth of research and accessible texts now exist to provide a far more comprehensive and 'rational' model of how economies really work. One of the leading lights in this domain is Michael Mainelli at London's Gresham College, who has written lucidly on the topic, (a rare ability):

"Financial markets are about perceptions and the perceptions are the reality." (Mainelli, 2005)

The new approach of Complexity Economics is to consider economic patterns as 'emergent' phenomena, i.e. they arise spontaneously as a function of the nonlinear interactions occurring within all economic activity. A simple model that illustrates this is the Beer Distribution Game, created in the 1950s at MIT by Jay Forrester. The model simulates the interaction across a supply chain composed of a manufacturer, distributor, wholesaler and retailer. The game was originally played between students, but is now available as a computer simulation, which can be played online, or downloaded from http://beergame.mit.edu/. (A very nice demo of the game can also be found at http://www.backspaces.net/models/beergame.html. This was created by an old friend of mine Owen Densmore; a wicked Java guru who used to work for Sun, and now hangs out in downtown Santa Fe sipping lattes.) During a simulated beer game orders flow up the supply chain and supplies of beer cases flow down the chain. Players incur costs for holding inventory, or for running out of beer. The winner is the player with the least costs at the end of a

206

number of rounds. Sounds simple enough, and under classical economic theory such a system should exhibit some dynamic behaviour, i.e. variations in stock levels across the supply chain, and costs incurred by each player, but should rapidly settle into an equilibrium state where a steady flow of beer exists across the supply chain, and each player is paying a constant economic cost. (No direct communication between the players is allowed, except the information in each order placed.) Also the critical element is that orders take a finite time to arrive and for each order to be processed. Hence there are time delays in the system. The system is initialized with a steady and constant flow of orders, so the model starts and stays in equilibrium, however at some random point in time the number of input orders doubles, and then stays constant. According to old-school economists the system *should* move to a new equilibrium state.

Of course the actual results from runs of the game are not as expected, whether played by humans, or simulated on a computer. What actually happens is that oscillating waves of over-ordering and under-ordering swing across the supply chain, with similar oscillations in the beer stocks held at each point in the chain. Damaging boom-bust cycles thus emerge spontaneously in even a very simple, but realistic economic model. The key ingredient is the existence of time delays between the entities in the model, whether manufacturer, distributor, wholesaler or retailer. These make accurate forecasting of the future system state impossible, and lead to amplification of the errors in the order process. A classic nonlinear feedback loop is formed, that can only lead to chaos and the highly dynamic behaviour as witnessed.

Such a simple model illustrates the power computers offer, by allowing real-time experimentation on complex economic models. Specifically, the ability to visualize the results has made a huge contribution to our understanding of the subtle and complex connections that often lie hidden in the simplest of models. I would strongly recommend a studying of Beinhocker's text, or the online papers around the Beer Game, for deeper insights. In his summary Beinhocker states, the obvious conclusion:

"If the economy is something like a giant Beer Game, then one implication is that the standard solution of interest-rate cuts and increased government spending do not address the root causes of the cycle; they merely address the symptoms. We may never be able to eliminate business cycles entirely (and in fact we might not want to, as periodic contractions flush out inefficient uses of resources and spur innovation), but if governments wanted

to attenuate cyclical effects in a more fundamental way, then they would need to look at the structure of the economic system itself."

(Beinhocker p.172.)

Political leaders across the spectrum would do well to study this simple game and this conclusion. Of course, it remains in their own interest to foster the belief that central government still possesses immutable levers of power, in the form of interest rates and money supply, which are all powerful. The truth is the only real lever they have is public spending, in a Keynesian manner, to kick-start the economy in the down cycle. With all of the known risks that entails for inflation, currency risk and higher taxation. Such public expenditure again creates time-delayed signals and injects even more feedback into the system, with long-term consequences. As an article in the Guardian reports: "Flawed model 'blinded' King to credit crisis":

"Former members of the monetary policy committee will this week call on Mervyn King to tear up the Bank of England's complex mathematical model of the economy, as the Bank is accused of having exacerbated the recession by failing to cut interest rates fast enough when the credit crunch hit. As King prepares to issue the Bank's latest economic forecasts this week, three former MPC members, Sushil Wadhwani, Willem Buiter and DeAnne Julius, have agreed to join an extraordinary experiment by number-crunchers at consultancy Fathom to build a rival to the Bank of England Quarterly Model (BEQM), its main forecasting model. Interest rates have now been slashed to an unprecedented low of 1% to cushion the economy against the worsening downturn; but they were left on hold for much of last year, as MPC members fretted about the risk that rising oil prices would affect the public's "inflation expectations", which would in turn lead to surging wages. Critics say using BEQM to guide its decisions had blinded King and his colleagues to warning signs in the outside world. Using information gleaned from publicly available documents and Bank insiders, Fathom's number-crunchers have constructed a replica of BEQM. It shows that the model actually stops working when interest rates hit zero - an increasingly pressing possibility - and fails to allow for the impact of a credit shortage on the economy."

(http://www.guardian.co.uk/business/2009/feb/08/bank-of-england-governor)

Another reference in this area is by Michael Mauboussin, (Mauboussin, 2006), which offers an introductory view of complex systems, as applied to Economics. As an investor and economist he is well placed to make this analysis, and it is a readable book with some useful insights from psychology and studies of investor behaviour.

Risk Analysis

The 2008 credit crisis has been discussed ad nauseam, but it is pertinent to the theme of this chapter, so here is a brief overview of some interesting factors. The first dimension is the obvious coupling of behaviour across the population of investors and fund managers. A second key factor was that many were using the same risk analysis tools, such as the equation developed by David Li, (see the fascinating Wired article Feb. 2009.) However, the risk filter they were applying was fundamentally flawed, and these flaws were then amplified by the herd mentality of the market.

"The effect on the securitization market was electric. Armed with Li's formula, Wall Street's quants saw a new world of possibilities. And the first thing they did was start creating a huge number of brand-new triple-A securities. Using Li's copula approach meant that ratings agencies like Moody's—or anybody wanting to model the risk of a tranche—no longer needed to puzzle over the underlying securities. All they needed was that correlation number, and out would come a rating telling them how safe or risky the tranche was. As a result, just about anything could be bundled and turned into a triple-A bond—corporate bonds, bank loans, mortgage-backed securities, whatever you liked. The consequent pools were often known as collateralized debt obligations, or CDOs. You could tranche that pool and create a triple-A security even if none of the components were themselves triple-A. You could even take lower-rated tranches of other CDOs, put them in a pool, and tranche them—an instrument known as a CDO-squared, which at that point was so far removed from any actual underlying bond or loan or mortgage that no one really had a clue what it included. But it didn't matter. All you needed was Li's copula function."

(Wired Feb., 2009)

So here we have a classic collapse of diversity, combined with a positive feedback cycle, which delivered a devastating blow to the global economy. What it also illustrates is the danger in labeling complex entities and blindly applying advanced mathematics, without being able to translate what the equations mean into tangible forces, which human beings can visualize and comprehend. Worse still the process was infectious, and the traders assiduously copied what appeared to be a recipe for instant profit:

"The Gaussian copula soon became such a universally accepted part of the world's financial vocabulary that brokers started quoting prices for bond tranches based on their correlations. "Correlation trading has spread through the psyche of the financial markets like a highly infectious thought virus," wrote derivatives guru Janet Tavakoli in 2006...As Li himself said of his own model: "The most dangerous part is when people believe everything coming out of it.""

Looks like the 'copula' function was very aptly named! The next section looks at the potential of agent-based modelling tools as a means of understanding the processes acting in Complexity Economics.

Trust in Agents

This section discusses some of the research the author has conducted using agent-based computer models of complex systems, in order to understand the forces that impact cohesion. Specifically, this work was concerned with the impact of trust on the cohesion of agent groups, and their ability to withstand the impact of defection by other agents. Before we begin however, we need to question why this approach is useful. In a seminal presentation by one of the leaders in the field, Joshua Epstein, (based at the Brookings Institute in Washington,) asked exactly this in: *"Why Model"*, a keynote address to the Second World Congress on Social Simulation. Epstein provides an illuminating argument on the value of scientific models in general and agent-based models in particular.

"Simple models can be invaluable without being "right," in an engineering sense. Indeed, by such lights, all the best models are wrong. But they are fruitfully wrong. They are illuminating abstractions. I think it was Picasso who said, "Art is a lie that helps us see the truth." So it is with many simple beautiful models: the Lotka-Volterra ecosystem model, Hooke's Law, or the Kermack-McKendrick epidemic equations. They continue to form the conceptual foundations of their respective fields. They are universally taught: mature practitioners, knowing full-well the models' approximate nature, nonetheless entrust to them the formation of the student's most basic intuitions (see Epstein 1997). And this because they capture qualitative behaviors of overarching interest, such as predator-prey cycles, or the nonlinear threshold nature of epidemics and the notion of herd immunity. Again, the issue isn't idealization—all models are idealizations. The issue is whether the model

offers a fertile idealization. As George Box famously put it, "All models are wrong, but some are useful."".

A deep, but rather technical reference that covers the detail of human social cohesion from a mathematical and network perspective is also provided by Douglas White in his paper, *"Dynamics of Human Behaviour"*, (SFI research paper, 2008-09-042.) The best online reference for detailed, but readable papers, on the application of agent modelling to social issues is the Journal of Artificial Societies and Social Simulation. It is available online at:

http://jasss.soc.surrey.ac.uk.

Using a similar model to the one introduced in detail in chapter 3, it has been possible to study how the process of trust and reciprocity between agents, affects the resilience and cohesion of social groups. While agent reputation systems (Abdul-Rahman and Hailes, 2000), and (Yu and Singh 2002) have been extensively reviewed, there is still a lack of understanding in terms of how processes of trust and reputation evolve dynamically over time. These ideas were motivated by the need to improve computer security models, as traditional approaches are primarily technical and ignore the most vital element, i.e. the social dimension. Some excellent work that outlines this issue is set out by Yu and Singh:

"Social mechanisms complement hard security techniques (such as passwords and digital certificates), which only guarantee that a party is authenticated and authorized, but do not ensure that it exercises its authorization in a way that is desirable to others."

(Yu and Singh, 2003)

First let's define the game being played and see how it maps onto real world situations. Imagine for example, we are running an online auction web-portal and want to reduce the number of users cheating or being malicious. What we need is an automated mechanism that enables users to score the reliability of other traders, and filter out those that defect, or reduce the frequency with which they are allowed to interact with users that do cooperate. This process was modeled as a computer simulation in which the following processes were set up.

The simulation assumes that for any agent there is a variable probability that it may defect or cooperate. The agent then decides which action to take at each step based on its expected payoff from that action. Using a spatial model in which local interactions occur between individuals occupying neighboring nodes on a square lattice, then stable population states for the prisoner's dilemma depends upon the specific form of the payoff matrix. Depending on the exact payoff matrix values, the dynamics of local interaction can lead to a world constantly in flux, or equilibrium. Regions occupied predominantly by Cooperators may be successfully invaded by Defectors, and vice versa. In this state, there is no "stable strategy" in the traditional dynamical sense. (See the seminal reference paper by (Nowak and May, 1992), for a detailed introduction to the topic.) If you have time I strongly recommend the related and more substantial text by (Nowak, 2006.) In particular the chapter on Spatial Games is the best explanation of this form of agent model and evolutionary dynamics. One bizarre example Nowak demonstrates is how small groups of cooperating, or defecting agents, can invade worlds dominated by the opposing strategy. Such groups can migrate through the world, and for some parameter values of the payoff matrix, if two such groups collide it can trigger a cascade or 'big bang' effect, within which the strategy explodes across the agent landscape. A highly recommended web site that allows interaction with many forms of evolutionary games can be found at: http://www.univie.ac.at/virtuallabs/.

In Nowak's summary some key points emerge. Firstly, cooperators tend to survive best in clusters, a principle termed "spatial reciprocity". Some thought makes this an intuitive result, as cooperating agents are mutually reinforcing, whereas defecting agents are mutually destructive. And second, cooperating agents can successfully invade a population of defecting agents when starting from a small seed cluster. Hence the two strategies, while they can coexist, are not the same in their dynamic evolution. More research is required to understand how these evolutionary game models actually map into real social networks, although in this chapter we make some wild and general observations.

First though, we need to understand what is meant by trust in the context of software agents? Much work has addressed the notion of trust in computational systems, (Marsh, 1999, or Castelfranchi and Falcone, 1998), or the early work on evidence based reasoning (Shafer, 1976.) Another dimension to the trust question stems from the study of agent group formation managed by processes of trust; such as that identified by (Griffths and Luck 2003.) A second important approach, considers the dynamic evolution and adaptation of trust within individual agents. For example:

"Each event that can influence the degree of trust is interpreted by the agent to be either a trust-negative experience or a trust-positive experience. If the event is interpreted to be a trust-negative experience the agent will lose trust to some degree, if it is interpreted to be a trust-positive, the agent will gain trust to some degree".

(Jonker and Treur, 1999)

The research we conducted was similarly concerned with how an agent dynamically modifies its own trust perception of social interactions and events. Of course this agent simulation first requires mechanisms that enable the formation of cooperating groups. In related work (Ghanea-Hercock, 2004), we used a tag based selection scheme in order to enable agents to determine whether to trust other agents, with cost as the criteria. Where a tag may be defined as any unique attribute displayed by an agent (Holland, 1993.)

Basically, the research proposed that it is economically efficient for most agents to utilize a "passive trust" process. By this is meant that an agent preferentially selects which agents to interact with on the basis of a similarity metric applied to the other agent. Hence trust is reinforced by cooperative interactions, and degraded by defections. In the human realm we call it experience. In effect it models the way in which humans generally prefer to trade and socially interact with those from a similar social group, i.e. one in which they can easily identify the social 'tags', e.g. clothes, cars, football shirts, or anything that labels an individual as belonging to a group. Of course the group may also have specific sociological traits, i.e. caste, faith, gender, or race.

An agent's interaction in any complex environment requires a continuous reassessment of the degree of trust it should assign to external agents and events. The underlying assumptions made in the model were:

a) Trust is assigned as a continuous variable internal to each agent.
b) Positive events result in an agent increasing its degree of trust.
c) Negative events result in an agent decreasing its degree of trust.
d) Agents apply a threshold parameter to determine whether to trust another agent.
e) Agents shift their probability of cooperation or defection based on the expected behaviour of the majority of its neighbours, i.e. if the majority of neighbours play defect then each agent will increase the probability that it defects, and the same for cooperation.

A population of agents was then created with the following attributes:

- Vision – integer range of local cells the agent can perceive and directly interact with.
- Credit parameter – the value of an agent's current energy parameter.
- Resource – an integer parameter defining a tradable commodity.
- Metabolism – agents consume credit at a rate specified by the metabolism.
- Trust threshold parameter – defined as the degree to which an agent will trust agents within its vision.
- Probability to defect – probability that agent will defect, range [0.0 – 1.0].
- Probability to cooperate - probability that agent will cooperate, range [0.0 – 1.0].

The simulation selects a number of agents at random each time step and calls the execution method of each agent. The rules applied by an agent are:

i)   Create a new message requesting a resource and an offered credit price for the resource.
ii) Broadcast the message to all agents within the neighbourhood defined by its vision.
iii) Parse all messages from the mailbox and respond.
iv) For each message, if the predicted trust rating of the sending agent is higher than the internal trust threshold, of this agent then interact, else ignore message.
v)   If interaction occurs then select to play cooperate or defect, based on internal probabilities for each.
vi) If agent cooperates the sending agent increases its degree of trust for future interactions.
vii) Else if agent defects the sending agent decreases its degree of trust for future interactions.
viii) If an agents credit or resources is < 0 then reset the agent to an initial random state.

Clearly the iteration of this process can lead to cycles of positive or negative feedback for each agent, which leads to either a global low or high trust regime. (Related work on trust dynamics, has also considered the evolution of trust on small-world type networks. Thus mimicking the spread of trust interactions over realistic social network patterns.)

Hence the agents become more trusting if the majority of interactions are cooperative, and more likely to defect if the majority of recent interactions were defections. Clearly if agents experience a sequence of cooperative interactions they will tend to form stable high-trust groups, but otherwise will move rapidly to a low trust state with no stable groups of trusting agents. In the simulation results we see this displayed with strong bi-modal distributions of cooperating and defecting agents. What is most interesting from these simulation studies is that the population converges on quite different trust regimes from almost identical initial conditions, i.e. small variations in the initial propensity of agents to be trusting or distrusting, has a significant impact on the equilibrium state. The model in general will converge on a dominance of either cooperators or defectors, but it is virtually impossible to predict in advance which strategy will win.

It is interesting to compare this to studies of the historical evolution of social capital and trust in Italy, as outlined in chapter 3. If we looked at pre-renaissance Italy, it would have been difficult to predict the economic and social polarization of the state into a wealthy North and impoverished South. However, studies of the models as discussed, though extremely crude, do indicate that once a population experiences even slightly biased degrees of trust or distrust, within that region, then the population rapidly shifts into a stable state of cooperation of defection. What is more, the model also demonstrates that such states are very resistant to further changes. In the experiments we have to change the rules of the game significantly, in order to perturb the agent communities out of their equilibrium condition. This appears to be reflected in many real world states, including Italy, where efforts at economic stimulus and social reform appear to make little if any impact (Putnam, 1993.) In the real world one recent example of this type of process, is reputation control on eBay. However, while the eBay reputation system works well most of the time, (actually amazingly so), homo economicus has quickly figured out how to game the system:

"A new study concludes that some eBay users are artificially boosting their reputations on the Internet auction Web site by selling items for practically nothing in exchange for positive feedback from the buyer. Sellers with good reputations can seek higher prices on items they sell, according to the study out of the University of California at Berkeley's Haas School of Business."

(http://news.cnet.com/8301-10784_3-6149491-7.html)

A final word from Epstein and Axtell is a pertinent summary of this emerging discipline, (and most of science):

"Just as the community of biologists had to learn to fully exploit the microscope when it was first invented, so we have only begun to explore the use and limits of the artificial society as a scientific tool. We can only hope that the field itself will display the evolutionary process it studies – new agents join, and intellectual heterogeneity grows; social networks of scientists endogenously take shape; selection pressures operate; and from the social enterprise of agent-based social science, interesting things emerge!"

(Epstein and Axtell, p.178, 1996)

5. Case Studies

It is time to briefly review some well known companies from the perspective of innovation and cohesion. And ideally try to extract some common principles that have sustained their success. The examples happen to be companies whose products I like, which means it is completely biased and subjective! At least I'm being honest. (Tip for the day, never hire an engineer for your marketing or sales division.)

Boeing

Let's kick off with an overview of a major manufacturing company, Boeing. First however, let's analyse the main competitor company, i.e. Airbus. This may appear to be a bizarre diversion, but consider the Airbus A380. It ticks all the wrong boxes in terms of cohesive management and innovation development i.e.:

- Distributed construction process,
- Distributed management responsibility.
- Poorly defined objectives and commercial focus.

A product of several competing European states, who were compelled to merge airliner production, the result is a state directed mess. In the case of the A380 there was a disquieting set of drivers; firstly to build something that would be technically and physically imposing, and second to maximize profit by cramming as many bodies as possible into the smallest space. I for one will not be flying in this oversized cattle truck. It also fails from a commercial perspective in requiring a major investment in the supporting infrastructure, with expensive gates at the few airports it can even land in. This violation of existing standards is a fatal flaw to make when developing any new network-based technology. (Which is what air transportation fundamentally is.)

"The hubbub now surrounding the world's largest airliner might lead casual observers to believe the Airbus A380 is actually the world's largest lemon....It is true that Airbus has failed to solve stubborn problems with A380 wiring, suffers from French-German jealousies, made blunders in product choices, failed to predict the popularity of Boeing's new Dreamliner and then produced a meek rival aircraft - the A350 - that the industry determined to be inadequate and that Airbus is now scrambling to revamp. No one is saying that Airbus is a candidate for brilliant industrial management of the year. The problem that has delayed the A380's entry into commercial service for more than a year falls into the highly annoying category. For reasons that have defied simple explanation, the massive wiring harness for each plane keeps showing up with serious defects that can leave them useless. Because many of the bundles are made in Hamburg and then shipped to Toulouse, France, accusations have flown between the French and German plants as to whose fault this is."

(http://www.iht.com/articles/2006/06/28/business/transcol29.php)

Major new aircraft projects reflect the delivery of major IT programmes, once a project crosses some mysterious threshold of complexity then trouble is a certainty. Guess what, the counter examples of major projects being on time and to budget, are all from organizations operating with a cohesive social and technical network, and with good usage of corporate memory. Returning to the example of Boeing, let's consider the new Boeing Dreamliner 787. It was designed for fuel efficiency and passenger comfort; the two key selling points as far as airline operators are concerned, as they engage in ferocious competition.

Can we divine anything in the history of Boeing that enables it to successfully produce highly complex modern airliners? Boeing was founded back in 1917, but made its name with the creation of the Boeing 314 Clipper flying boat in 1938. The largest civil aircraft of the age, able to carry 90 passengers. In the same year, Boeing completed work on the Model 307 Stratoliner. This was the world's first pressurized-cabin transport aircraft, and it was capable of cruising at an altitude of 20,000 feet. Collins and Porras also pick Boeing as one of their worthy examples of good companies, pointing out its idealized view of its self-identity, as the driving force in its major decisions.

Once again the companies focus was on delivering pioneering developments in its field, i.e. aviation, and not on pure profit.

So Boeing is over 90 years old, and the future looks secure. From Pan Am Clippers to the Dream liner 787. The 787 has an impressive array of features, from the new giant passenger windows to the higher cabin pressure. All made possible via the all-composite airframe. This all plastic structure was a radical and bold move, an innovative risk in action.

Update: well seems like I spoke too soon again. As of summer 2009, the Dream liner is two years behind schedule. The plastic composite shell really has been a disruptive innovation. The problem is actually interesting, from a broader perspective. Most large aircraft since the 1920's have used the same method for linking the aircraft panels together, i.e. small rivets that fasten the metal sheets together; (millions of them in the case of a 747.) This method is not as strong, as say, a welded joint and much more expensive to make, but it has a single requisite feature. It is very resilient. The rivets allow the airframe to flex, expand and contract, as any plane undergoes immense stresses, and large temperature variations from ground level to high altitude. Since the 1970's some light aircraft have been made using composite materials, e.g. carbon fiber, to reduce weight and fabrication costs. This works fine for a small aircraft, as the stresses on the plane are much lower, and they don't fly at the higher altitudes reached by commercial airliners. Boeings bold attempt to scale the same processes up to an airliner are really pushing the envelope of aircraft technology. So no surprises that they are being forced to invent additional reinforcement methods as they proceed. The point is however, at least they are trying.

A final caveat to this was the revelation that the computer network in the Dreamliner's passenger compartment, designed to give passengers in-flight internet access, is also networked to the plane's control, navigation and communication systems. Not clever. Boeing is apparently looking into a solution, which had better be very good.

In retrospect the history of air travel in 20th century created a complex virtual network; (in chapter 2 we reviewed the topology and physical characteristics of the air route network.) The emerging web of air routes in the inter-war (1920-39) years stitched together the continents at a physical and social level, and transformed the political and commercial dimensions of the world to a greater extent than any previous age in history.

Apple Computers

My favourite technology company by far is Apple, or Apple Computer Inc. as it was previously known. This was not always the case however, since the 1980's I had only occasionally used a Mac, as they were generally expensive, (actually bloody expensive), and the universities or companies I worked in had standardized on cheap PC's. Basically I admired their slick design and interface, but lamented the companies pricing strategy. Finally in 2005 I acquired a Mac Book G4 laptop which started my conversion to the Apple camp; (plus my company was footing the bill.) What finally tipped the balance I think for many was the adoption in early 2006 of the Intel processor, and the ability to run Windows natively on the Apple platform.

This illustrates one of the two major gambles Apple made, the first was the migration of its operating system to a Unix core model in OS X, which risked losing market share and alienating its developer community. The second was the migration from the original Power PC chip to Intel CPUs. Both risks however, were driven by the long term perspective, a key strategy for any healthy company. Of course in the early pre-iPod days, they made some real screw ups, which we will review. Ok, first let's skim over the 30 years of Apple history, so we can then attempt to deduce how the company embodies the TCC principles we are looking for.

"The Apple I, Apple's first product. Sold as an assembled circuit board, it lacked basic features such as a keyboard, monitor and case. The owner of this unit added a keyboard and a wooden case. Apple was founded on April 1, 1976 by Steve Jobs, Steve Wozniak, and Ronald Wayne (and later incorporated January 3, 1977... They were hand-built in a garage of Jobs' parents, and the Apple I was first shown to the public at the Homebrew Computer Club. Eventually 200 computers were built. The Apple I was sold as a motherboard (with CPU, RAM, and basic textual-video chips) — not what is today considered a complete personal computer. The user was required to provide two different AC input voltages (the manual recommended specific transformers), wire an ASCII keyboard (not provided with the computer) to a DIP connector (providing logic inverter and alpha lock chips in some cases), and to wire the video output pins to a monitor or to an RF modulator if a TV set was used.

The Apple II was succeeded by the Apple III in May 1980 as the company struggled to compete against IBM and Microsoft in the lucrative business and corporate computing market. The designers of the Apple III were forced to comply with Jobs' request to omit the cooling fan, and this ultimately resulted in thousands of recalled units due to overheating. An updated version was introduced in 1983, but it was also a failure due to bad press and wary buyers."

(http://en.wikipedia.org/wiki/Apple_Computer)

Ok, so first lesson, if you are designing a new computing product and your CEO tells you to not bother with a cooling fan, as its noisy and expensive, think twice before saying yes. Personal exuberance and market vision do not make the best engineering qualifications! A second error that's easy to judge with hindsight was the exit of Steve Jobs in 1985, which was subsequently corrected in 1997 when Apple bought the NeXT computer company Jobs had founded, and made him CEO again. However, what Apple has got right, is the ability to constantly reinvent themselves as a company. They have become market definers, not just leaders, which is the quintessential quality of the very best. Sometimes they also demonstrated the qualities of TCC.

"If we want to move forward and see Apple healthy and prospering again, we have to let go of a few things here. We have to let go of this notion that for Apple to win, Microsoft has to lose. We have to embrace a notion that for Apple to win, Apple needs to do a really good job. And if others are going to help us that's great, because we need all the help we can get, and if we screw up and don't do a good job, it's not somebody else's fault, it's our fault. So I think that is a very important perspective. If we want Microsoft Office on the Mac, we should treat the company that puts it out with a little bit of gratitude; we like their software. So, the era of setting this thing up as a competition between Apple and Microsoft is over as far as I'm concerned. This is about getting Apple healthy, this is about Apple being able to make incredibly great contributions to the industry and to get healthy and prosper again".

(Steve Jobs, http://en.wikipedia.org/wiki/History_of_Apple)

So let's ask, what are the future prospects of the company. In the authors opinion Apple stock is a good long term investment. Based on the points already made, they have precisely the right focus and corporate ethos, i.e. make the customer happy. And do so by selling an experience, not a piece of technology. In contrast to the prevailing philosophy in the PC business, of cut costs and hope no one notices. Or worse, stuff the product with bloated

220

applications that add minimal value to the user experience, and consume CPU resources. The proof of this, as of early 2009, is that Apple stock is relatively stable, while the tech markets suffer a severe battering in the current economic crisis.

Google – not yet evil

The final example we will consider is the search engine company Google. In September 1998 Google sets up a workspace in Susan Wojcicki's garage at 232 Santa Margarita, Menlo Park. (Garages are such useful spaces.) The company easily fits in the Collins & Porras model of a company built to last, as its own web site proudly boasts the companies' ten founding principles. The most discussed among these is the principle, "6. *You can make money without doing evil.*" summarized in the motto *"Don't be evil"*. And refers to the ideal of offering users search results that are unbiased by sponsorship. This was almost certainly the key factor that distinguished them from the mass of search engine competitors that thrived around the turn of the millennium, e.g. Alta Vista, Yahoo, Excite or Ask Jeeves.

Once again a garage start up becomes a global enterprise. And yet again it is a company driven by high ideals and a core-ideology; (and on some odd days even profit.) One of those ideals is to give the customer what they want, not what you can maximize profit from. This is so often neglected by companies, that it is exceptional to find a major company that truly operates this way. The heat of market pressure can so easily bend and distort the best of ideals.

"Google's success came from an understanding of what Chris Anderson refers to as "the long tail," the collective power of the small sites that make up the bulk of the web's content. DoubleClick's offerings require a formal sales contract, limiting their market to the few thousand largest websites. Overture and Google figured out how to enable ad placement on virtually any web page. What's more, they eschewed publisher/ad-agency friendly advertising formats such as banner ads and popups in favor of minimally intrusive, context-sensitive, consumer-friendly text advertising."

The Web 2.0 lesson: *leverage customer-self service and algorithmic data management to reach out to the entire web, to the edges and not just the center, to the long tail and not just the head.* Hence the key competencies of Web 2.0 companies can be stated as:

- Services, not packaged software, with cost-effective scalability
- Control over unique, hard-to-recreate data sources that get richer as more people use them
- <u>Trusting</u> users as co-developers
- Harnessing <u>collective</u> intelligence
- Leveraging the long tail through customer self-service
- Software above the level of a single device
- Lightweight user interfaces, development models, AND business models

In the above points we see our old friend *trust* rear its head again. In this context it is the fundamental point that any company's users are your most important stakeholders. They will shape and co-evolve your products far more effectively than most organizations realize or accept. It appears to be a fear of losing control that motivates enterprise internal departments to keep customers out of the design and development loop. Companies that embrace real partnerships with their client base, will have a clear advantage in the crucible of networked globalization. One final note about Google, they are likely to remain a successful company, not because of the quality of their search engine, but rather as a result of statements such as the following: *"Google considers diversity a business imperative."* Note the choice of words, *business imperative*, not 'it's useful', or 'it's central to our customers', but imperative to our survival. As illustrated in the earlier section on diversity, it is a key driver in the process of innovation, and more importantly in the construction of real corporate social cohesion.

It now appears the battle is one between Google and Microsoft for control of the computing front-line. Microsoft is busily engaged in efforts to reinvent themselves and become more agile; (although Vista has not been the best example of agile computing!) As both sides maneuver to control the Cloud, web apps and online services, it should prove to be quite a spectacle in the coming decade.

Footnote: I was also going to offer Starbucks as an example of innovation, as I think they are a great company, but I know this triggers spasms of emotional outbursts from the green lobby that will fill my inbox, with examples of Ethiopian farmers starving as a result of coffee exploitation. My appreciation for them stems from the fact that they created a new culture of coffee houses that were pleasant places to socialize on the high street. In contrast, in Britain up until the Starbucks phenomena in the late 1980's, the only options were the local pub, with free gratuitous violence. Or an Olde Worlde tea shop, with some sticky buns and tea that tasted like boot polish. If I have time I might return to this later. If I haven't, then I didn't.

Visionary Companies

So visionary companies with a core-ideology and values do well and prosper over extended periods of time. A valid query might be, isn't it only the big successful companies that can afford such 'luxuries'? Collins and Porras also address this point and provide the example of Sony corporation. In the case of Sony, the founder Masaru Ibuka started with just $1600 in savings, in a bombed out building in downtown Tokyo. While he thought about cash flow and customers, he also codified an ideology for his fledgling company, part of which follows:

"If it were possible to establish conditions where persons could become united with a firm spirit of teamwork and exercise to their heart's desire their technology capacity...then such an organization could bring untold pleasure and untold benefits...",

(Collins and Porras, p.50)

Even more amazing are some of the management guidelines he set out:

"We shall eliminate any unfair profit-seeking, persistently emphasize substantial and essential work, and not merely pursue growth. We shall place our main emphasis on ability, performance, and personal character so that each individual can show the best in ability and skill."

This spirit has animated the company for many decades and helped deliver many world firsts. In electronics and computing, the Sony Walkman of 1979 was the classic example. A superb example of this spirit is the Sony Aibo robotic dog. In my early research career engaged in autonomous robots, I witnessed the development and progressive refinements of the Aibo, from a primitive skeletal-like machine to an amazingly sophisticated robotic system. While it was eventually shut down in 2006, and almost certainly made a loss, it perfectly demonstrated the founding ideals of Sony and inspired a generation of engineers into robotics and technology. It also illustrates the difficulty in measuring indirect gains to an organization. While the Aibo venture was never going to make a profit, it generated a vast amount of positive media attention and PR for Sony. And more importantly deepened internal corporate morale, (the most important element). In the past decade the competition in the consumer electronics market has also been intense. In order to retain its brand reputation, it was not enough to merely produce quality products, it also needed to capitalize on projects such as the Aibo to sustain belief in the brand.

Unfortunately, the credit crunch of 2008 has shaken many trees, and Sony has discovered that they have over-relied on past glories, at the expense of genuine innovation. A January 2009 article in the Financial Times put it succinctly with the caption, "*Sony has lost what made it special – ability to innovate*", (FT p.20, 23-1-09.) The article highlights the woes of a company that is still making commodity electronic products in a high-cost state i.e. Japan. The new company CEO, Howard Stringer, a westerner, is pushing to migrate the company to a focus on networked service oriented products such as the Playstation, but he faces intense resistance within the old guard in the Japanese corporate offices. One former Sony Engineer, summed the mood up in a book, titled 'Lost Technical Competence', in which he draws the conclusion that Sony became reliant on its brand image and let its core technical skills deteriorate. Not smart when the technology, and especially the PC computing and home electronics landscape was undergoing seismic shifts, from 1990 to the present. It remains to be seen at this point whether the new boys will kick-start sufficient innovation within the company. In March 2009 the sacked workers in one French Sony Factory, basically kidnapped the French Chief Executive of the company, and held him hostage overnight, which illustrates the depth of the companies woes. (An excellent overview of how corporate culture operates, and its associated norms, is also provided by Beinhocker, p.370.)

It is interesting, in this context, to witness the rise of the Global Business Schools, such as Harvard, or the Judge Institute in Cambridge and the newer Said Business School in Oxford. These have historically offered boxed vanilla MBA programmes for aspiring executives, but have lately realized they have the potential to function as catalysts for innovation and real economic growth in the corporate space. The younger Oxford Said School in particular, is demonstrating a real entrepreneurial spirit in fostering innovation between companies and organizations. One example of their research groups that intersects the topics of this text is the Complex Agent-Based Dynamic Networks group, (or CABDyN for short). It is managed by an ever jovial character, by the name of Felix Reed-Tsochas. Their web site is well worth a visit if you are seeking to understand complex networks. (But it is deep science so be prepared.)

The folk at Sony and other struggling enterprises could do worse than refresh their vision of where innovation can arise from. It is rarely from within your in-house R&D department any more. Occasionally, when an internal R&D group is set completely free, such as within a Skunk-works type structure, then great innovation can occur. However, the dilemma then is how to integrate the very disruptive outputs back into the core business. The truth is innovation flourishes at the intersection of ideas and organizations. The best aspect of the current downturn is precisely that it will pressure lofty executive boards to look at the wider world. And ideally stop pressing their faces up so close to spreadsheets, that no longer have any real meaning. Graphs really mean nothing.

Summary

Historically the development of human commerce was a direct expression of the emergent social structures surrounding the early city-states and nations, and the early trading routes. The constant exchange of goods, people, and services has since bound together every human society. In much the same way as nuclear matter is bound by the constant exchange of virtual particles. As with cities and nations, individual companies are limited in the size they can grow to by the underlying technological base and infrastructure. (Between 1955 and 2003 the average number of employees in a Fortune 500 company grew from 16,000 to 48,000. Clearly as a function of the communications revolution over this time frame.) With the advent of modern communications in the early 19th century, and rapid transport links, (compared to any preceding forms), the first true multi-national corporations were formed. Such communication links enabled small boards of directors to manage vast empires of commerce at a global scale, which remains the case today.

The hypothesis of this chapter has been that the key to long term survival and growth for any organization, whether commercial or otherwise, is the degree of trust, (specifically TCC), that exists between its participants and its customers. On a positive note, current international measures of good corporate behaviour, such as the green ICT movement, bode well for the future. Such measures are a very positive step and would have been unthinkable as a corporate topic even 20 years ago. There is now a vast array of programmes and organizations operating under the general banner of corporate social responsibility, such as: http://www.csreurope.org/, www.joinred.com, or http://www.sustainability-indexes.com/. Another excellent UK based group is 'Business in the Community', whose web site is well worth a visit, http://www.bitc.org.uk/.

Unfortunately, there is still an obsession within many companies to see trade as a win-lose game, rather than expect that win-win situations may be the norm. Competitors will always exist, but increasingly in a diverse sense, such that they also act as customers and partners at the same time. A classic example is Microsoft vs. Apple. In one sense they are archetypal rivals, in another they are mutualistic partners, as Apple has long sold MS Office for its platform. And MS rely on the Jobs team to ward off the anti-trust lobby. In addition, since the migration of OS X to the Intel platform and the release of Bootcamp in 2006, Apple hardware can now support MS windows. (In truth, Microsoft are rather more concerned with their real nemesis, Google.)

Staying on the Apple theme, the iPod story offers some useful morals. Firstly, it is often cited in corporate training sessions as the perfect business model. Its success stems from the seamless integration of content, via iTunes, and the hardware of both the sexy iPod design and easy docking connection to the host computer. This is true, but I feel it is more to do with the ethos within the Apple organization, and the vision and positive collective belief that has lead to this point. The result is the goal of all marketing departments, i.e. a customer base that doesn't just like your products, but will queue in pouring rain for days to buy one. Heck, many of them would queue in the rain while being beaten with sharp sticks! I suspect back in 2001, mp3 players were not on Microsoft's future watch list as innovative threats to its Windows OS. Yet the iPod halo effect has massively reinforced and stimulated Apples OS X.

Hence some divisions of two enterprises may be fiercely competing, while other divisions are solid partners in joint product development. This raises the question, where are the boundaries of the company/organism? It is no longer a simple question. As discussed earlier, this issue is also reflected in the cyber security policies of an enterprise, where it can be horrendously difficult to know where the boundary of trust resides. Is it within the customer's database, in partner's networks, or only within an organizations internal firewalled systems? Returning to the main theme of the chapter, TCC is a long term strategy that requires a concomitant investment. Secondly, focusing on a dominant strategy makes your management and marketing strategies myopic to subtle shifts in the market and edge effects.

In brief, you need to cultivate, trust, diversity and group spirit. Short-sighted policies of customer lock-in, market dominance and optimized business processes are the products of a childish mind-set. First, your customers are not stupid; (not unless you are selling military hardware). A useful reference in this regard is the Cluetrain Manifesto by Locke *et al*, which graphically spells out the empowerment of modern users and customers. A little too graphically at times, but the authors have a valid point to make. In particular, their message that the market is, and always was, an ongoing conversation, is precisely correct. The network age finally restores the human voice to people, and that is the driving force of real innovation and organizational success. The Internet has created a global bazaar for trade and services. Most of all it is messy, organic and complex. (Their list of 95 useful theses is also messy and too complex; humans can only remember 5 things, and that's on a good day.) However, a nice quote summarizes their thoughts:

"The idea that business, at bottom, is fundamentally human. That engineering remains second-rate without aesthetics. That natural human conversation is the true language of commerce. That corporations work best when the people on the inside have the fullest contact possible with the people on the outside."

(Locke *et al*, p.xvii)

Corporate thinking is just beginning to accept this as ground truth, and build new organizational frameworks around it. One manifestation of this is the concept discussed earlier of 'Open Innovation', where R&D groups accept that they have most to gain by fusing with teams from other organizations. (Check out the site on this topic at http://www.openinnovation.eu/). The best method to achieve this is to take your senior research staff, and send them to a remote hotel venue with a similar team from a potential partner organization. In addition, on *no account* send any product managers or legal representatives. The whole idea is to freely share ideas. Legal advice is the kiss of death to any innovation process. As Shakespeare famously remarked, and which always was his best advice: *"The first thing we do, let's kill all the lawyers."*

The most detailed study of how companies should be designed to survive and thrive in the long-term is the seminal work by Collins and Porros, which we briefly reviewed in this chapter. The same story emerged again and again, i.e. what matters is the values and ideology of a company, not its focus on profit or average dividend. The success of GE being a classic example, where great emphasis was placed on nurturing strong culture and values. Its most famous CEO Jack Welsh, referred to this deep linking of people, values and culture as GE's "social architecture", which provided it with an intrinsic ability to adapt and transform itself. What that reference doesn't explicitly define however, is that it is the product of the right ethos, i.e. the formation of broad social networks, and hence group cohesion, which ensures long-term survivability. The single reference in this domain, that is essential reading however, is the concise and brilliantly written *Harnessing Complexity*, by Axelrod and Cohen. They eloquently set out the lessons that can be learnt from studies of complex adaptive systems, and applied in real commercial and policy domains. It is a useful toolkit of techniques and measures. For example, in their summary of systems and interaction mechanisms, they summarise as follows:

"Build networks of reciprocal interaction that foster trust and cooperation. One way to do this is to promote the informal associations that provide the basis of social capital." and similarly, *"Use social activity to support the growth and spread of valued criteria."* (p.156)

Finally, without real diversity and a deep team spirit, you are building on quicksand, as employees will have no allegiance to the organization and cohesion is unattainable. If you are a CEO and need the message distilling even further, Trust = Cohesion = profit! Finally, in chapter 6 we arrive at the obligatory overview of the whole text.

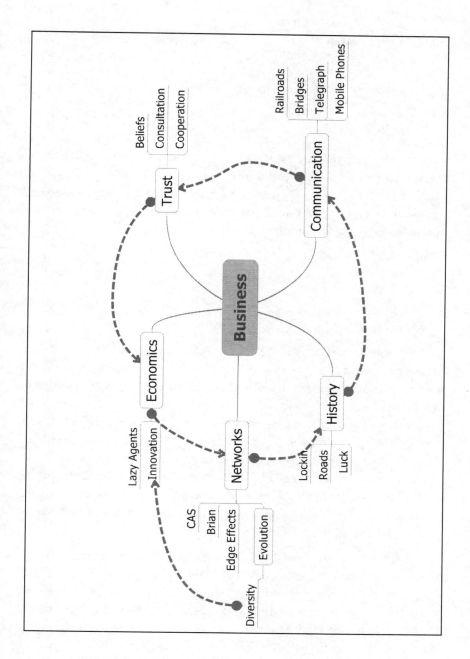

Mind map for chapter five.

Chapter 6

Conclusion: Bridges

"Every civilization carries the seeds of its own destruction, and the same cycle shows in them all. The Republic is born, flourishes, decays into plutocracy, and is captured by the shoemaker whom the mercenaries and millionaires make into a king. The people invent their oppressors, and the oppressors serve the function for which they are invented."

(Mark Twain, *Eruption*)

1. Overview

The above quote by Mark Twain perfectly summarizes the cyclic nature of human organizations, as they perpetually form and disintegrate. In this manner they reflect the underlying processes of cohesion we have attempted to describe and explain. Change and revolution are pervasive forces in both the human and physical realms. Often stated, yet less often understood. We have a deep psychological desire to make simple and predictable mental models of the world. Mark Twain, (real name Samuel Langhorne Clemens), had no such illusions, as he well understood the revolutionary nature of life. This chapter aims to summarize the key themes of the book, and also to inject a little revolutionary thought into the increasingly dull and politically correct worlds of academia and politics.

In writing this text I sought to avoid another concatenation of interesting ideas from the field of Complex Systems. There is an excess of texts in this area, each offering a slightly different slant on self-organization, fractals and power laws; or some equally fascinating aspect of complex adaptive systems. The aim was to develop the perspective that emergent cohesive order, is an intrinsic process within human society. In this, I am following concepts laid out in earlier work by Stuart Kaufmann and many others. Hopefully by using a single overarching theme, i.e. cohesion, we have captured one of the fundamental threads, which run through the domain of complex systems. It is not a novel theory, merely a position from which to categorize, and conceptualize the diverse processes at work. Such an effect may be best defined as one of *consilience,* i.e. a binding together, or unity, of knowledge.

"The greatest enterprise of the mind has always been and always will be the attempted linkage of the sciences and humanities. The ongoing fragmentation of knowledge and resulting chaos in philosophy are not reflections of the real world but artifacts of scholarship."

(Wilson, *Consilience,* 1998, p.8)

Should you be so inclined to put this book down and browse another in your wandering through the shelves, I heartily recommend you buy Wilson's text; it is by far the best book on popular science written in the past forty years. (Ideally buy both!) First though, let's return to the original questions posed in the first chapter.

The first question we addressed was, why do any complex social structures form at all? From the discussion in chapter 2 we saw that a number of physical conditions determine the degree of cohesion and integrity in complex systems. Firstly, this includes the topology of the internal networks of the system, as this influences the resilience of the network under attack or degradation. Second, the weighting of the network edges is important, in terms of weak versus strong ties. The third aspect is the point that complex adaptive systems need diversity and the capacity to adapt, in order to sustain a cohesive structure.

The attribute of structural stability is also an intrinsic aspect of self-organizing complex systems. Although, it is often problematic to determine the actual boundaries of any real complex system, as we saw in chapter 5; as in the case of large commercial organizations. Of course there must also be an energy flow through the system in order for it to sustain itself. Using this model, a city is a classic complex adaptive system. It has a large number of interacting agents, each of which is adaptive. There is a complex physical infrastructure and multiple communication pathways within and to/from the system. The city as a whole displays adaptive and resilient properties, and it evolves over time. We are only just beginning to understand the degree of complexity within such a system. Hence researchers in the field of complexity prefer to focus on relatively simple organizational structures, such as ant hills. It is quite apt that one of the most inspirational scientists of the past fifty years, Edward Wilson, wrote the definitive text on the humble Ant, and also the brilliant compositional work on socio-cultural evolution, *Consilience*. Wilson's definition of consilience as a fusion process in complex systems is one we will invoke within the chapter. Later we will consider the evolution of major cities, and how they may remain cohesive in the face of significant future perturbations.

The second set of questions we posed was: what makes stable social structures? and: can we increase the degree of social cohesion? These are far more difficult questions, but represented the original motivation for writing this text. In chapter 3 we discussed some of the key topics that impact the question of social stability and cohesion. The truth is this requires a full spectrum approach from psychology, sociology, economics and politics, through to applied physics. A number of texts have attempted to address the first part of the query, i.e. what social forces engender stable societies. However, the second aspect, can we therefore engineer societies with greater cohesion, has received far less attention from a scientific perspective. It does however remain a constant source of political machinations in many states. In most western countries a constant diatribe is heard from politicians of all parties, lamenting the demise of social capital; (they usually label it by some other term e.g. 'Back to Basics', but what they really mean is social capital. See chapter three for a definition.) A plethora of socio-political theories have been expounded on how social cohesion may be restored. But they typically lack any scientific basis or framework.

The study of social structure and the norms that compose cultures, is one starting point for a framework that may be amenable to intelligent discussion, and one that is sufficiently free from cultural bias and political misrepresentation. The economist Beinhocker in his synopsis on the origin of wealth, looks at how a 'norm' based analysis, can offer insights into improving the economic prosperity of states. These norms are broadly categorized as follows:

- Norms related to individual behaviour: E.g. those supporting strong work ethics, and individual accountability.
- Norms related to cooperative behaviour: e.g. the belief that life is a non-zero sum game and that cooperation pays.

It also includes norms for reciprocity and fairness, and the sanctioning of free-riders. (Interestingly Beinhocker makes the point that societies that are weak in these norms also tend to be in a state of low mutual trust, which as we discussed will tend to reinforce poor reciprocity and cooperation; thus completing a negative cycle.)

A third category is norms that are related to innovation: this is reinforced by belief systems that tend to rational rather than superstitious views of the world. In particular, a culture needs to be able to tolerate heresy and experimentation. The final requirement, being a positive attitude towards risk-taking and entrepreneurship. The UK is an interesting case in point in this regard. As a culture we strongly encourage the mad inventor and the right to be different or eccentric. Yet we fail to applaud those who take economic risks, or even those who actually achieve commercial success. Numerous attempts to inculcate the latter mind-set have been fostered by successive British governments with limited success. A final category of norms is how a society views time: some cultures have a fixation on history, over the present, which results in multiple problems, such as a low work ethic. Conversely societies that focus on the future, tend to invest and save more, and value work as a cultural expression. (This is one of the strengths of US culture; it tends to be future-focused.)

Beinhocker makes the case that these are not moral judgments, for or against any particular set of norms, but rather suggests that economic success is predicated by the relative orientation of a culture across the set of norms. Societies can choose whether that is the only metric they wish to live by. At this point I must disagree with his conclusion. Firstly, an individual living within a particular culture that scores poorly by the economic yardstick of norm 'quality', is seriously disadvantaged by them. They also have minimal choice over which norm set they would prefer to live by. Cultures that score poorly on this scale tend to be oppressive. Second, Beinhocker argues himself for society's ability to evolve new and thus improved norms by selecting new fitness functions. At the end of the day we collectively make moral judgments on the value of a particular norm to the future well being of society. Of course this is a difficult task within a state, or single cultural boundary, and does become a moral minefield when we try applying such judgments to the norms of other communities. This issue is further complicated by the problem that we need to maintain a diversity of cultural norms; as this makes the global collective more resilient and keeps future options open. Looking back at chapter three and the examples of empire building, the most extensive frequently made efforts to accommodate a diversity of cultural norms. At least for some periods of their history. (The peak of the Islamic age in Andalucía, is one example of an harmonious and multicultural, yet imperial era.)

Another question is what constitutes a useful cultural norm? It is increasingly argued that the western obsession with work, and economic growth, are in fact a fundamental problem, due to the resulting environmental and climatic impact. In contrast to those cultures that seek a stable and harmonious relationship with their environment. A culturally loaded question then, is does increased economic prosperity automatically result in greater group cohesion? The answer is far from simple. In western states, such as the United Kingdom, post-war economic growth from 1945 to the present has been at the expense of the fragmentation of family structures, a widening wealth gap, and a deep-seated sense of lost common cultural values. However, there is clearly a lower threshold of economic activity, below which the stress of survival causes poor social cohesion; as witnessed in many sub-Saharan states. The remainder of this chapter reviews each of the major themes of the book, and aims to articulate some of the future patterns now emerging, as technology and history collide.

2. Building Bridges

The bridge metaphor has been used across the chapters, as an embodiment of the cohesion theme, and as a conceptual framework. Hopefully this has been of some value in binding the strands of the text together. In this section we return to the bridge viewpoint and some related examples that reinforce this point. It is interesting to note that early bridges have frequently been the geographical seed of many major cities; London, Paris, New York, Rome, Boston. These have all emerged around the oldest fording points of the coastal, or inland river systems that supported and attracted human settlement in the first place. Cities have emerged like growing crystals around the bridges that bound together the earliest settlements.

They have also frequently been the focal points of the greatest conflicts, as people have fought bitter struggles to gain control of key bridges. The modern examples of Arnhem and the Rhine bridges serve as cases in point. And more recently, in the invasion of Iraq, the fiercest fighting occurred on the Tigris at the key road bridges. It is probably the case that throughout recorded history more people have died in conflict on, or around bridges, than any other type of physical structure. (Particularly, if we include the draw-bridges of castles and forts.) They are also of course a favourite location for people to jump from, as a means of committing suicide. In chapter 5 we looked at the economic impact of some classic bridges. As in the case of the Golden Gate bridge; a graceful expression of architecture and engineering excellence, that functions as a vital link in the region's economic and social integration.

Social Bridges

As we discussed in chapter two, an important aspect of the study of social networks is that some individuals act as social 'bridges'. Research has highlighted the 'weak ties' argument, by showing the value in how different parts of multiple social networks are bridged, (Burt, 1992). Hence, strategic advantage may be enjoyed by individuals with ties into multiple networks, which are largely separated from one another. This fits nicely with the bridge theme.

"The Strength of Weak Ties. More novel information flows to individuals through weak than through strong ties. Because our close friends tend to move in the same circles that we do, the information they receive overlaps considerably with what we already know. Acquaintances, by contrast, know people that we do not, and thus receive more novel information. This outcome arises in part because our acquaintances are typically less similar to us than close friends, and in part because they spend less time with us. Moving in different circles from ours, they connect us to a wider world. They may therefore be better sources when we need to go beyond what our own group knows, as in finding a new job or obtaining a scarce service. This is so even though close friends may be more interested than acquaintances in helping us; social structure can dominate motivation. This is one aspect of what I have called "the strength of weak ties."
(Granovetter, 1973)

A recent study at the Said Business School in Oxford using large databases of mobile phone data, has illuminated in detail the nature of social ties, and the impact different strength ties have on social structure and information flow.

"Here we examine the communication patterns of millions of mobile phone users, allowing us to simultaneously study the local and the global structure of a society-wide communication network. We observe a coupling between interaction strengths and the network's local structure, with the counterintuitive consequence that social networks are robust to the removal of the strong ties, but fall apart following a phase transition if the weak ties are

removed. We show that this coupling significantly slows the diffusion process, resulting in dynamic trapping of information in communities..."

(Onnela *et al*, 2007)

Studies of this kind are particularly illuminating in their ability to help visualize the human and information flows across cities. The availability of large-scale communication and computing networks, now offers a precise and accurate means of measuring social interactions as never before. This represents a revolution in the social and political sciences; the full consequences of which are yet to be realized. (The security and privacy implications of the fine-grained monitoring of peoples phone calls and location, are also proving to be a social challenge!) As we discussed in chapter two on digital networks, the relative strength of connections also has a significant impact on the cohesion of information networks. There are also virtual bridging edges and sub-networks that bind large-scale information networks together. This may be stretching the bridge metaphor too far, but for want of a better alternative we can run with it. Also the web itself is an overlay network that is shaped by the economic, social and cultural forces that act out upon it. So it is hardly surprising to find similar power laws and bridging structures, to those prevailing in the social network domain.

The greatest expression of a physical bridge is a title that has many contenders; such as the Golden Gate Bridge, or London Tower Bridge. However, my personal favourite is the recently completed Millau Bridge in southern France that spans the River Tarn. This has to be the ultimate example of art, architecture and engineering in a bridge form. In a delightful way, it is a totally over the top and exuberant structure, (nearly a full 1000 feet tall), to achieve a purpose that could have been realized with a far simpler and classical suspension format. Of course its parent was a British architect, Sir Norman Foster. Equally true is that, unfortunately Britain would never have actually built such a grandiose thing. It required the merging of the best norms from British and French culture to achieve this particular vision.

Cultural Bridges – Religions

And an old priest said, Speak to us of Religion

And he said:

Have I spoken this day of aught else?

Is not religion all deeds and all reflection,

And that which is neither deed nor reflection, but a wonder and a surprise ever springing in the soul, even while the hands hew the stone or tend the loom?

(Kahlil Gibran, *The Prophet*)

An interesting concept we initially explored in chapter three, was to consider the role played by the world's major faiths over the past two millennia, in acting as bridges between disparate cultures. In this sense, religions have arguably made a positive impact in increasing trade, cultural exchange and the flow of innovation. Of course this has frequently been accompanied by violent friction between the cultures involved, and we can't escape the often negative dimensions of religious expansionism. In the later section on revolutions and cultural clashes we will return to this theme.

A recent article in The Times offered a fascinating and provocative piece on the value of faith in economic development within Africa. The author Matthew Parris, an avowed atheist, concluded that the single most influential and lasting impact on social development across Africa is still the impact of Christianity; through missionary and associated activities. It is an entirely subjective conclusion, but one based on a childhood spent in Malawi and his many subsequent travels across the continent. He expresses it best as follows:

"Christianity, post-Reformation and post-Luther, with its teaching of a direct, personal, two-way link between the individual and God, unmediated by the collective, and unsubordinate to any other human being, smashes straight through the philosophical/spiritual framework I've just described. It offers something to hold on to too those anxious to cast off a crushing tribal groupthink. That is why and how it liberates."

Even more profound, and in keeping with the mantra raised throughout this text, is the statement that: *"Those who want Africa to walk tall amid 21st century global competition must not kid themselves that providing the material means or even the knowhow that accompanies what we call development will make the change. A whole belief system must first be supplanted."*

(*The Times*, p.17, 27/12/2008.)

This is a crucial conceptual shift that applies globally, not just in rural Africa, i.e. the root of all economic development and social stability, are the belief systems that live in people's hearts and minds. Returning to the powerful influence of norms, it is the author's contention that these arise as a side-effect of practiced beliefs. However, this is not to be confused with a simple liturgy for the value of western mono-theism. For example, the cohesion of societies, across the Orient, from India to Japan, has been sustained for millennia by the belief systems expressed within Buddhism, Hinduism, Taoism and Confucianism. What appears to be of pivotal value, is the ability of strong belief systems to foster healthy norms; which in turn inculcate personal values, social responsibility, and a sense of connection to the wider society. These are precisely the attributes that are lacking within some cultures, and that have been seriously eroded within many developed western states.

On this topic, an illuminating report was produced in the summer of 2008, by the Von Hugel Institute in Cambridge, (*Moral but no Compass*), which revealed the depth of concern among UK Christian groups; in that government ministers fail to understand the Church's broad role in providing social services. It rightly pointed out that institutions established and operated by the Church of England, and many other religious orders, have for centuries provided vital social services, from hospitals, to schools and welfare to the poor. These efforts, the report states, have been marginalized by increasingly secular governments, which have assimilated control of all such roles under the mantle of the state. I suspect the concerns raised in this report will go unheeded, as the issues will simply appear too diffused and difficult to integrate into government policies.

Science and Faith

This topic is a perennial matter for debate, and the God versus Evolution discussion bubbles on endlessly. However, there have been a number of noted publications of late that have raised the temperature. (We touched on this topic in chapter three and will expand here.) Richard Dawkins work "The God Delusion" stands out as a rigorous defence of the pro-reason and anti-faith alliance. While, one of the best countering texts is *Darwin's Angel*, by John Cornwell. He actually conveys a high regard for Dawkins writing, and has referred to him as *"one of the most brilliant living natural historians"*. Yet, Cornwell finds the God Delusion harmful in its failure to tackle the problem of extremism and wrong on many important issues. In this book, Cornwell adopts the persona of the Guardian Angel of Charles Darwin, who is now looking after Richard Dawkins. He pens a letter to Dawkins in 21 short chapters. One nice example of which is the section on "Is God Supernatural?" where Cornwåll argues with Dawkins's apparent image of God as, "A Great Big Science Professor in the Sky", which is not what most theists believe in. Similarly the idea that believers are encouraged not to understand the Trinity is refuted by the many books in Divinity Faculties trying to achieve precisely this. It is certainly a worthy text to study for a reasoned perspective on the question of science vs. religion.

A strong case for the harmony of reason and faith can also be found in the work of Polkinghorne. He describes his view of the world as Critical Realism and believes strongly that there is One World, with science and religion both addressing aspects of the same reality. He suggests that the simple mechanistic explanations of the world, which have continued from Laplace to Dawkins, should be replaced by an appreciation that most of nature is cloud-like, rather than clock-like. On the matter of evolution he raises a key point that is increasingly supported by the systems level view of biology, (Noble, 2008):

"…the fact that we share 98.4% of our DNA with chimpanzees shows the fallacy of genetic reductionism, rather than proving that we are only apes who are slightly different. After all I share 99.9% of my DNA with J. S. Bach, but that fact carries no implication of a close correspondence between our musical abilities".

(Polkinghorne, 2005)

In addition he makes some strong arguments for the rationality of religious faith. In particular, he does not claim that God's existence, or not, can be demonstrated via logic, but simply that theism makes more sense of the world, and of human experience, than pure atheism.

"The intelligibility of the universe: One would anticipate that evolutionary selection would produce hominid minds apt for coping with everyday experience, but that these minds should also be able to understand the subatomic world and general relativity goes far beyond anything of relevance to survival fitness. The mystery deepens when one recognises the proven fruitfulness of mathematical beauty as a guide to successful theory choice."

(Polkinghorne, *From Physicist to Priest*, p.107)

In the UK the dialogue brewed up in 2008, with a number of high profile figures wading in for a series of public debates. One of the classics took place in the Guardian newspaper, where the philosopher Daniel Dennett took on

Robert Winston, the British fertility guru. This particular debate really is a must read, but can be summarized by the following quotes:

"True, you don't have to be religious to be crazy, but it helps. Indeed if you are religious, you don't have to be crazy in the medically certifiable sense in order to do massively crazy things." (Dennett).

To be fair Dennett does also correctly argue that:

"This imperviousness to reason is, I think, the property that we should most fear in religion." Quite so, when any religion advocates blind faith at the expense of reason, then we are all better off without such. However, as Winston then brilliantly articulates,

"Religion is built into human consciousness and there is plentiful evidence of it being a cohesive force...In reality, both religion and science are expressions of man's uncertainty. Perhaps the paradox is that certainty, whether it be in science or religion, is dangerous. The danger of Dennett's relatively gentle brand of certainty is that it increases polarization in our society. With inflexible positions on both sides, certainty surely is the biggest threat to rationality, and to science."

(Robert Winston, *The Guardian*, p.14, 22-4-08)

In truth, the aim of all such debates should be to build a bridge between the two camps. This is what the whole of humanity desperately requires. We cannot, and must not, race into the coming century without such a reconciliation in place. The raw secular science, as espoused by Dawkins and Dennett, takes no account of the Promethean power that is being unleashed on humanity. The nano-bio-computing dream will become an Orwellian nightmare, if we fail to build a new foundation of ethical and moral values. The roots of which, must necessarily, stem from the heritage of the world's great religions. Returning to the words of Wilson, who while formally rejecting his Christian church, still pays homage to the values faith provides:

"Still, I had no desire to purge religious feelings. They were bred in me: they suffused the wellsprings of my creative life. I also retained a small measure of common sense. To wit, people must belong to a tribe; they yearn to have a purpose larger than themselves. We are obliged by the deepest drives of the human spirit to make ourselves more than animated dust...Perhaps science is a continuation on new and better-tested ground to attain the same end. If so, then in that sense science is religion liberated and writ large."

(Wilson, 1998, p.7)

The truth is we now need a new shared set of beliefs. For example, Beinhocker advocates the need for a shared platform or "common layer", i.e. a bridge across cultures within a multi-cultural state such as the UK. Many political and social commentators have picked up on this theme. Unfortunately, no one appears to have the faintest idea what such a common set of beliefs should look like, or where it might arise from, or who has responsibility to make it happen, or how, etc. Basically this is the challenge of the 21st century; we stand or fall on this battle for a common cultural nexus.

"Science faces in ethics and religion its most interesting and possibly humbling challenge, while religion must somehow find the way to incorporate the discoveries of science in order to retain credibility. Religion will possess strength to the extent that it codifies and puts into enduring, poetic form the highest values of humanity consistent with empirical knowledge."

(Wilson, p.290, 1998)

Ok, that's all a bit deep and contentious, so in order to inject a constructive dimension to this search, let's begin with one of the practical social process, which can catalyze positive cultural interactions, i.e. trust.

3. Trustworthiness

This point was expounded at length in chapter 3 and in the commercial examples in chapter 5, where the pivotal role of trust was demonstrated. The hypothesis, as advocated, is that trust is the central pillar of the many bridges that bind society together. It is ubiquitous in all functioning organizations and institutions. Whenever and wherever it is eroded, then systemic failures of the associated social organization is inevitable. (As an exercise for the reader, pick up any newspaper from late 2008, or early 2009, and count the instances of the word trust.) As an example, one UK building society, the Nationwide, just placed a large national press advertizement, with the following strap-line: *"Honest. Open. Trustworthy…More trusted than any other bank or building society"*. In a world riven with economic scandal and moral laxity, trust has become the new 'gold standard'. It is now worth cold hard cash.

Trust is fundamentally the critical factor in generating social or organizational cohesion. Specifically, the degree of trust that exists between the agents in a system is what counts. It really is a lubricant that permits the smooth transaction of trade and public services, (Putnam, 1993.) In situations of low trust, conflict becomes possible, and the cost of all transactions is greatly increased. In states of high trust the inverse is the case. A recent article makes the point clear:

"Today's financial crisis is, at heart, a crisis of trust. A few years ago, banks knew how badly they managed their own risks, how aggressively they had priced their own assets, and how much their own bonuses depended on these aggressive valuations. "If we are acting so irresponsibly, think how much more irresponsibly other banks must be acting," they thought. Thus, when repricing started, projections of social norms indicated that the repricing and credit terms should be more negative than market norms indicated. The banks failed to trust each other."

(Mainelli, 2009)

It is pertinent to consider that the antithesis of trust is corruption. In many states the failure to build a high-trust society, inevitably leads to the endemic practice of corruption and bribes. The human cost of this process is immense, and has received insufficient academic study in economic circles. One individual example from Kenya is the following episode:

"Each morning Wambui Kamau boards a matatu taxi bus to get to the city centre. This morning, like every other, it is flagged down at a police checkpoint, where the driver hands an officer 100 shillings. At lunchtime, Wambui heads to the Minsitry of Immigration to pick up a new passport. It miraculously surfaces when she offers the clerk 100 shillings. Heading home, the matatu is stopped at the same checkpoint and another bribe paid."

(The Times p.26, 18-2-09)

One World Bank survey ranked corruption, as the single greatest impediment to economic development and prosperity. It can reduce a countries growth rate by up to 1% a year. The total value involved is staggering; by one estimate the total amount in bribes paid worldwide is in excess of 1 trillion US dollars, according to the World Bank Institute. (Based on 2001-02 economic data.) Fukuyama also addressed this issue in his work on: *Institution formation, State-Building: Governance and World Order in the 21st Century*, (Fukuyama, 2005.)

Figure 6.1 illustrates the remarkable correlation between the level of trust between individuals within a state, and its economic prosperity: as measured by GNP per capita. (However, this nice data set hides some significant variations in the measurement of GNP/capita. The data for the Nordic states in particular displays a wide statistical deviation; hence the graphed value, for these states, was averaged over the available data sources.) (This figure may be directly compared with similar findings by Harrison and Huntington (2000); based on 1995 GNP/capita and trust survey data.)

The data presented in figure 6.1 is not just a snapshot of the correlation between trust and economic performance; it is of far more importance than that. What we also can infer is the likely future economic state of the listed countries. For example, outlier data points such as Vietnam, Indonesia and China, have relatively high trust scores. And as we witness they are moving up the GNP scale, as they undergo rapid economic development.

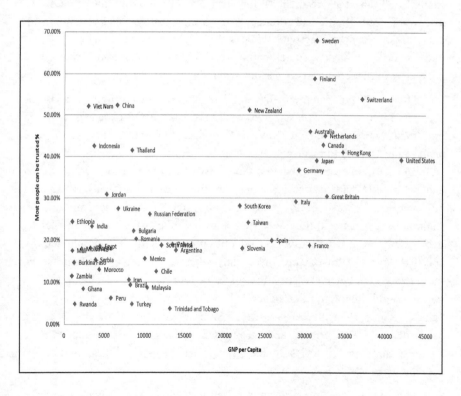

Figure 6.1 Relationship between Trust and Economic Performance, GNP per capita from World Bank estimates of purchasing power parity, in 2005 US dollars. The trust values are from interview survey data at: http://www.worldvaluessurvey.org/. (Based on the question: can most people be trusted?)

In contrast the US has a relatively low trust score compared to its premier economic status. As Robert Putnam famously argued in *Bowling Alone*, this is likely a consequence of the US living off the social capital invested by previous generations, and the falling trust score indicates an imminent decline in the economic fortunes of the US. I would strongly agree with this conclusion. (For example, California is currently issuing IOUs as its deficits soar.) An even starker example from the figure, however, is the data from France; with the lowest trust score of the developed nations on the chart. France is gripped in a deep economic malaise as successive governments fail to implement overdue economic reforms to liberalize the market and enable a more mobile workforce. This is amplified by the poor trust score, which is exemplified in the recurring riots in French metropolitan areas, as disenfranchised Islamic and ethnic cultural groups protest their exclusion from main-stream economic activity. Unless there is a genuine infusion of effort into restoring France's social capital and cultural integration, the future prosperity of that country is in serious jeopardy.

The third dimension of figure 6.1 is the obvious religious divisions between high and low trust regimes. The qualitative differences between traditionally Protestant, and Confucian, high-trust communities on the one hand, and other cultural groups is striking. Clearly each faith has its unique cultural norms and these impact on the ability of people to form bonds of trust and reciprocity with others in society. A finer grained analysis is required however. In the case of Protestantism since its historical separation from Catholicism, and the following three centuries of conflict, it has inculcated many of the norms that have been identified as promoting economic activity and high levels of trust. More specifically where it has factionated into sects, these have often been a reaction to a perceived corruption of such core values by the church hierarchy; and hence led to the forming of groups where such values became even more reinforced. Examples of note being the Quakers, Methodists, Presbyterians and Mormons. All of these groups have demonstrated long histories of high reciprocity, trustworthiness and hence economic growth.

This also touches on a question raised by Beinhocker on what should be the criteria of social success? Certainly, not mere cash flow. Many Islamic states are struggling with the issue of equitable wealth distribution, specifically in the oil rich regions of the Middle East. However, on a recent four week stay in Dubai, one thing became immediately apparent, it felt safe. Wandering along the sea front in the late evening with my family was a relaxing experience. Few major western cities can claim the same social benefit. In contrast within the economically prosperous UK, there is little sense of security within its crime ridden metropolitan areas. As for wandering around most US cities at night, I have only ever done so in small provincial Santa Fe in New Mexico, and once in New York, when I was much younger and very naïve. An orthodox faith, such as Islam can therefore create a very ordered social structure that leads to a positive environment for all, with cohesive extended families. Hence, apart from trust there are clearly other social metrics that determine how successful a particular region or community may be judged; the level of perceived fear being a prime example.

It is a personal belief of the author that individual faith is the root and mainstay for the development of trust, and hence social capital. Attempts by well meaning, but secular policy makers in all states, or cultures, are doomed to failure. This is very apparent in the UK where initiative after initiative to reform the economically deprived inner cities has failed. You can ask people to change, and fiddle with welfare programmes for eternity, but unless people have internalized a value system that creates positive norms of behaviour, then you are simply wasting time.

The only mechanism that has achieved such personal transformation throughout history, has been the transmission and assimilation of a belief system. Of course people have a fixation on whose god is the truth, which has always been a childish and fruitless argument. As mentioned previously, that is precisely why we need a whole new level of interfaith dialogue. (A great set of mini-essays appeared in the New Scientist, by a set of vanguard thinkers on the limits and power of reason, as a means of understanding the universe. The best of which is the article by Keith Tyson, an artist, in which he wrote:

"This makes me feel nostalgic for the days when there was no differentiation between being a natural historian or an artist-theologian. The lives of Newton or da Vinci seem much richer. The specification and reductionism of knowledge has given us many technological advancements, but I feel that we've lost a holistic synthesis. That's not a cerebral question, it's an emotional one." (New Scientist, 26-7-08, p.41)

4. Revolutions and the Nature of Change

"Revolutions always come around again. That's why they're called revolutions."

(Terry Pratchett, *Night Watch*)

This section reviews the kinds of change society is experiencing and the challenges to cohesion over the next fifty years. In chapter 1 we briefly covered the qualitative kinds of change possible in complex adaptive systems. These included some weird techno babble such as punctuated equilibria, and the ever ubiquitous phase transition effect. Such is the nature of growth, disruption, and reconstruction in complex systems. Ok, but what does it all mean, you ask. So let's try to ground it in some non-technical examples.

Clashes of Everything

A frequently debated topic is the '*Clash of Civilizations*' proposed by Samuel Huntington (Huntingdon, 1996.) This infamous thesis advocates that the near future of mankind will be defined by an ongoing conflict, both cultural and physical, between the major world cultures. Many have rightly argued that this is an overly simplistic stance, which glosses over important details in the composition and philosophy of most cultures. For example, Edward Said in an essay entitled, '*The Clash of Ignorance*' (Said, 2001), argues quite correctly, that Huntington's categorization of the world's fixed 'civilizations', completely ignores the dynamic interdependency and interactions between cultures. This is spot on, as what we define as a specific 'culture', is in reality a nebulous mixed bag of social norms, beliefs, politics, and historical baggage. Any culture is the epitome of a nonlinear complex adaptive system. It is certainly not a Newtonian billiard ball, with precisely calculable trajectories. Of course, it's simply easier to formulate policy, if one can label them as such.

Nevertheless, since the 9/11 attacks in New York, Huntington's argument has become a motif for the interaction between the USA and the Islamic world. This is hopefully a temporary state of affairs, as the stance is not constructive, nor conducive to social cohesion at any scale. More specifically, it represents an old-world zero-sum game mentality, where for one party to win someone else must loose. All cultures have something of value to contribute, and likewise all cultures have deeply entrenched negative 'norms' of behaviour, or belief, that must be addressed and adapted.

Clash of Culture - Orient and Occident

One of the most hotly debated clashes of this age is the strident emergence of China onto the world stage. Napoleon is famously quoted as saying *"When the sleeping dragon awakes, he will shake the world."* The Chinese model of surging economic development at over 8% annual growth, while retaining a one party political game, is certainly shaping much thought in Asian policy circles. There is unfortunately a disquieting murmur in American politics that the world can only have one superpower. This reflects the mindset of the cold war and the futile view of the world it engendered. The US will have to face the new reality of Sino-Asian dominance in many facets of global policy shaping. The Western powers would do well to consider their historical roles in China's recent history, and the blood that was spilt enforcing Western hegemony, (e.g. the Opium wars, Boxer Rebellion, etc.). The fact is the world is now a single economic and manufacturing enterprise. China can't grow without foreign markets and the west has no real inclination to reestablish its manufacturing base again. It is telling indeed, that the current US secretary of State Mrs Clinton, dashed to China in her first outing, in order to enkindle the economic activity, so urgently required by the two powers. The Chinese are also less than thrilled at the Trillions of US Treasury bills they currently hold, whose value looks a little precarious. Joint US Sino economic development is clearly a win-win game.

The future is ever deeper and stronger partnerships between the orient and occident, if we both wish for peaceful coexistence. The bleak alternative is best portrayed in a semi-mythical Russian proverb that was common in the 1990's; as Russia underwent vast economic and social perturbation: *"The optimists are learning English, the pessimists are learning Chinese and the realists are learning Kalashnikov."*

For China, what must happen is the same cultural process that occurred during the 1970s' and 1980s', in which Japan ceased to be perceived by the west as an economic threat, and simply migrated to its current role as an integral component of the worlds markets, and global economic structure. All growth curves are really S curves, and every developing state will reach a plateau of output and economic maturity. For some reason policy makers and military strategists fear systems/cultures in the growth part of the curve. Invariably such fear is misplaced. Of course a foreign power that holds several trillion dollars in US currency reserves requires circumspection and careful diplomacy on the part of the US. However, as mentioned in chapter 5, the pressure created by the engines of change i.e. China and India, also necessitates a revolution in the educational systems of many western states; in order to sustain economic competitiveness.

A fascinating article on the current economic woes of Japan appeared in the New York Times, on Japan's Crisis of the Mind, by Mararu Tamamoto. Discussing the current collapse in Japan's vast economic machinery, Masaru identifies the fundamental problem as being psychological in nature, rather than a function of poor policies, or finance. Referring to its historical progression since the Second World War, he reflects on what happened since the 1970's:

"So what happened once we caught up? Over the past two decades, the answer has largely been paralysis. Japan's ability to imitate outside models was mistaken for progress. But if progress is defined by pursuing a vision of a desirable future, then the Japanese never progressed. What we had was a concept of order and placement, which is essentially stasis...If we want to survive as a nation, we must shed our deeply rooted resistance to immigration. Contrary to widespread prejudices in favor of keeping Japan "pure," we desperately need to dilute our blood. Our aging nation will need millions of university-educated middle-class immigrants with high productivity, people who will put down roots and raise families, whose pride and success will be the affirmation of new Japanese values."

(New York Times,2-3-2009)

It is interesting to recall from chapter 5, that the very emblem of Japanese technical prowess, the Sony corporation, was held up as a paradigm of an organization with vision and pride in its early years. What this quote reflects is that any organization, whether commercial or cultural, needs to continuously regenerate its vision, and infuse renewed values into itself, in order to avoid stagnation. In Japan's case the missing vital ingredient, as the quote implies, is diversity. It remains a 'pure' monoculture, which is never a healthy condition.

Multiculturalism

In the UK since the London tube bomb attacks on 7th July 2005, many political and media commentators have lambasted the policy of multiculturalism, on the basis that it has fueled the isolation of Muslim communities and other minority groups. This is a simplistic response to what is a complex problem. We need to look at the cultural norms outlined in the previous section to see why some cultures have successfully migrated across national boundaries (e.g. the Chinese and Hindus into the UK), while others have formed isolated communities cut-off from the main-stream of their host culture. The point is not to compare cultures, but rather to see how education, communication and collective realization across communities can lead to a more positive social outcome for all. All cultures, whether in the majority or minority, need to face some hard facts about what their aspirations are, and how they can adapt to the process of community cohesion. I just avoided using the term community integration, as it has overtones of assimilation, but it is a valid expression of what needs to be done. This issue is not going to be resolved today or tomorrow. More conflict is probably a safe bet, hence greater efforts by everyone is a requisite, if a stable and cohesive future is to be created for all communities.

In this particular regard the USA is arguably doing a better job than much of Europe. A nice example was a report in the Economist, in an article entitled '*An age of transformation*'. The article highlights the amazing cultural transformation that has swept across the US suburbs. One example of which is a suburb called Willingboro:

"*FIFTEEN miles east of Philadelphia, Willingboro's Grand Marketplace is a chaotic place. Merchants hawk Christian T-shirts, Amish quilts, Chinese food, massages and Afrocentric literature. Salsa music blasts from a CD stall. Most of the shoppers are black; the shopkeepers are a variegated mix of blacks, Latinos, Asians, Arabs and whites, including Pennsylvania Dutch farmers in traditional garb. Welcome to bland, homogenous suburbia.*"

However, it is a strained and multi-faceted process,

"*Weak government is a particular problem because, as suburbs become less homogenous, they are also losing some of their cohesiveness. A big complaint in Willingboro is that neighbours are less sociable than they used to be. Levitt's ideal of self-contained neighbourhoods is largely forgotten: most of the pools have closed, and children may no longer attend their local school. Jim Gray, a longtime resident, complains it is ever harder to rustle up volunteers for civic events. On the other hand, the same could be said of almost anywhere in America. Willingboro has managed to arrange about a dozen events to celebrate its 50th birthday.*"

(The Economist, p.33, 31-5-08)

The process in the US is further complicated by the trend to migrate to neighbourhoods that are a close cultural match to peoples own beliefs and ideology. This has been highlighted in a recent book by Bill Bishop. Bishop argues that it is not just the process of migration into segregated cultural zones that is polarizing individuals views, but also the impact of modern media that enables people to easily filter out opinions that they find disagreeable, e.g. via Internet blogs and channel preferences in a multi-channel age. Bishop makes the strong assertion that this is 'tearing' America apart. But at least for the present, the deep multi-cultural tolerance and inclusivity that has shaped American history is still a dominant force that overrides the cultural zoning that is occurring in some sectors of US society. Whether that cohesive legacy will continue to operate as the dominant social process is another question. If we compare this effect across states there are significant differences, for example in the UK there is less internal migration than the US on average, but there remains a persistent North to South movement, as people move to the more economically prosperous South East regions. This has also led to some distinct cultural segregation; especially in the major urban conurbations of London, or Bristol.

It is interesting to compare this effect to the work in Epstein and Axtell's work on artificial societies, in which one common result is that a simulated agent society can spontaneously exhibit segregation into culturally isolated groups, merely by the process of agents choosing neighbourhoods based on cultural 'tags'. (See chapter 3 for a more detailed discussion on this topic.) So the universal challenge is blending cultures in a heterogeneous mix, whilst retaining and building social cohesion. It is a skill that the US has manifestly and dexterously accomplished throughout its history. *E pluribus unum*, once more.

Digerati & Technorati - (Clash of Education)

The author of Brave New World, Aldus Huxley, was profoundly astute in his predictions; in the western world, if one is pessimistic, we now have a society of educated Alphas and drugged Deltas. A new polarization of the traditional three tier class system has occurred, into those with, and those without education. The educated have access to the full economic benefits of a global online society. While those who are failed by their respective educational system, are condemned to a life of ignorance, state welfare or burger flipping. I am particularly thinking of the UK in this regard, where this process is acutely apparent, but it is mirrored on a global scale in many industrialized nations. What is important is that this process cuts across cultures, faiths, and prior class backgrounds. Education is increasingly a fundamental currency in the management of society. In the new world order a quality education is life itself. (It is another debate entirely as to what constitutes a 'quality' education. It is not necessarily an expensive or private one. Of greater significance I feel, is the cultural and moral ethos it transmits to the young, i.e. what is the value system being instilled.)

This is not an issue in many of the rising BRIC countries, as they have a long standing and deeply ingrained belief in the value of education. (I have worked as a teacher in China and as a Lecturer in the UK.) Hence poverty per se is not a barrier to education, as is often falsely held to be the case in the west. What matters is whether your family and peers promote the value of education. (To be sure however, poverty makes the process a damn sight harder. My Chinese students had to sit in classrooms over the winter at temperatures of minus 15 degrees C, as the city Hefei at that time, had no resources to heat public buildings.)

My solution to this problem would be to implement the following policy in those states where the process is defective, (e.g. the UK):

a.   Give teachers absolute authority in the classroom. I mean a return to good old fashioned Victorian values.

b.   Make parents sign a social contract, agreeing to support the educational process, where the rights of both parties are clearly defined.

c.   Higher education must be funded via a graduate tax scheme, where each year in higher education increases your future base tax rate by some percentage value. No tuition fees or loans. Higher education is a right in a modern society, but you pay via future taxable income.

d.   Reward excellence, good teachers get good pay, and more importantly respect.

e.   Punish failure, bad teachers get fired. (If you wish to restore a sense of balance, have the students they failed beat them with canes!)

That's it, quite simple and it will work. Of course the liberal voices will denounce my right wing agenda, and that's their democratic right. (In truth, the authors political views are in general pretty liberal, but not on education policy.) An excellent example of what I mean is the KIPP schools programme in the US, where education is a values driven process; http://www.kipp.org/. I strongly recommend a visit to their web site.

Clash of Party Politics

In order to reach a more ordered and cohesive society, existing western political systems, and the party focused model must be restructured. Given the deeply entrenched nature of western party politics, however, I suspect a radical phase transition will be necessary to realize such a new paradigm of political expression. Political commentators have frequently concluded that North American unity was established only following the process of a bitter civil war that engulfed the early US. Or that modern European unity was forged out of the First and Second world wars. More recently, as Russia emerged from the Soviet bloc era during the 1990's, we all watched with baited breath as tanks shelled the Russian White House. Fortunately, the situation stabilized, although that game may be about to begin again, as economic tensions once more deeply polarize Russian politics. If we at least recognized the nature of such transitional periods within human systems, then our institutions ought to be better equipped to handle the resulting social shockwaves.

Following the analysis by Surowiecki, it is clear that our present political models lack diversity in both leadership and the range of options available to the voting public. Of course this state of affairs is a product of people's desire for a small number of simple choices. Of course we do have some diversity in the operational process of government, via all-party committees, as commonly used in most EU states and the US. Unfortunately, the conclusions of these committees is generally ignored, no matter how wise and erudite the findings. Power remains in the hands of the executive who perceive the world through party filters, the ballot box threat and media pressure. (Using Surowiecki's model, the political aggregation mechanism is basically broken. In like manner, were the failings of the US intelligence agencies pre and post 9/11; who used distributed and semi-autonomous processes to aid the intelligence process, but lacked an information aggregation process.)

A more insidious problem is the current erosion of the democratic checks and balances resulting from the war on terror in the US and UK. The systematic undermining of the classic checks and balances model within both Parliament and Congress is a real and present danger to our common democracies. Some argue it is an inevitable consequence of the Clash of

Civilizations, which is logical, but glosses over the societal changes taking place within the states concerned. They have been struggling since the 1950's with the transformation into pluralistic and rapidly changing societies. (A fiery account of the war on democracy raging within the US at present can be found at the following site, http://words-of-power.blogspot.com/. The site is maintained by a superbly able and eclectic friend of mine, Richard Power. Some of it though is very hard in-the-face discussion, so be prepared.) The following quote makes the best case against the prevailing arguments for the war on terror:

"Out of unity comes security. I don't think you can impose security from on top. Just look at Yugoslavia. For years it seemed as if everything was quiescent...So I think we want to put unity first. Out of real unity--which can only be based on understanding and mutual respect--will come the kind of security that we really want.."

(Aung San Suu Kyi)

If we establish the norms that best lead to a cohesive and united society, such a collective will be intrinsically resilient. Clearly this overlaps with the issues raised in the clash of faiths section. Without a meaningful and sincere interfaith dialogue then no modern state can achieve such a harmonious and integrated society. This is patently a non trivial exercise and might need a few centuries work! In the short term it requires politicians to place such dialogue at the top of the agenda. Constant and broad ranging societal efforts will be needed to design and engineer the social bridges needed between the major faiths, and across cultural divides in general. Ultimately, failure in this Endeavour means war, to be blunt. Since the current cost estimate for the Iraq conflict alone stands at $700 billion, (or $4 trillion depending on how creative your accounting is), this seems to be a rather expensive way to resolve our differences.

Clash of Economics

A number of excellent texts have been produced in recent years, which define and explain the new age of complexity economics; (as detailed in chapter 5.) The point of this section is not to repeat their findings, but to examine what the impact is on the topic of social cohesion. First just to restate the essence of the subject, our traditional economic models are based on a Newtonian world view that is linear in cause and effect. In stark contrast the new complexity based model, views the economy as a non-equilibrium system and accounts for the non-linear and semi-rational behaviour of the human actors. Regarding human rationality, it is quite clear that few economists have ever been to a real auction or market. I have frequently witnessed in UK auction houses, buyers paying more for second-hand goods than the goods would cost new in the high street. Real human beings are not rational, trust me. Instead Economists have redefined human behaviour to fit the kind of mathematical model they have the ability to solve and model. (A little bit like the early astronomers who attempted to fit the orbits of the planets to circular models, as these were neater to imagine, and fitted their theological and earth-centric view of the cosmos. A parallel Copernican revolution is now just beginning within the stale world of Economics.)

From a societal perspective, the problem is most central banks and treasuries don't appear to have read these wonderful new economic textbooks! In the UK it is certainly the case that classical linear economic and control theory is still being applied by the bank of England to manage the economy. This failure of economic practice, is a criminal state of affairs, as such a failure of basic knowledge is causing widespread economic hardship. It would be excusable for a developing state to lack awareness of contemporary economic theory, but it is difficult to perceive why most western states are failing in this regard. The failure of the economic sphere to embrace, or even acknowledge, the presence of the well-founded approach of complexity economics is therefore having a significant negative impact on the cohesion of many societies. We can only hope that as awareness spreads, then the necessary paradigm shift will take place in the corridors of power. To be fair even when such a process has occurred it will be difficult for chancellors and chief economists to explain to the wider public that there is no longer a magic lever they can pull, (i.e. interest rates), that will make life better. Indeed given the importance of beliefs within the new economic model, it is paradoxical that the mass of economic players do still need a leader figure to give just such a simple message.

Future Visions

This section has two questions to address; first will the immediate future be socially cohesive? Second, if so, in what forms, and to what extent? Attempting to answer the first part has been the quest of this book, and the conclusion I believe, is that we will achieve a higher degree of social unity in the near future. Answering the second part is a little more difficult. The question of what form will such a cohesive society take, and over what fraction of humanity, has a number of facets. Lets attempt to tease apart some of these elements; in the certainty that futurology is part science, part voodoo and part astrology.

Visions of Order

Firstly, there is the perpetual fear that it will arise through some imposed cultural homogeneity. This is a reasonable and valid concern given the horrors of the 20th century. (I have personally visited the Auswitchz camp in Poland and my sub-conscious still blocks out even the memories of that passing visit.) Orwell's fears of the rise of Fascism were very well founded. The future is still menaced by the clouds of political extremism of left and right, or even the centre 'middle-way'. Commentators in the US are rightly worried that Fascism may sprout in North America and will arrive, 'wrapped in the flag and carrying a cross'. This was exactly the portentous vision, (written way back in 1964) of the iconoclastic Sci-Fi author Robert Heinlein in his book *Revolt in 2100*. In that book he vividly portrays an America that has been consumed with a far right Christian orthodoxy that uses Orwellian tactics to suppress the population. I would strongly recommend any readers living in the US to read a copy of this novel. It may help prevent it coming true, as the current signs are not good.

A parallel fear is the current obsession with Islamic extremism and the perceived threat to Western interests. This issue requires some balanced reasoning on all sides. For the West, the need for dialogue and greater cultural awareness and understanding should be the order of the day. There needs to be a wider acceptance that our oil dependence is causing enormous social tensions within the Middle East. In addition, a failure to address the Palestinian issue is also a cause for deep seated resentment, and a pervasive sense of injustice in the region. However, looking at the future visions we are addressing here, there must also be a broader movement within Islamic communities to embrace change and create a future focused mind-set. This needs to be illuminated by the vastly expanded interfaith dialogue we discussed earlier. The rapid social and economic development of some Gulf States has clearly demonstrated how Islamic states can flourish and maintain their religious and cultural identity, while accepting increasing social diversity.

As a race we can no longer afford the consequences of this religious-cultural divide. Europe made some of its most significant progress when it was stimulated by the infusion of Islamic knowledge and culture, via Spain from the 9th to the 14th centuries. For example, Cordoba and Toledo in the 10th century were the world centers for academic knowledge, and the development of new crafts, in ceramics, textiles, and metalwork.

Globalization Again

Another common fear is that globalization will bring bland cultural homogeneity, via the Starbucks and MacDonald's process. We touched on this in chapter 5, but skirted the social consequences. Globalization is inevitable, and is an inseparable function of the global communication links we discussed in chapter 4. As the world shrinks everyone experiences the same commercial offerings and markets converge. To be frank this is inescapable, but need not mean the loss of cultural diversity. What it means is that cultures will need to evolve far more rapidly than ever in order to adapt. Interestingly, since the late 1990s there has been a grass roots rejection of the homogenized offerings of the multi-nationals, and a desire to engage directly with alternative and diverse cultural products. Once in Beijing, I recall sitting in a MacDonald's, munching a burger, right on the corner of Tiananmen Square in 1993. This has since been bulldozed, as the Chinese felt it was a deep cultural affront; (and more importantly was far too valuable a plot to sell burgers from.) The striking arguments within the Cluetrain Manifesto represent the key point, that in the global village people really want a voice again. The conversation between trade and craft is returning as the global network links makers and consumers.

This topic links us back to the question of education. Where people have knowledge they can make wise choices. Also where positive cultural norms have been inculcated, people may forgo short term personal gain in order to benefit alien people living in distant lands. We are all too fond of cheap goods from Chinese and Asian sweat shops. I lament how few western shoppers pause, even for a second, to consider how it is possible for them to purchase a cotton T shirt for $2. Constant social pressure is required to raise awareness and explain the costs of our actions. Many positive examples of this exist, such as the Fair Trade movement for coffee, chocolate and tea. One excellent example is the Divine chocolate company, (www.divinechocolate.com). It started life in 1998, and brought fair-trade chocolate to the UK market, with a direct share of profits returning to the Ghana farmers co-operative that produces it. This was not an easy achievement as the chocolate market is a global corporate business with intense competition between the big producers. It required close cooperation between the Ghanaian co-operative managers and farmers and the foreign fair trade company, Twin Trading, to make it work. What is even more amazing was the goal they set, of not just selling chocolate direct, but realizing that their beans were some of the best in the world, they decided to aim for the premium market. This required real consultation and cooperation between the co-operative stakeholders, who clearly had vision and determination, to be fused with the experience and marketing skills of the parent company.

It is interesting to reflect back on the origins of globalization as we now understand it. It really began long before the 20th century, or even the 19th. It might best be dated to the early 17th century, when the awakening British Empire was harvesting the world for coffee, tea, tobacco, silk and all manner of goods. As expressed in Niall Ferguson's epic text on Empire:

"Taken together, the new drugs gave English Society an almighty hit: the Empire, it might be said, was built on a huge sugar, caffeine and nicotine rush – a rush nearly everyone could experience."

(Ferguson, p.15)

Referring to the political consequences that shadowed this commercial explosion in trade on a global scale, not seen since the days of the Roman Empire, he continues:

"Today we call the spread of this process globalization, by which we mean the integration of the world as a single market. But in one important respect seventeenth-century globalization was different. Getting the bullion out to India and the goods home again, even the transmission of orders to buy and sell, meant round trips of some twelve thousand miles, every mile made hazardous by the chance of storms, shipwrecks and pirates.

The biggest threat of all, however, came not from ships flying the Jolly Roger. It came from other Europeans who were trying to do exactly the same thing. Asia was about to become the scene of a ruthless battle for market share. This was to be globalization with gunboats." (ibid, p.17)

It is remarkable that international shipping from Asia to the west is still the subject of pirates out of the horn of Africa today, in the ungoverned waters there. At least the gunboats have gone, and instead new international mega-corporates battle it out on the trading floors of markets from New York to Shanghai. No less ruthless though.

Mega Cities

Another facet is where will the homogenized masses live? The simple answer is already apparent in the giant sprawling mega cities we now see: e.g. Mexico City, Tokyo, Shanghai, or Sao Paulo. First let's look at the historical rise of such vast urban conurbations. To my mind the first modern depiction of a mega city is the dystopian vision painted in Fritz Lang's 1926 film 'Metropolis'. In this film the city is a huge technology dominated social hive, in which deprived human workers slave to support an all-powerful corporate elite. (A bit like present day London, but with a working transport infrastructure.) Unsurprisingly, Lang's techno-future vision attracted the keen interest of the Nazi elite of the time in his home country, which prompted the visionary Lang to pack his bags and relocate to the New World.

Let's ask some basic questions about the mega city phenomena. First why do they arise and second are they in fact a dominant expression of human social cohesion? Taking the first question, the process really got started around the middle years of the 20th century. The combination of mass transport systems, communication networks and the pressure to find work, have all acted to drive ever increasing numbers into the urban centers that form the heart of these mega cities. What is interesting is that they fall into two clear categories with some common features. The first type is exemplified by Tokyo with approximately 13 million people, or 35 million if we consider the Greater Tokyo region; (it's difficult to count them as they don't stand still long enough!) Seriously, the issue of where to define the boundaries of a mega-city is a complex problem, and often the subject of political interference, for financial/economic reasons. In the Tokyo case it has an extensive central business district (CBD) and a huge urban hinterland that surrounds it. This extended urban region, however, is relatively prosperous with an average annual GDP of $1200 billion dollars; (based on a report by PricewaterhouseCoopers from 2007.) The second category is typified by Mexico City with 22 million inhabitants. Here we see a similar high-rise shiny CBD, with a GDP around $315 billion. However, now the vast hinterland is fractured into small zones of relative economic wealth, and much larger regions of extreme poverty. Similarly, the share of urban population in Brazil increased from 58 to 80 percent between 1970 and 2000, a huge increase. In terms of which ranks the largest, the prize as ever goes to China, with the Yangtze River Delta Metropolitan Area, (incorporating Shanghai, Hangzhou, Nanjing, Ningbo, and Suzhou). This has a combined population of ~ 88 million. This is clearly stretching what we mean by the word city.

Regarding the second question, i.e. are such cities the natural evolutionary product of human gregariousness and the action of commerce, we may draw divergent conclusions. On the one hand they are clearly still growing and will dominate cultural and economic development in the 21st century. The trend is manifestly towards ever larger super-conurbations that span entire regions. On the other hand, they pose significant challenges in terms of sustaining the resource base they require and the environmental impact they have at a global scale. (One example is Beijing, which is currently engaged in a vast programme of water diversion via the South-to-North Water Transfer Project. This is planned to tap the Yangtze River and its tributaries by 2010 and will supply northern China, whose urban growth has depleted many rivers and aquifers.) The over exploitation of the worlds fossil water reserves, in most developing states is a tragedy in the making, and one which needs urgent action to avoid disaster.

An alternative conclusion is that the ability to interact and trade in cyber space will greatly reduce the need to centralize economic activity. And the ability to socialize online will further reduce the human need to congregate in the same physical space. Hence the future may witness a reversal of the urbanization process, as many choose to live in smaller village/town structured settlements. In the USA this process is already apparent to some degree, as vast numbers flow into the suburbs and exurbs; far from the CBD and core urban zones. I suspect the future, as usual, will be a complex mixture of both processes. In states with high GDP/capita levels and well developed national infrastructures, many are migrating to the rural or small town settlements. However, in developing states with extensive rural poverty, the pressure on city growth is inexorable and is going to demand some highly creative resourcing within the mega cities.

One example of the pressures resulting from unchecked population growth is the current civil conflict within Pakistan. Most commentators focus exclusively on the tribal and religious dimensions of the conflict. Occasionally, a reporter will discuss the chronic economic problems and the state of underdevelopment in the Swat valley and Northern regions of the country. However, very few have made the simple inference that since 1951

259

the population of Pakistan has increased fivefold. When combined with a low literacy rate of ~ 50%, it is not surprising that civil conflict has broken out. This point is made clear by Wilson in *Consilience*, where he gives the example of Rwanda and the genocide there. Once again, all commentators focused on the tribal nature of the process, which is true, but as Wilson points out the country also experienced massive population growth in the preceding forty years. With an eightfold reduction in the area of arable land available per family unit. When faced with chronic shortfalls in food and resources, the normal conflict resolution mechanisms of a culture will start to fail.

The positive way of viewing such population driven conflicts is that people actually don't wish to fight, or engage in warfare. The innate drive of most human beings is to seek a peaceful coexistence, which is a dynamically stable state when the local population matches the resource capacity of the area. Deep social unrest is invariably a reflection of imposed resource contention, either as a result of excess population, or some external factor, (such as famine, inter-state war, or colonial activity); that is overriding the normal processes of trade and civil negotiation. Given the predicted pressures on key resources over the next fifty years, we must raise the debate on population control once again. It is not a new topic and in the 1970s was a dominant issue, leading to many apocalyptic reports on the imminent crash of civilization; (such as the Club of Rome reports). The projected outcomes failed to materialize, as the technology revolution in agricultural production and transport enabled the population growth to be absorbed at the global scale. Local famines plagued Africa, but these were seen as local aberrations, due to wars or climatic shifts. Unfortunately, the projections of extreme resource contention and social unrest were correct, just wrong on the date. The green revolution through the 1970-80s simply shifted the curve to the right over time by thirty years. Some voices are now calling for a new green revolution to feed the nine billion souls on the planet that will exist soon. This is certainly a requirement, but it must be in parallel with a major drive to reduce the population levels in most states.

Clash of Ages

Of course nothing is ever so simple. The preceding section argued strongly for a reduction in the global human population, however, there is another dimension we need to address. Many commentators rightly point out that the world's population is rapidly aging. In both developed and emerging countries the percentage of retired and elderly people is on a steep curve upwards. For now the percentage of the world's population over 60 is ~ 11%, but by 2050 it will have risen to double that i.e. 22%. Even worse the mix in the developed world will be closer to 33% over 60. Based on current state welfare models, this is simply an economic disaster in the making.

One simplistic argument is therefore to encourage people to have more children, so that the ratio of working age adults to retired folk stays balanced. Indeed, some EU states such as France have adopted this strategy with generous childcare benefits and encouragements for mothers to mix a career with having children. Yet this approach retains all of the problems we discussed earlier, and stresses the social and physical networks we depend upon. A smarter philosophy is to accept that this demographic shift is a natural process and reshape our cultural practices to accommodate the grey wave.

Firstly, we need a new economic model that accurately calculates the economic value generated by the elderly. Most of those aged 60-75 are actually engaged in part-time work, voluntary and charity efforts, or most importantly helping with childcare. This relieves the state of a huge economic cost. The state can help the situation by pushing forward legislation banning age-discrimination, and encouraging flexible working schemes via tax incentives. The majority of people really do not wish to switch off at 65 and watch televison, they would rather remain employed and active, but in a flexible manner. To be sure, the age shift will increase the support and health care costs incurred by the state and society. However, by enabling the majority to remain economically active the burden could be managed.

The real problem in most western states is people's failure to take responsibility for their own state of health. The above model only works, if a majority of the elderly has a sufficient level of fitness to do part-time work (paid or voluntary). The real demographic threat is not aging, but deteriorating standards of fitness, due to obesity and associated life-style diseases. For example, Japan has had a high percentage of elderly citizens for many years, but many of them are physically active due to the balanced low fat diet they consume. Hence the problem is manageable. (China faces a real problem, though for a different reason, its one-child policy now means that a single child will have two parents and up to four grandparents to care for.) In contrast the UK and USA are already experiencing severe strains on the healthcare and elderly support systems; precisely because a large percentage of the population are obese. If policy makers in the West truly fear the future, now would be a good time to get serious about forcing healthy food on people. Of course this presumes everyone can afford good quality food, or possess sufficient education to distinguish healthy products on supermarket shelves. The question of future resources leads us onto the next topic of climate change and technology impact.

5. Visions of Ice and Snow

The titanic problems we face in managing the environment, global climate change and resource distribution will stress society for many decades. To answer this question, of resources and distribution, we need to consider the major forces likely to shape society. In summary, I think these boil down to the parallel impact of climate change and technology in overdrive.

Climate

The first of these is climate change. My personal interpretation of the reports on climate change over the next 30 years, are that the most pessimistic predictions will be accurate. (Sorry, bad news.) I have no political bias on this topic, and have traveled widely enough to observe the signs in many countries. The Greenland ice cap is melting rapidly at the fastest predicted rate; this alone will likely disrupt the North Atlantic Gulf Stream and cause seismic shifts in the weather patterns of Northern Europe. On a global scale we will see extreme climate forces affecting many coastal regions in particular. Since this is where the majority of the mega-cities are located, this will require some really creative planning. Either the affected populations will need relocating inland to new metropolitan zones, or the existing infrastructures will need vast flooding defences; which are technically possible as the Dutch have demonstrated over centuries. (Although, they did have substantial economic resources and a small, but profitable empire).

The more important aspect, however, is the impact on global food supply, which will be severely disrupted. As one example, the 2007 drought in Australia decimated the countries cereal production. Intense competition for staple foods and commodity resources will drive new and aggressive regional alliances. The double-digit inflation in global food and commodity prices from 2005 to 2008 is the first harbinger of the trends to come. The 2008/09 economic storm has only temporarily suppressed this process. Some of the mega-cities as a consequence of climate and resource pressure are therefore likely to fail; in the same sense that we have failed states now. The lamentable conditions in New Orleans post-Katrina are a case in point. Where even within a Super Power, there is insufficient political will to rescue a major city. What was most amazing about the whole Katrina episode was seeing which US organization was first on the scene with food and assistance. Just as an exercise, guess who it was: the US Coastguard? the Marines? the Navy? Nope. Based on media reports at the time, the most immediate and effective response was by the Salvation Army. A charity run Christian group, with no fanfare, or grandiose media posturing; they simply called in their volunteers, packed supplies and went to help. Demonstrating once again the power of faith to truly motivate individuals in times of need.

A parallel development will therefore be an explosive growth in the impoverished shanty regions that surround such cities. Lacking in the most basic services, the likelihood of access to good educational provision seems remote, thus isolating these communities from the future networked service economy. However, human ingenuity thrives under pressure and current examples illustrate how such communities can rapidly improvise and develop. For example, in Bangladesh the establishment of a Grameen style phone banking network in 2007 quickly attracted over 15 million customers.

On a positive note, in many countries there is a drive to use wind power on a micro scale to supply energy to individual homes and local buildings. One problem slowing the development of this technology is the intermittent nature of wind power, which makes small wind turbines an unreliable power source. The standard approach is to store the power in large batteries, or to deliver any surplus back into the local grid. A better alternative is to analyse what the major uses of energy are in any home; specifically the provision of hot water and heating. If the electrical energy from a domestic wind turbine was used to heat the water in a well insulated hot water tank, then the water would act as a low cost, (and green), energy store. I am not aware of any current systems that utilize this method, which is a shame. (Email me if you know of any.)

Technological Advances

The master of the cyber punk genre, William Gibson has famously said *"the future is here already, it's just not evenly distributed."* This strikes a strong resonance within me, as my life-time has spanned the information age, and I have been fortunate enough to participate in exciting research work in Robotics and IT. My travels across China also make this quote stand in relief, as you can travel from cities pushing the envelope of 21st century design and living, to a countryside trailing a 100 years in the past, where indoor sanitation is rare, (trust me I know). I suspect, and fear, that this state of affairs will continue into the next century as well.

So what technological developments will shape the distribution of future wealth? Well the simplest visions of most futurologists, envisages that portable ubiquitous computer power will be virtually free, with high bandwidth communication links to the net. Most likely, paid for by advertizing, and occasionally by state subsidies. Nicholas Negroponte and his one laptop per child, is one example of this process, and has great potential to revolutionize life in the poorest regions. Further advances in nano-technology mean that such devices will also be universally available. Being an eternal optimist I like to believe that such universal communications access will primarily lead to new flourishing economic models and cooperative norms, which will enrich vast numbers of people. The real revolution however, lies in the potential to enable remote learning and education provision across broad swathes of the poorer regions.

An alternative future dystopia is famously portrayed in Stephenson's *Snow Crash*, where 'burbclavs' and mind viruses are one future scenario, and where multi-culturalism is taken to an extreme conclusion. In most novels in this genre the future is bleak, as the masses are unable to utilize the global network for personal economic advantage. But rather act as consumer fodder for the mega global corporates that rule the new earth. (The Snow Crash hero "Hero Protagnist" sits in his impoverished container home, jacked into the net via fibre optics and a super computer, but he is still living in squalor.) Personally, I don't think this will entirely be the case as the second key enabler will be online micro payments. Using these it becomes possible for someone in a shanty town to sell some local service, or knowledge, for tiny amounts of cash, but to a global market. (This was touched upon in chapter 5, on the power of current mobile phones in Africa to transmit digital cash vouchers.) This could enable a global digital Grameen banking mechanism, which could have profound and positive results for developing states.

Nanotechnology

This is a specific technology domain that demands a separate discussion piece. It is a well worn cliché, but if you are not scared, or at least deeply concerned by this technology you really should be. I don't believe the worst

264

case 'Grey Goo' scenario is a threat, or the hunter-killer drones in Michael Crichton's frankly awful novel 'Prey', are going to materialize any time soon. However, the potential for economic and social disruption by the imminent arrival of advanced nanotechnology manufacturing systems is of the utmost concern. On the economic front, imagine the ability to setup a supercomputer assembly plant in your garage. Or militarily, the ability for a terrorist group to create an entire air force of autonomous micro scale planes with potent weapon systems on board. In the personal space the threat to privacy will be extreme as video sensors shrink to dust like proportions. The fundamental issues though, stem from the impact on basic manufacturing. This is already apparent in the ICT sector. As alluded to earlier, the reduction in costs of computing power will have immense social consequences. As an example in 1994 I purchased memory chips for £30 per megabyte. By 2009 I just ordered 2 gigabytes of memory for a laptop for the sum of £15. It doesn't sound so big a deal, but work it backwards, that means in 1994 the same amount of memory would have cost £60,000! Push the same trend forward for computing power and storage, and we get virtually free supercomputers. These can either drive immersive 3D games, or design new biological weapons. Of course that's true today, but the scale, speed, and complexity of the process will be several orders of magnitude greater.

Looking at the longer term, in the seminal text by Eric Drexler (Drexler, 1990), the argument that nanotech will revolutionize human affairs is fundamentally an accurate one. Some of the technical hurdles are glossed over slightly; specifically the issues of power supply and heat dissipation and the serious AI challenges. But as a vision of what may be technically feasible it is brilliant. Drexler's dream of some global agreement and policies for controlling advanced nano-technology, however, are simply unrealistic and quite naive. In this regard Gibson and Stephenson are the better guides to the near future. Nano-technology will be used globally by all cultures for good and evil. We cannot push these genii back in the bottle; the die was set from the publication of Richard Feynman's paper in 1959, (*There's Plenty of Room at the Bottom.*) This is one of the primary reasons why we must resolve our differences now. In the immediate future everyone's neighbour will have access to awesome technology, and unfortunately our moral evolution has yet to catch up. (Go read Neil Stephenson's other major work '*Diamond Age*' if you really wish to know what such a future holds. The concept of global tribal/cultural identities, bound together by cyber links is an especially powerful metaphor.) For an up-to-date reference on the technical issues surrounding advanced nanotechnology, the work by Richard Jones (Jones, 2004), is a useful introduction. Jones makes the point that as computing devices shrink they will be embedded in every form of manufactured goods. The current RFID tags we now see in high-value goods and clothes are one example. Imagine these as small as dust, and with the computing power of a present day laptop.

Summary

I am currently looking out of my home office window on a sunny day, after weeks of torrential rain in the UK. Across the road is a familiar sight, an old wooden telegraph pole festooned with brown ceramic insulator pots and copper wires reaching out to the local homes. What strikes me is that a Victorian engineer would be quite comfortable with such physical technology. And yet it carries a virtual world of hyper-dimensional information, at light speed, that would stun a mind from even a few generations ago. I suspect the future will hold equally bizarre juxtapositions of old and new technologies. The problem is that this aspect will be compounded by the educational divisions mentioned earlier, such that the digitally excluded, while living in the same timeframe, will simply be unaware of the flow of services and technological power around them. Of course this is an age old Sci-fi theme from Metropolis to Blade Runner. Such visions of the possible are what science fiction is all about, and represent its real value to society. On a more upbeat note, Star Trek is the classic example of a future with an ever expanding integration of diverse alien cultures into a cooperative whole. It is hopefully a reflection of where we may trend to as a single species. (As the true visionary Gene Rodenberry clearly intended.)

The original questions we have attempted to address have been: what makes stable social structures and can we increase the degree of social cohesion? The title of the book presupposes that society is the dynamic product of countless interwoven cohesive forces. This final chapter has attempted to summarize the key issues that underscore this hypothesis, and expounded on the challenges facing our immediate collective future. One of the challenges has been avoiding use of the term 'unity', as this has quite negative connotations for many. Yet unity is precisely the degree of coherent social organization we need to emerge in the near future. Not uniformity, but a consilient, yet diverse federated networking of social norms that enhances all human cultures. (One aspect of the problem that has not been addressed in the text, however, is the impact of gender on the processes of social cohesion. The role of women in this regard is a major topic and could easily fill another book. This is a planned future project.)

One of my family's most treasured possessions is a small bed quilt that was hand made by a dear friend of ours, as a present for our first daughter. It is a simple square mosaic of many different brightly coloured fabrics stitched together. For me, it is the perfect expression of the value inherent in the merging and blending of disparate patterns, and more importantly cultures. One final question of course, must be has the cohesion theme proved useful in understanding the topics addressed? Well you the reader must decide that, but social cohesion is a critical issue that must be addressed in a frank and open manner across all cultures, if we are to survive.

I feel humanity has a glorious future just within its grasp. In the blink of an eye, by evolutionary or even historical time-scales, we can achieve an age of peace and global cooperation. Not wishful dreaming, merely simple extrapolation from the major trends in recent history, and the forces inherent in the technological revolution at work. Of course there are some minor issues like global warming, food supply and poverty, etc. I sincerely believe we will overcome these issues, and build a global politically federated, yet culturally diverse society. The evidence from all of the fields considered in this text suggests that given a sufficient degree of communication, then the co-operative assembly of such a meta-system is inevitable. More importantly, however, is the motivating belief behind this book, which is that when human beings cooperate in a positive spirit, then anything is possible. Only a united and socially cohesive world is going to take us to the stars and beyond.

"The Earth is but one country and mankind its citizens"
Baha'u'llah

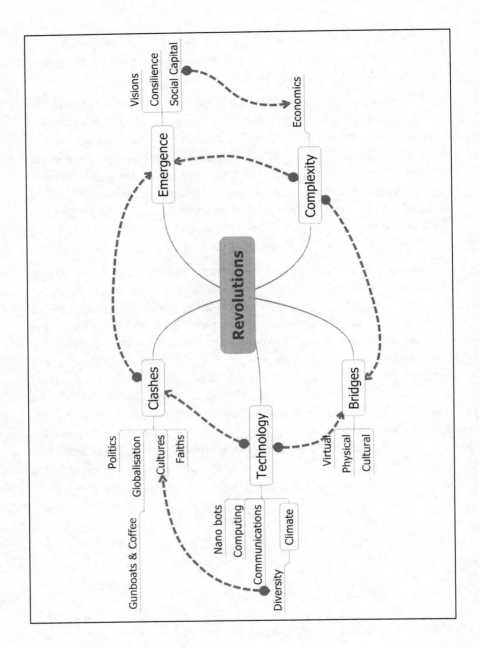

Mind map for chapter six.

Bibliography

Abdul-Rahman, Alfarez, Hailes, Stephen, *Supporting Trust in Virtual Communities*. Proceedings of the 33rd Hawaii International Conference on System Sciences, HICSS, 2000.

Adami, C., *What is complexity?*, Bioessays 24 (12): 1085-94. PMID 12447974, 2002.

Adamic, Lada, A., Huberman, Bernardo, A., *The Web's hidden order*, Communications of the ACM archive, Volume 44 Issue 9 September 2001.

Adams, Scott, *The Dilbert Future: Thriving on Business Stupidity in the 21st Century*, (Paperback), Collins Business,1998. (Not just for the laughs, it points up the serious issues surrounding IT in the commercial world.)

Alberts, David, S., and Hayes, Richard, E., *Power to the Edge: Command and Control in the Information Age (Information Age Transformation Series)*, pub. Cforty Onesr Cooperative Research, 2003. (Online: http://www.dodccrp.org)

Albert R., Jeong H., and Barabsi, A.L., *Error and attack tolerance in complex networks*. Nature, 406:378, 2000.

Amin, Masoud and Schewe, *Preventing Blackouts*, Scientific American, pp. 60-67, www.Sciam.com, May 2007.

Anderson, Ross, J., *Security Engineering: A Guide to Building Dependable Distributed Systems*, (Wiley Computer Publishing), (Paperback), John Wiley & Sons, April 2001.

Ankerl, Guy, *Coexisting Contemporary Civilizations: Arabo-Muslim, Bharati, Chinese, and Western*, Geneva:Inupress, 2000.

Arthur, Brian, *Self-Reinforcing Mechanisms in Economics*, in The Economy as an Evolving Complex System, pp. 9-33, K. J. Arrow and P. Anderson (eds.), Wiley, New York, 1988.

Arthur, Brian, *The End of Certainty in Economics*, Talk delivered at the conference, Einstein Meets Magritte, Free University of Brussels, 1994. Appeared in Einstein Meets Magritte, eds., Kluwer Academic Publishers, Holland, 1999.

Arthur, Brian, *Myths and Realities of the High-Tech Economy*, Talk given at Credit Suisse First Boston Thought Leader Forum, Sept. 10, 2000.

Ashby, William, Ross, *An Introduction to Cybernetics*, Chapman & Hall, 1956.

Ashworth, Tony, *Trench Warfare, 1914-18: The Live and Let Live System (Pan Grand Strategy)*, Pan Books; New edition, 2004.

Aspray, W., *John von Neumann and the Origins of Modern Computing*, Cambridge, Mass.: MIT Press, 1990.

Atkinson, Simon, Reay and Moffat, Jim, *The Agile Organisation*, CCRP http://www.au.af.mil/au/awc/awcgate/ccrp/atkinson_agile.pdf, 2005.

Axelrod, Robert, Hamilton, and William D. *The Evolution of Cooperation*, Science 211: 1390–96, doi:10.1126/science.7466396, 1981.

Axelrod, Robert, and Cohen, Michael, *Harnessing Complexity: Organizational Implications of a Scientific Frontier* (Hardcover) pub. Freepress, 2000.

Babbage, C. (ed. by Campbell-Kelly, M.), *Passages from the Life of a Philosopher*, New Brunswick: Rutgers University Press, 1994.

Balbiak, Paul, and Hare, Robert, D., *Snakes in Suits (When psychopaths go to work)*, pub. Collins, 2006.

Ball, Philip, *The Self-Made Tapestry, Pattern formation in nature*, Oxford University Press, 1999.

Ball, Philip, *Critical Mass, How One Thing Leads to Another*, pub. Farrar, Straus and Giroux, 2004.

Barabasi, Albert-Laszlo and Reka, Albert, *Emergence of scaling in random networks*. Science, 286:509-512, October 15, 1999.

Barabasi, Albert-Laszlo, *Linked: How Everything is Connected to Everything Else and What it Means for Business and Everyday Life*, pub. Plume, 2003.

Barber, Benjamin, R., *Jihad vs. McWorld*, Paperback: Ballantine Books, 1996.

Beinhocker, Eric, *The Origin of Wealth: Evolution, Complexity, and the Radical Remaking of Economics* (Paperback), Random House Business Books, 2007.

Bennett, S., *F.C. Williams: his contribution to the development of automatic control*, National Archive for the History of Computing, University of Manchester, England. (This is a typescript based on interviews with Williams in 1976.)

Bishop, Bill, and Cushing, Robert, G., *The Big Sort: Why the Clustering of like-minded America is Tearing us Apart*, Houghton Mifflin Company, 2008.

Blankley, Tony, *The West's Last Chance: Will We Win the Clash of Civilizations?*, Washington, D.C., Regnery Publishing, Inc., 2005.

Braynov, S., Sandholm, T., *Contracting with Uncertain Level of Trust*, Proceedings of the first ACM conference on Electronic commerce, November 3-5, 1999.

Bridge, Maureen, and Pegg, John, *Call to Arms*, Focus publishing, 2001.

Brooks, Rodney, A. *A Robust Layered Control System for a Mobile Robot*, IEEE Journal of Robotics and Automation, Vol. 2, No. 1, March 1986, pp. 14–23; also MIT AI Memo 864, September 1985.

Brown, Shona L. & Eisenhardt, Kathleen M., *Competing on the Edge: Strategy as Structured Chaos,* Harvard Business School Press, 1998.

Brownowski, Jacob, *The Ascent of Man*, pub., Little Brown & Co, 1974.

Burke, James, *Connections*, Simon & Schuster; Reprint edition, 2007.

Burt, Ronald, *Structural Holes: The Social Structure of Competition.* Cambridge: Harvard University Press, 1992.

Buzan, Tony, *Use Your Head: Innovative Learning and Thinking Techniques to Fulfil Your Potential,* (Paperback) by Tony Buzan, BBC Active; New edition, 2006.

Byrd, Jacqueline, *The Innovation Equation - Building Creativity & Risk Taking in your Organization*, San Francisco, CA: Jossey-Bass/Pfeiffer – Aprint, 2003.

Callaway, Duncan, S.,Newman, M. E. J., Strogatz, Steven, H. and Watts, Duncan J., *Network Robustness and Fragility: Percolation on Random Graphs*, Phys. Rev. Lett. Vol.85, no.25, pp.5468--5471, Dec. 2000.

Carey J., Gross N., Port O., and Stepanek M., *Software Hell*, Business Week, Dec. 6, 1999.

Carpenter, B.E., and Doran, R.W. (eds), *A. M. Turing's ACE Report of 1946 and Other Papers*, Cambridge, Mass.: MIT Press, 1986.

Castelfranchi C., and Falcone R., *Principles of trust for MAS: Cognitive anatomy, social importance, and quantification.* In Proceedings of the Third International Conference on Multi-Agent Systems (ICMAS-98), pages 72–79, Paris, 1998.

Centola, Damon, Eguiluz, Victor, M., *Cascade dynamics of complex propagation*, Physica A 374, p.449-456, Elsevier Pub., 2007.

Chakravorti, Bhaskar, *The Slow Pace of Fast Change: Bringing Innovations to Market in a Connected World*, Boston, MA: Harvard Business School Press, 2003.

Chesbrough, Henry, William, *Open Innovation: The New Imperative for Creating and Profiting from Technology*, Boston, MA: Harvard Business School Press., 2003.

Christakis, N.A., and Fowler, J.H., *Connected: The Surprising Power of Our Social Networks and How They Shape Our Lives,* (Hardcover), Little, Brown and Company, 2009.

Christensen, Clayton M., *The Innovator's Dilemma: When New Technologies Cause Great Firms to Fail*, Harvard Business School Press, Cambridge, 1997

Christopher, Martin and Peck, Helen, *Building the Resilient Supply Chain*, International Journal of Logistics Management, Vol. 15 No. 2, 2004

Cohrane, Peter, *Tips for Time Travellers*, McGraw-Hill Companies, 1998.

Collins, James, C., and Porras, Jerry, I., *Built to Last: Successful Habits of Visionary Companies,* (Hardcover), Random House Business Books, New edition, 2005.

Copeland, B.J. (ed.), 1998, *The Turing-Wilkinson Lecture Series on the Automatic Computing Engine,* in Furukawa, K., Michie, D., Muggleton, S. (eds), Machine Intelligence 15, Oxford University Press: 381-444, 1998.

Cornwell, John, *Darwin's Angel: An angelic riposte to The God Delusion,* (Paperback), Profile Books, 2008.

Darryl, Henderson, *Cohesion the Human Element in Combat,* National Defense University Press, 1985. (Online at:

http://www.au.af.mil/au/awc/awcgate/ndu/cohesion/ch01.pdf)

Davila, Tony, Epstein, Marc J., and Shelton Robert, *Making Innovation Work: How to Manage It, Measure It, and Profit from It,* Upper Saddle River: Wharton School Publishing, 2006.

Dawkins, Richard, *The God Delusion* (Paperback), Black Swan; New Ed with additions edition, 2007.

De Atkine, Norvell, B., *Why Arabs Lose Wars,*

http://www.unc.edu/depts/diplomat/AD_Issues/amdipl_17/articles/deatkine_ar abs1.html#Anchor_bio, 2002.

de Beer, G. ed. 1960. Darwin's notebooks on transmutation of species. Part III. Third notebook [D] (July 15 to October 2nd 1838). Bulletin of the British Museum (Natural History). Historical Series 2, No. 4 (July):119-150.

deGeus, A., *The Living Company,* Cambridge: Harvard Business School Press, 1997.

Dosi, Giovanni, *Technological paradigms and technological trajectories,* Research Policy 11 (3): 147-162, 1982.

Drexler, Eric, K., *Engines of Creation: Nanotechnology - the Next Scientific Revolution* (Hardcover), Fourth Estate, 1990.

Dreyer, Edward, *Zheng He: China and the Oceans in the Warly Ming Dynasty,* 1405-1433 (Library of World Biography) (Paperback), Prentice Hall, 2006.

Elton, H.W., *Warfare in the Roman World,* Oxford Classical series, Clarendon Press, 1996.

Epstein, Joshua, M., and Axtell, *Robert, Growing Artificial Societies Social Science From the Bottom Up,* Brookings Institution Press and MIT Press, 1996.

Epstein, Joshua, M., Why Model?, Journal of Artificial Societies and Social Simulation, vol.11 no.4 http://jasss.soc.surrey.ac.uk/11/4/12.html, 2008.

Evans, C., *The Pioneers of Computing: an Oral History of Computing,* London Science Museum, 1976.

Ettlie, John, *Managing Innovation*, Second Edition. Butterworth-Heineman, an imprint of Elsevier. ISBN 0–7506–7895-X., 2006.

Evangelista, Rinaldo, *Sectoral patterns of technological change in services, economics of innovation*, Economics of Innovation and New Technology 9: 183–221. doi:10.1080/10438590000000008, 2000.

Fagerberg, Jan, *Innovation: A Guide to the Literature*, in Fagerberg, Jan, David C. Mowery and Richard R. Nelson: The Oxford Handbook of Innovations. Oxford University Press, 1–26., 2004.

Fairbank, J.K., *China: A New History* (Paperback), Harvard University Press; 2nd Revised edition, 2006.

Farmelo, Graham, (Ed.) *It Must be Beautiful: Great Equations of Modern Science* (Paperback), Granta books, 2003.

Ferguson, Niall, *Empire: How Britain Made the Modern World* (Paperback), Penguin; New edition, 2004.

Fifer, S., *Analog Computation: Theory, Techniques, Applications*, New York: McGraw-Hill, 1961.

Fiksel, J., *Designing Resilient, Sustainable Systems*, Environmental Science and Technology, December 2003.

Forrest, S., Perelson, A.S., Allen, L., & Cherukuri, R., *Self-Nonself Discrimination in a Computer*, In Proceedings of the 1994 IEEE Symposium on Research in Security and Privacy, Los Alamitos, CA: IEEE Computer Society Press, 1994.

Freeman, Chris, *Prometheus Unbound*, Futures 16 (5): 494–507.. doi:10.1016/0016-3287(84)90080-6., 1984.

Freeman, Chris, *The Economics of Industrial Innovation*, Frances Pinter, London, 1982.

Freeman, Chris, *A set of measures of centrality based on betweenness.* Sociometry, 40:35, 1977.

Fukuyama, Francis, *Trust: The Social Virtues and the Creation of Prosperity.* New York: Free Press, 1995.

Fukuyama, Francis, *State Building: Governance and World Order in the 21st Century: Governance and World Order in the Twenty-first Century* (Paperback), Profile Books; New edition, 2005.

Fuller, Buckminster, R., *Critical Path*, St. Martins Press, New York, 1981.

Gell-Mann, Murray, *The Quark and the Jaguar: Adventures in the Simple and the Complex*, pub. Abacus, 1995.

Ghanea-Hercock R., "Applied Evolutionary Algorithms in Java", Springer Pub., New York, 2003.

274

Ghanea-Hercock, Robert, *Phobos: An Agent-based User Authentication System*. IEEE Intelligent Systems, 18(3): 67-73 (2003), June 2003.

Ghanea-Hercock, Robert, *The Cost of Trust*. Seventh International Workshop on Trust in Agent Societies, held at Autonomous Agents & Multi-Agent Systems Conference, New York, 2004.

Gladwell, Malcolm, *The Tipping Point: How Little Things Can Make a Big Difference*, Pub. Back Bay Books, 2002.

Glass, Robert L., *Software Runaways: "Lessons learned from massive software project failures"*, Prentice Hall, ISBN 0-13-673443-X , 1998.

Gleick, James, *Chaos: Making a New Science* (Paperback), Vintage; New edition, 1997.

Granovetter, M., *The Strength of Weak Ties*, American Journal of Sociology, Vol. 78, Issue 6, May 1360-80, 1973.

Granovetter, M., *The Impact of Social Structure on Economic Outcomes*, republished from the Winter 2004 Journal of Economic Perspectives, (Vol 19 Number 1, pp. 33-50), 2004.

Griffiths, Brian, *Markets can't be improved by rules. Only by personal example*, The Times, Opinion piece, p.30, 9th April, 2009.

Griffiths N., and Luck M., *Coalition Formation through Motivation and Trust*, International Conference of Autonomous Agents and Multi-Agent Systems, Melbourne, Australia, 2003.

Grimal, Nicolas. *A History of Ancient Egypt*. Librairie Arthéme Fayard, 1998

Haken, Hermann, *Synergetics: Introduction and Advanced Topics* (Physics and Astronomy Online Library) (Hardcover), Springer; 3rd Revised edition, 2004.

Hamel, Gary and Valikangas, Lisa, *The Quest for Resilience*, Harvard Business Review, September 2003.

Hammond, Ross A., Models of social dynamics: Corruption, migration, and prejudice, PhD, UNIVERSITY OF MICHIGAN, 2007; 3253279.

Hare, Robert, *Without Conscience, The disturbing world of the psychopaths among us*, pub., Guilford Press; 1 edition,1999.

Harris, Lee, *Civilization and Its Enemies: The Next Stage of History*, New York, The Free Press, 2004.

Harrison, Lawrence, E. and Huntington, Samuel, P. (eds.), *Culture Matters: How Values Shape Human Progress*, New York, Basic Books, 2001.

Heather, Peter, *The Fall of the Roman Empire: A New History* (Paperback), Pan Books; New edition edition, 2006.

Henderson, Darryl, W., *Cohesion: the Human Element in Combat*, 1985, full text online at: http://www.au.af.mil/au/awc/awcgate/ndu/cohesion/ch01.pdf

Hinsley, H., and Stripp, A. (eds), *Codebreakers: The Inside Story of Bletchley Park*, Oxford University Press, 1993.

Hoff, Benjamin, *The Tao Of Pooh*, Penguin Books; New edition, 1983.

Hoffman, Robert, *Twenty Years on: The Evolution of Cooperation Revisited*, Journal of Artificial Societies and Social Simulation vol. 3, no. 2, http://www.soc.surrey.ac.uk/JASSS/3/2/forum/1.html, 31st March 2000.

Holland J., *The Effects of Labels (Tags) on Social Interactions*, Santa Fe Institute Working papers 93-10-064, Santa Fe, NM, 1993.

Holland, John, *Emergence: From Chaos To Order*, pub. Basic Books, 1999.

Hollnagel, Erik (Editor), Woods, David D. (Editor), Leveson, Nancy (Editor), *Resilience Engineering: Concepts and Precepts*, pub. Ashgate, 2006.

Huntington, Samuel P., *The Clash of Civilizations?*, in *Foreign Affairs*, vol. 72, no. 3, Summer 1993, pp. 22-49, 1993.

Huntington, Samuel P., *The Clash of Civilizations and the Remaking of World Order*, New York, Simon & Schuster, 1996.

Jackson, M.O. and Watts, A., *The Evolution of Social and Economic Networks*, Journal of Economic Theory, 106(2), pp. 265-295. 2002.

Jones, Richard, *Soft Machines nanotechnology and life*, Oxford University Press, 2004.

Jonker C., and Treur J., *Formal analysis of models for the dynamics of trust based on experiences*. In Multi-Agent System Engineering, Proceedings of the 9th European Workshop on Modeling Autonomous Agents in a Multi-Agent World, MAAMAW'99. LNAI 1647, 1999.

Kaufman, Alfred, *Curbing Innovation: How Command Technology Limits Network Centric Warfare*, Institute for Defense Analyses, Argos Press, 2004.

Kauffman, Stuart, *At Home in the Universe: The Search for Laws of Self-organisation and Complexity* (Penguin science) (Paperback), Penguin Books Ltd; New edition, 1996.

Kelly, John, and Etling, Bruce, *Mapping Iran's Online Public: Politics and Culture in the Persian Blogosphere*, April 05, 2008, online at:

http://cyber.law.harvard.edu/publications/2008/Mapping_Irans_Online_Public

Kelly, Kevin, *Out of Control, the New Biology of Machines*, Pub. Fourth Estate, 1994.

Kepel, Gilles, *Bad Moon Rising: a chronicle of the Middle East today*, London, Saqi, ISBN 0-863-56303-1, 2003.

Keser, C., Leland J., and Shachat J., *Trust, the Internet, and the Digital Divide*, IBM Report RC22511, 2002.

Khare R., and Rifkin A., *Weaving a Web of Trust*, working paper, World Wide Web Journal archive, Volume 2 , Issue 3, Special issue: Web security: a matter of trust Pages: 77 – 112, 1997.

Khursheed, Anjam, *The Unviverse Within*, Pub. One World, 1995.

Kleinberg, J., *The small-world phenomenon: An algorithmic perspective.* Proc. 32nd ACM Symposium on Theory of Computing, 2000.

Köchler, Hans, *The "Clash of Civilizations": Perception and Reality in the Context of Globalization and International Power Politics,* Tbilisi (Georgia), 2004

Koestler, Arthur, *The Ghost in the Machine*, (Paperback), Arkana; New ed., 1989.

Kohler, W., *Gestalt Psychology* (Paperback), W. W. Norton & Co.; 2nd Revised edition, 1992.

Krebs,Valdis, *Uncloaking Terrorist Networks*, First Monday 7(4):, 2002.

Kurant, M., and Thiran, P., *Trainspotting: Extraction and analysis of traffic and topologies of transportation networks.* Physics/0510151, 2005.

Kurant, M., and Thiran, P., *Layered complex networks.* Physics/0510194, in Phys. Rev. Lett., 2006.

Levy, Steven, *Artificial Life: A Report from the Frontier Where Computers Meet Biology.* New York: Vintage, 1993.

Locke, Christopher, Levine, Rick, Searls, Doc, Weinberger, David, *The Cluetrain Manifesto: The End of Business as Usual,* (Paperback), Basic Books, 2001.

Mainelli, Michael, *Perceptions rather than rules: The (mis)behaviour of markets,* Gresham College Lecture, London, http://www.gresham.ac.uk, 2005.

Mainelli, Michael, *If only the banks had trusted each other, we might all be better off,* commentry article in The Independent newspaper, 5th March 2009.

Mauboussin, Michael J. *More than you Know – Finding Financial Wisdom in Unconventional Places*, pub. Columbia University Press, 2006.

McCain, Roger A. *Game Theory: A Non-Technical Introduction to the Analysis of Strategy* (Hardcover), South-Western, Div of Thomson Learning; illustrated edition, 2003.

McGeough, Kevin, M., *The Romans*, Oxford University Press, 2004.

Metropolis, N., Howlett, J., Rota, G.C. (eds), *A History of Computing in the Twentieth Century*, New York: Academic Press, 1980.

Mitchell, Melanie, *An Introduction To Genetic Algorithms* (Paperback), Prentice Hall India; 1st edition, 1998.

Milgram, Stanley, *Obedience to Authority: An Experimental View*. New York: Harper/Collins, 1974.

Mitnick, Kevin, and Simon, William L., *The Art of Deception: Controlling the Human Element of Security* (Paperback), John Wiley & Sons; New edition, 2003.

Momen, Moojan, *Baha'u'llah: A Short Biography* (Paperback), Oneworld Publications; illustrated edition, 2007.

Moravec, Hans, P., *A Non-Synchronous Orbital Skyhook*, Journal of the Astronautical Sciences, Vol. 25, October-December, 1977.

Morgenstern, O., and von Neumann J., *The Theory of Games and Economic Behavior*, Princeton University Press, 1947.

Myerson, Roger B., *Game Theory: Analysis of Conflict*, Harvard University Press, Cambridge, 1991.

Newman, Mark, E.J, *The structure of scientific collaboration networks*. Proceedings of the National Academy of Sciences 98: 404–409. doi:10.1073/pnas.021544898, 2001.

Nilsson, J. *Shakey The Robot*, Technical Note 323. AI Center, SRI International, 333 Ravenswood Ave., Menlo Park, CA 94025, April 1984.

Noble, Denis, *The Music of Life: Biology beyond genes* (Paperback), OUP Oxford, 2008.

Nowak, M.A., and May, R.M., *Evolutionary Games and Spatial Chaos"*, Nature, 359(6398), 29th October, pp. 826-829, 1992.

Nowak, Martin, *Evolutionary Dynamics: Exploring the Equations of Life,* (Hardcover), Belknap Press, 2006.

Onnela J.-P., Saramaki, J., Hyvonen, J., Szabo, G., Lazer, D., Kaski, K., Kertesz, J., and Barabasi, A.-L. *Structure and tie strengths in mobile communication networks*, PNAS May 1, 2007 vol. 104 no. 18 7332-7336, 2007.

Padgett, John., and McLean, P., *Economic and Social Exchange in Renaissance Florence*, http://www.santafe.edu/research/publications/wpabstract/200207032, 2002.

Page, Scott, E., *The Difference: How the Power of Diversity Creates Better Groups, Firms, Schools, and Societies* (New Edition), Princeton University Press; New edition, 2008.

Parry, Chris, Strategic Trends Review, MoD DCDC report, http://www.mod.uk/NR/rdonlyres/5CB29DC4-9B4A-4DFD-B363-3282BE255CE7/0/strat_trends_23jan07.pdf, 2007.

Polkinghorne, John, *Exploring Reality: The Intertwining of Science and Religion* (Hardcover), Yale University Press, 2005.

Polkinghorne, John, *Theology in the Context of Science* (Paperback), SPCK Publishing, 2008.

Putnam, Robert, *The Prosperous Community: Social Capital and Public Life*, The American Prospect 13 (Spring 1993), 35-42, 1993.

Putnam, Robert, *Making Democracy Work: Civic Traditions in Modern Italy*, Princeton, NJ.:Princeton University Press, 1993.

Putnam, Robert, *Bowling Alone: The Collapse and Revival of American Community* (Paperback), Simon & Schuster Ltd; New edition, 2001.

Putnam, Robert, Social *Capital and Public Affairs*, The American Prospect, no.13 (1993b):1-8.

Putnam, Robert, *E Pluribus Unum: Diversity and Community in the Twenty-first Century -- The 2006 Johan Skytte Prize*. Scandinavian Political Studies 30 (2), June 2007

Randell, B., *On Alan Turing and the Origins of Digital Computers*, in Meltzer, B., Michie, D. (eds), Machine Intelligence 7, Edinburgh: Edinburgh University Press, 1972.

Randell, B. (ed.), *The Origins of Digital Computers: Selected Papers*, Berlin: Springer-Verlag, 1982.

Rosvall, M., Trusina A., Minnhagen P., and Sneppen K., *Networks and Cities: An Information Perspective*, Phys. Rev. Lett., 94:2 028701, cond-mat/0407054, 2005.

Saffre, Fabrice, and Ghanea-Hercock, Robert, *Simple Laws for Complex Networks*, Journal of the Institution of British Telecommunication Engineers, vol.21. No. 2, April 2003.

Sagan, Carl, *Cosmos*, Abacus; New edition edition, 1983.

Said, Edward, *The Clash of Ignorance*, The Nation, October 2001.

Salmon, Felix, *Recipe for Disaster: The Formula That Killed Wall Street*, Wired Magazine, 23rd Feb. 2009.

Samuel, Shah and Hadingham, *Mobile Communications in South Africa, Tanzania and Egypt: Results from Community and Business Surveys*, Online, http://www.idrc.ca/en/ev-121698-201-1-DO_TOPIC.html, February, 2005.

Shafer, G. *A Mathematical Theory of Evidence*. Princeton University Press, Princeton, NJ, 1976.

Shapiro, Carl, and Varian, Hal, R., *Information Rules: A Strategic Guide to the Network Economy* (Hardcover), Harvard Business School Press; illustrated edition, 1998.

Sherman, Amy, L., *Reinvigorating Faith in Communities*, Hudson Institutec. 104pp., 2002.

Silverman, David, P., (Ed.) Ancient Egypt, Duncan Baird, London, 1997.

Singh, Simon, *The Code Book: The Secret History of Codes and Code-breaking* (Paperback), Fourth Estate, New edition, 2000.

Skinner, B. F., *Beyond freedom and dignity*. New York: Vintage Books. ISBN 0-553-14372-7. 1972.

Smith, John, Maynard, *Evolution and the Theory of Games*, Cambridge University Press, 1982.

Standage, Tom, *The Victorian Internet: The Remarkable Story of the Telegraph and the Nineteenth Century's Online Pioneers*, Weidenfeld & Nicholson, London, 1998.

Stephenson, Neal, *Snowcrash*, Penguin, New Ed., 2002.

Surowiecki, James, *The Wisdom of Crowds: Why the Many Are Smarter Than the Few and How Collective Wisdom Shapes Business, Economies, Societies and Nations* (Hardcover), Doubleday Books, 2004.

The Economist, p.67, 'The Big Sort', June 21st 2008.

Turing, Alan, *The chemical basis of morphogenesis*, from *Philosophical Transactions of the Royal Society of London*, Series B, No.641, Vol. 237, 14 August 1952.

Turing, A.M., *On Computable Numbers, with an Application to the Entscheidungsproblem*, Proceedings of the London Mathematical Society, Series 2, 42 (1936-37): 230-265

Turing, A.M., 1947, *Lecture to the London Mathematical Society on 20 February 1947*, in Carpenter and Doran, 1986.

von Neumann, J., *First Draft of a Report on the EDVAC*, reprinted in full in Stern, N. From ENIAC to UNIVAC: An Appraisal of the Eckert-Mauchly Computers Bedford, Mass.: Digital Press (1981), pp. 181-246, 1945.

Waldrop, Mitchell, *Complexity: The Emerging Science at the Edge of Order and Chaos*, Penguin Books Ltd, 1994.

Walker, David, *U.S. Heading For Financial Trouble? Comptroller Says Medicare Program Endangers Financial Stability*, CBS News, 60 Minutes, July 8, 2007.

Walker, David, *Transforming Government to Meet the Demands of the 21st Century*, www.gao.gov/cghome/d071188cg.pdf, GAO report, GAO-07-1188CG, August 2007.

Walter, William, Grey, The Living Brain, [1953], Penguin, London, 1967.

Watts, Alan, *Tao: The Watercourse Way*, Pantheon Books,1977.

Watts, D.J., Strogatz, S.H., *Collective dynamics of 'small-world' networks*. Nature 393 (6684): 409–10, 1998.

Watts, Duncan, J., *Six Degrees: The New Science of Networks*, pub. Vintage, 2004.

Waverman, Meschi and Fuss, *The Impact of Telecoms on Economic Growth in Developing Countries, Africa: The Impact of Mobile Phones*, Vodafone Policy Paper Series 2, March 2005.

Weber, Max, *The Protestant Ethic and the Spirit of Capitalism*, The original edition was in German and was entitled: Die protestantische Ethik und der 'Geist' des Kapitalismus. 1905. (Routledge; 2nd edition in English, 2001).

White, Douglas, R., Dynamics of Human Behaviour, Santa Fe Institute Working paper, 2008-09-042, 2008.

Willams, *The Relationship between Mobile Telecommunications Infrastructure and FDI in Africa*, Online, http://www.idrc.ca/en/ev-121698-201-1-DO_TOPIC.html, February 2005.

Williams, F.C., *Early Computers at Manchester University*, The Radio and Electronic Engineer, 45: 237-331, 1975.

Wilson, D.S., *Darwin and the Cathedral*, University of Chicago Press, 2002.

Wilson, Edward, *Consilience: The Unity of Knowledge*, pub. Knopf. 1998.

Woolley, Benjamin, *The Bride of Science: Romance, Reason, and Byron's Daughter*, McGraw-Hill Companies, 2002.

Woods, D. D. *Creating Foresight: Lessons for Resilience from Columbia*. In M. Farjoun and William Starbuck (eds.), Organization at the Limit: NASA and the Columbia Disaster. Blackwell, 2005.

Yu, B., and Singh, M., *An Evidential Model of Distributed Reputation Management*, International Conference of Autonomous Agents and Multi-Agent Systems, Bologna Italy, 2002.

Yu, B., and Singh, M.P., *Detecting Deception in Reputation Management*, Proceedings of Second International Joint Conference on Autonomous Agents and Multi-Agent Systems, 2003.

Web References

The following web links are a smattering of useful references and material, intended to aid the reader in studying or researching the cohesion topic:

http://www.cpn.org/topics/community/index.html -The Civic Practices Network, a Learning Collaborative for Civic Renewal.

http://www.mod.uk/DefenceInternet/MicroSite/DCDC/OurPublications/StrategicTrends+Programme/ - The UK MoD Global Strategic Trends Programme 3rd Edition.

http://www.redfish.com/ - A cool web site, for Java and agent-based models of complex systems.

http://www.santafe.edu/sfi/publications/wpabstract/199804027 - A basic Game Theory Tutorial.

http://www.technologyreview.com/computing/13893/page3/ - *What went wrong in Iraq*, online reference at Technology Review, 2004.

http://www.bahai.org - An introductory web site on the Baha'i Faith and its teachings.

http://ccl.northwestern.edu/netlogo/ - Netlogo: a very easy to use and free agent-based modelling tool to understand complex systems and many of the topics covered in the book.

http://repast.sourceforge.net/ - Repast: a more sophisticated agent modelling tool for complex systems.

http://www.bbc.co.uk/history/ancient/egyptians/egypt_end_01.shtml - An introductory reference for Ancient Eygpt.

http://www.commissionforafrica.org/english/report/background/scott_et_al_ba ckground.pdf - Commission for Africa report, 2004.

http://www.rossashby.info/ - An overview of the history of Cybernetics, and a free electronic copy of the early work of Ross Ashby is available from: http://pespmc1.vub.ac.be/ASHBBOOK.html

http://blogs.law.harvard.edu/idblog/2009/06/11/mapping-irans-blogosphere-on-election-eve/ - Article and diagrams on: Mapping the Iranian Blogosphere.

http://www.google.com/corporate/tenthings.html - Google Corporate Philosophy,

http://www.pbs.org/wgbh/pages/frontline/shows/pentagon/interviews/vanriper. html - Van Riper story on Network Centric Warfare; online article, 2004.